THE NATURE OF CONSTITUTIONAL RIGHTS

What does it mean to have a constitutional right in an era in which most rights must yield to "compelling governmental interests"? After recounting the little-known history of the invention of the compelling-interest formula during the 1960s, *The Nature of Constitutional Rights* examines what must be true about constitutional rights for them to be identified and enforced via "strict judicial scrutiny" and other, similar, judge-crafted tests. The book's answers not only enrich philosophical understanding of the concept of a "right," but also produce important practical payoffs. Its insights should affect how courts decide cases and how citizens should think about the judicial role. Contributing to the conversation among originalists, living constitutionalists, and legal realists, Richard Fallon explains what constitutional rights are, what courts must do to identify them, and why the protections that they afford are more limited than most people think.

Richard H. Fallon Jr. is Story Professor of Law at Harvard Law School and Affiliate Professor in the Harvard Government Department. A former Rhodes Scholar, Fallon served as a law clerk to Justice Lewis F. Powell of the United States Supreme Court. Fallon has written extensively about Constitutional Law and is the author of multiple books including, *The Dynamic Constitution* (2d ed. 2013) and *Law and Legitimacy in the Supreme Court* (2018).

D1601245

CAMBRIDGE STUDIES ON CIVIL RIGHTS AND CIVIL LIBERTIES

This series is a platform for original scholarship on US civil rights and civil liberties. It produces books on the normative, historical, judicial, political, and sociological contexts for understanding contemporary legislative, jurisprudential, and presidential dilemmas. The aim is to provide experts, teachers, policymakers, students, social activists, and educated citizens with in-depth analyses of theories, existing and past conditions, and constructive ideas for legal advancements.

General Editor: Alexander Tsesis, *Loyola University, Chicago*

The Nature of Constitutional Rights

THE INVENTION AND LOGIC OF STRICT JUDICIAL SCRUTINY

RICHARD H. FALLON JR.

Harvard Law School, Massachusetts

CAMBRIDGE
UNIVERSITY PRESS

CAMBRIDGE
UNIVERSITY PRESS

University Printing House, Cambridge CB2 8BS, United Kingdom

One Liberty Plaza, 20th Floor, New York, NY 10006, USA

477 Williamstown Road, Port Melbourne, VIC 3207, Australia

314–321, 3rd Floor, Plot 3, Splendor Forum, Jasola District Centre,
New Delhi – 110025, India

79 Anson Road, #06–04/06, Singapore 079906

Cambridge University Press is part of the University of Cambridge.

It furthers the University's mission by disseminating knowledge in the pursuit of
education, learning, and research at the highest international levels of excellence.

www.cambridge.org
Information on this title: www.cambridge.org/9781108483261
DOI: 10.1017/9781108673549

© Richard H. Fallon Jr. 2019

First published 2019

Printed and bound in Great Britain by Clays Ltd, Elcograf S.p.A.

A catalogue record for this publication is available from the British Library.

ISBN 978-1-108-48326-1 Hardback
ISBN 978-1-108-70391-8 Paperback

For Libby, Joseph, Doug, and Maggie

Contents

Acknowledgments

In writing this book, I have drawn liberally on ideas developed, and sometimes on language included, in articles published over the past dozen years. Chapters 1 and 2 both echo, though they also revise, *Strict Judicial Scrutiny*, 54 U.C.L.A. L. Rev. 1267 (2007). Chapter 3 builds on, but very substantially reworks and augments, a much earlier article, *Individual Rights and the Powers of Government*, 27 Ga. L. Rev. 343 (1993). It also picks up themes from *Judicially Manageable Standards and Constitutional Meaning*, 119 Harv. L. Rev. 1274 (2006). Chapter 5 makes use of *Constitutionally Forbidden Legislative Intent*, 130 Harv. L. Rev. 523 (2016). Chapter 6 weaves together ideas and repeats some language from *The Linkage between Justiciability and Remedies – and Their Connections to Substantive Rights*, 92 Va. L. Rev. 633 (2006); *Asking the Right Questions about Officer Immunity*, 80 Fordham L. Rev. 479 (2011); *The Fragmentation of Standing*, 93 Tex. L. Rev. 1061 (2015); and *Fact and Fiction about Facial Challenges*, 99 Cal. L. Rev. 915 (2011). Chapter 7 adapts arguments and borrows some language from *The Core of an Uneasy Case for Judicial Review*, 121 Harv. L. Rev. 1693 (2008).

I am grateful to Alexander Tsesis for suggesting that I write a book based on some of the themes that this one develops. Without his suggestion and encouragement, this book never would have come to pass. John Berger of Cambridge University Press also made suggestions that made this book better than it would have been otherwise. Reports by two anonymous outside readers lead to multiple revisions, including the addition of an entire chapter.

Because this book synthesizes and revises ideas that have developed over many years, it would be impossible for me to thank all of the many people who have assisted me along the way. I owe special debts for help with one or more pieces of the argument to Mike Dorf, Heather Gerken, Debbie Hellman, Vicki Jackson, Michael Klarman, Daryl Levinson, Gillian Metzger, Martha Minow, John Manning, Dan Meltzer, Frank Michelman, Henry Monaghan, David Shapiro, Fred Schauer, Mark Tushnet, and Adrian Vermeule. Steve Schaus provided not only invaluable research assistance, but also wise substantive and editorial advice. Isaac Park and Adam Savitt provided further excellent research help to get me through the home stretch, as did Grayson Clary at the very end.

As always, I am grateful to my wife Jenny for all manner of support and encouragement. While I was first thinking about and then writing this book, our daughter Libby and her husband Joseph Weintraub blessed us with twin grandchildren Jeanie and Jamie, followed by Dolly less than two years later. Meantime, our son Doug and his wife Maggie Fallon had added Kenny to the roster of grandchildren. It will be a long time, if ever, before this book means anything to Jeanie, Jamie, Dolly, or Kenny. With gratitude for the grandchildren and much else, I dedicate it to Libby, Joseph, Doug, and Maggie.

Introduction

What are constitutional rights? We all know that we have constitutional rights. Most Americans could list some, probably proudly. But what does it mean to say that someone has a right? Are constitutional rights privileges to do or say whatever one wishes, regardless of the consequences? For example, if I have a right to burn the flag for purposes of political protests, can I do so at any time and any place, even if it would create a fire hazard? Do rights kick in only when the government acts for forbidden reasons or motives, such as to stifle political criticism or to subordinate some on the basis of race or religion? Are rights merely statements of ideals or aspiration that must yield to the common good whenever the common good is genuinely at risk? Or are they "absolutes" in some sense – and, if so, in what sense?

These are hard questions, not easy to answer. If hesitating, we might recall what St. Augustine said about the nature of time: "What . . . is time? If no one ask[s] of me, I know; if I wish to explain to him who asks, I know not."[1] We might imagine that we occupy a situation like that with respect to constitutional rights – one of knowing what constitutional rights are, even if we might stumble initially in explaining. Or, deploying the analogy in a different way, we might think that questions about the nature of constitutional rights have little practical significance. Even if most of us could not offer a good account of what time is (even or perhaps especially if we are acquainted with Einstein's famous claim that time is somehow relative to space, and vice versa), we get along well enough.

With constitutional rights, however, matters are different. Whatever time is, its nature lies beyond human control. By contrast, constitution-writers and courts have the power to change the rights that we have. They might give us new rights that we do not have now or take away some that we currently possess. More interestingly and challengingly, moreover, constitution-writers and courts can change the *nature* of constitutional rights. On this score, history leaves no doubt.

As I shall demonstrate in this book, the Supreme Court has altered the nature of constitutional rights within roughly the past three-quarters of a century.

[1] THE CONFESSIONS OF ST. AUGUSTINE, BISHOP OF HIPPO 301 (J. G. Pilkington ed. & trans., T. & T. Clark 1943).

Constitutional rights today are different not only in their subject matters, but also in their natures, from the constitutional rights that existed before 1937 and even before the 1960s. The signal development within the decade of the 1960s involved the invention of a judicial test, denominated as "strict judicial scrutiny," for defining, enforcing, and marking the limits on constitutional rights. When strict scrutiny applies, legislation will survive constitutional challenge only if it is "necessary" or "narrowly tailored" to promote a "compelling" governmental interest.[2] Today we cannot understand what constitutional rights are without understanding strict judicial scrutiny, even though, before the 1960s, there was no strict scrutiny to understand.

As every law student quickly learns, strict scrutiny forms one of two central pillars of the modern edifice of judicially protected constitutional rights. Since the collapse of the *Lochner* era at the end of the 1930s, the Supreme Court has relegated the protection of most ordinary "liberties" or "liberty interests" to the political process. Examples include the restraints on liberty that occur when legislatures impose highway speed limits, forbid trafficking in narcotic drugs, and require employers to pay their employees a minimum wage. Courts will uphold restrictions such as these pursuant to a "rational basis" test, which asks only whether a law is "rationally related to a legitimate government interest." The Supreme Court has described this test as "a paradigm of judicial restraint."[3]

Strict judicial scrutiny plays an equally paradigmatic role in defining and limiting constitutional rights, but one that puts the Supreme Court at center stage. The invocation of strict scrutiny signals that the Court takes the asserted right, and its role in protecting rights of that kind, extremely seriously. Under modern doctrine, the Court employs strict scrutiny to define and enforce many if not most of the constitutional rights that most Americans are likely to think most important. For instance, the strict scrutiny test applies to challenges under the Equal Protection Clause to statutes that discriminate on the basis of race or employ other "suspect" classifications.[4] It provides "the baseline rule"[5] under the First Amendment for assessing laws that regulate speech on the basis of content,[6] as well as for scrutinizing

---

[2]   *See, e.g., Cooper v. Harris*, 137 S. Ct. 1455, 1464 (2017); *Fisher v. Univ. of Tex. at Austin*, 136 S. Ct. 2198, 2208 (2016); *Reed v. Town of Gilbert*, 135 S. Ct. 2218, 2226–27 (2015); *Brown v. Entm't Merchs. Ass'n*, 564 U.S. 786, 799–800 (2011); *Citizens United v. FEC*, 558 U.S. 310, 340 (2010); *Parents Involved in Cmty. Sch. v. Seattle Sch. Dist. No. 1*, 551 U.S. 701, 720 (2007); *Johnson v. California*, 543 U.S. 499, 505 (2005); *Adarand Constructors, Inc. v. Pena*, 515 U.S. 200, 227 (1995); *Republican Party of Minn. v. White*, 536 U.S. 765, 775 (2002); *R.A.V. v. City of St. Paul*, 505 U.S. 377, 395–96 (1992); *Perry Educ. Ass'n v. Perry Local Educators' Ass'n*, 460 U.S. 37, 45 (1983).

[3]   *FCC v. Beach Commc'ns, Inc.*, 508 U.S. 307, 314 (1993).

[4]   *E.g., Fisher*, 136 S. Ct. at 2208; *Parents Involved*, 551 U.S. at 720; *Johnson*, 543 U.S. at 505; *Graham v. Richardson*, 403 U.S. 365, 372 (1971) (requiring strict scrutiny of "classifications based on alienage").

[5]   *Denver Area Educ. Telecomms. Consortium, Inc. v. FCC*, 518 U.S. 727, 800 (1996) (Kennedy, J., concurring in part, concurring in the judgment in part, and dissenting in part).

[6]   *See, e.g., National Inst. of Family and Life Advocates v. Becerra*, 138 S. Ct. 2361, 2371 (2018); *Reed v. Town of Gilbert*, 135 S. Ct. at 2226–27; *Brown*, 564 U.S. at 799–800; *United States v. Playboy Entm't*

content-based exclusions of speakers from a public forum.[7] In the domain of due process, the Supreme Court says that statutes that restrict the exercise of "fundamental" rights trigger strict scrutiny.[8] The same rule applies in cases involving rights that are deemed fundamental under the Equal Protection Clause,[9] as in equal protection cases involving challenges to majority-minority voting districts the design of which was predominantly driven by race-based concerns.[10] Statutes that impose substantial burdens on freedom of association also receive analysis under the compelling governmental interest test,[11] as do laws that single out religiously motivated conduct for governmental regulation.[12]

Not all constitutional rights are enforced either by strict scrutiny on the one hand or rational basis review on the other. We shall come to some other tests soon enough. But strict scrutiny and its archetypal alternative of rational basis review have vast importance in organizing constitutional doctrine and, by doing so, in defining and constructing constitutional rights. This book therefore makes strict judicial scrutiny, and the nature of the rights that strict scrutiny protects, a central focus. The lessons that emerge from close examination of that framework will prove to be generalizable in most important respects and usefully distinguishable in others.

The history of strict scrutiny's emergence is little known. The relative lack of attention to its development, which I seek to correct, is surprising. Given the widespread role of strict judicial scrutiny in modern constitutional doctrine, one might expect that it must have deep roots either in the Constitution's text or in longstanding interpretive traditions. Neither is true. The words "strict scrutiny" appear nowhere in the Constitution. Nor does that term embody traditional understandings about the nature of constitutional rights or the judicial role in protecting them. Accordingly, to describe strict scrutiny as an invention is not an overstatement. It is difficult to identify the first case to apply or define strict judicial scrutiny.

Grp, Inc., 529 U.S. 803, 813–14 (2000), *Simon & Schuster, Inc.* v. *Members of the N.Y. State Crime Victims Bd.*, 502 U.S. 105, 118 (1991).

[7] *See, e.g.*, *Minnesota Voters Alliance* v. *Mansky*, 138 S. Ct. 1876, 1885 (2018); *Ark. Educ. Television Comm'n* v. *Forbes*, 523 U.S. 666, 677 (1998); *United States* v. *Kokinda*, 497 U.S. 720, 726–27 (1990) (plurality opinion); *Widmar* v. *Vincent*, 454 U.S. 263, 270 (1981).

[8] *See, e.g.*, *Washington* v. *Glucksberg*, 521 U.S. 702, 720–21 (1997); *Reno* v. *Flores*, 507 U.S. 292, 301–02 (1993).

[9] *See, e.g.*, *Kramer* v. *Union Free Sch. Dist. No. 15*, 395 U.S. 621, 626–27 (1969); *Shapiro* v. *Thompson*, 394 U.S. 618, 634 (1969).

[10] *See, e.g.*, *Cooper* v. *Harris*, 137 S. Ct. 1455, 1464 (2017); *Miller* v. *Johnson*, 515 U.S. 900, 920 (1995); *Shaw* v. *Reno*, 509 U.S. 630, 643–44 (1993).

[11] *See, e.g.*, *Clingman* v. *Beaver*, 544 U.S. 581, 586 (2005); *Boy Scouts of Am.* v. *Dale*, 530 U.S. 640, 648–49 (2000); *Brown* v. *Socialist Workers '74 Campaign Comm.*, 459 U.S. 87, 91–92 (1982).

[12] *See Trinity Lutheran Church of Columbia, Inc.* v. *Comer*, 137 S. Ct. 2012, 2024 (2017); *Church of the Lukumi Babalu Aye, Inc.* v. *City of Hialeah*, 508 U.S. 520, 531–32 (1993). Prior to 1990, the Court also applied strict scrutiny to test the permissibility of substantial burdens on the free exercise of religion. But the Supreme Court effected a major retrenchment in *Employment Division* v. *Smith*, 494 U.S. 872 (1990). Under *Smith*, generally applicable laws that only incidentally burden the free exercise of religion no longer attract strict scrutiny. *See id.* at 882–89.

The modern formula evolved almost imperceptibly. Before the decade of the 1960s, strict judicial scrutiny as we know it today did not exist. By the end of the 1960s, it had achieved roughly the same reach that it possesses today. To understand the modern regime of constitutional rights, it is important to understand how and why strict scrutiny developed and spread.

The answers to those questions have profound continuing implications. The founders of the strict scrutiny regime were not constitutional or political theorists, at least self-consciously. Nevertheless, strict judicial scrutiny, willy-nilly, embodies a theory about the nature of constitutional rights. The crucial presuppositions emerge from the question: What do constitutional rights need to be like in order for the strict scrutiny test to be a coherent, well-adapted means for identifying and enforcing them? That question imagines a project of reverse-engineering. Taking strict scrutiny as a starting point, I work out what is or must be true about the nature of constitutional rights for them to be defined and applied in the way that the Supreme Court defines and applies them through the strict scrutiny formula.

The necessary analysis is partly conceptual. It should interest those who care about the relationship between constitutional law, on the one hand, and various philosophical theories about the nature of rights, on the other. But there are important practical payoffs too. When the assumptions that underlie strict scrutiny are laid bare, lawyers, judges, concerned citizens, and even Justices of the Supreme Court should have an enriched understanding of how courts could do better. Some of the sharpest implications involve the judicial role in devising remedies for constitutional violations and in determining who should have standing to sue. Rights and remedies are conceptually interconnected, I argue, and courts should exploit the connections to realize the values that underlie rights while limiting the sometimes inevitable social costs of rights enforcement.

My prescriptive conclusions, however, are less important than the lines of analysis that this book opens up. Most of us think it the glory of our Constitution that it guarantees our rights. Especially if so, and if the nature of constitutional rights can change, we have urgent reason to know what constitutional rights are today and what they might be or become instead. Roughly two centuries ago, the philosopher Jeremy Bentham derided appeals to natural rights as "nonsense upon stilts."[13] Rights, he thought, were no more real than ghosts, even if many people believed in both. We could easily imagine Bentham's barb as applying to constitutional rights. Nor should concerned citizens dismiss out of hand the Realists' manifesto that rights, at bottom, are whatever judges say they are. Beginning with the conceptual assumptions about the nature of rights that the prism of strict scrutiny reveals, this book depicts sense, not nonsense, at the foundations of our constitutional practice. But it depicts sense of a kind that will force many of those aligned

---

[13] Jeremy Bentham, *Anarchical Fallacies; Being an Examination of the Declaration of Rights Issued During the French Revolution*, in 2 THE WORKS OF JEREMY BENTHAM 489, 501 (John Bowring ed., 1843).

with the right, left, and center in modern constitutional debates to rethink their positions.

In contemporary debates, originalists equate rights with guarantees that the Framers embodied in the Constitution. But how does that view cohere, or does it fail to cohere, with the identification of constitutional rights through a strict judicial scrutiny test that judges invented only about a half-century ago? The legal philosopher Ronald Dworkin, who long carried the left-liberal banner in many constitutional debates, described rights as "trumps."[14] But doesn't the strict scrutiny formula assume that constitutional rights can be overridden by "compelling governmental interests"?

As these questions suggest, using the strict judicial scrutiny test as a prism through which to examine constitutional rights promises to generate insights not only about rights, but also about the judicial role in defining and enforcing rights. It will take patience to work out conclusions. But it is not too early to see that the strict scrutiny test requires distinctions among different kinds of rights, some of which may bear different relationships than others to original constitutional meanings, some of which may identify "trumps" in ways that others do not, and some of which might or might not be "living" or evolving.

By way of a down-payment, here is a first cut at some relevant distinctions. *Texas v. Johnson*[15] – a case to which I shall refer repeatedly – provides a useful paradigm. Gregory Lee Johnson was prosecuted for burning a flag under a statute that made it a crime to "desecrate" a "venerated object." The Supreme Court reversed his conviction on free speech grounds. Applying strict judicial scrutiny, the majority determined that Johnson had what I shall call an *ultimate right* not to be punished under the challenged statute, which the Court found not to be narrowly tailored to a compelling governmental interest. By an ultimate right, I mean one that the Court upholds or would uphold at the end of its inquiries, after applying all relevant law to the facts.[16] An ultimate constitutional right is a categorical constraint on the legitimate power of the government and its officials under identified circumstances.[17]

Significantly, however, much of the dispute in *Texas v. Johnson*, in which the Justices divided five to four, was not about compelling governmental interests and narrow tailoring. It was about whether strict judicial scrutiny should apply at all.

---

[14] *See, e.g.,* Ronald Dworkin, Taking Rights Seriously, at xi (1977) ("Individual rights are political trumps held by individuals.").

[15] 491 U.S. 397 (1989).

[16] It would be possible to draw further, potentially important distinctions within the category of ultimate rights. In perhaps the most influential categorical scheme in the jurisprudential literature, Wesley Newcomb Hohfeld, *Some Fundamental Legal Conceptions as Applied in Judicial Reasoning,* 23 Yale L.J. 16 (1913), distinguishes among claim rights to have others act in a particular manner, privileges, powers, and immunities. He also influentially contrasts those varieties of rights with their jural opposites (no-rights, duties, disabilities, and liabilities). I take no position on continuing controversies about the value of Hohfeld's analytical subdivisions. My interest in this book lies in distinguishing ultimate rights from other categories of rights with which the former can be usefully contrasted.

[17] *See* T. M. Scanlon, The Difficulty of Tolerance 151–52 (2003).

The dissenting Justices said no. In the vocabulary that I shall use throughout this book, their dispute with the majority involved the existence of a *triggering right*. In other words, the central question for the dissenters was whether the act of burning a flag under the law at issue properly elicited strict judicial scrutiny as a mechanism for protecting the freedom of speech. They concluded that it did not. As that disagreement among the Justices reveals, before a court determines whether a party has an ultimate right, it needs to make several analytically prior determinations (even if it does not pause to think about them in these terms).

Just to kick matters off, the Justices needed to decide whether a ban on flag-burning presented a First Amendment issue of any kind. Why wasn't burning a flag a form of conduct, not speech, and thus wholly outside the concern of the First Amendment? To answer that question, the Justices needed to have in mind what I shall term an *abstract* free speech right, reflecting the values, goals, or purposes of "the freedom of speech" that the Framers embodied in the Constitution and that the Constitution guarantees today. Being defined only by vaguely specified values, purposes, or historical understandings, an abstract right in this sense may be inchoate, as in *Texas* v. *Johnson*, and thus leave the Justices with a genuine question about whether to recognize a triggering right to any more sharply edged test of constitutional validity. We need the idea of an abstract right – to go along with the concepts of triggering and ultimate rights – to explain what the Justices were debating when they divided about whether to apply strict scrutiny in *Texas* v. *Johnson*: Was an abstract right to freedom of speech sufficiently infringed to call for exacting judicial review under the First Amendment?

There is just one more complication, in light of which it will sometimes be helpful to identify yet another category of constitutional rights. Because strict judicial scrutiny is not the only test of constitutional validity that the Supreme Court sometimes employs, a fully specified triggering right is defined by both (1) a threshold level or kind of infringement on an abstract right and (2) the particular test of constitutional validity that infringements of that kind make applicable. In *Texas* v. *Johnson*, a majority of the Justices concluded that strict scrutiny applied. But they also considered the possibility that a different test might be called for. A fully specified triggering right thus subsumes a *scrutiny right*, or a right to have a particular test employed. As this book will show, distinguishing among abstract, triggering, scrutiny, and ultimate rights, and among the judicial functions in making judgments within these varied categories, will clarify numerous constitutional debates. It will also illuminate the plausibility of various theoretical positions within those debates.

Even and perhaps especially when we distinguish among varieties of rights, examining constitutional debates through the prism of strict judicial scrutiny reveals a practical and conceptual puzzle that defines another large part of the book's agenda. This puzzle involves the relationship between rights and interests. Within the strict scrutiny formula, triggering rights – such as the free speech right to burn a flag that the Supreme Court identified in *Texas* v. *Johnson* – must be weighed against governmental interests, such as that in preserving the flag as a symbol of national unity, that courts must adjudge either compelling or not compelling. The juxtaposition of individual rights with governmental interests presents a question about the commensurability of rights and interests. To borrow a phrase from Justice Antonin Scalia, why isn't asking whether a governmental interest outweighs a right like asking whether a rock is heavier than a line is long?[18]

In response, I argue that rights themselves reflect, and are constructed out of, "interests." Along a myriad of often unrecognized dimensions, constitutional law requires the identification, specification, weighing, balancing, and accommodation of sometimes competing individual and governmental interests. The Supreme Court identifies, balances, and accommodates interests when it defines triggering rights by constructing them out of abstract rights. The triggering right to burn a flag for expressive purposes is a judicial construct in this sense. The Court performs a similar exercise when it devises tests such as strict judicial scrutiny and when, in applying the strict scrutiny formula, it balances triggering rights against governmental interests to determine the shape and scope of our ultimate rights, including our rights to freedom of speech and freedom from race discrimination.

The Supreme Court also takes competing interests into account when crafting and limiting remedies for constitutional rights. With respect to that issue, this book's central thesis cuts against the claims of those who view depict the Court solely as a "forum of principle"[19] and constitutional rights as "trumps" – as Professor Dworkin did – in a sense that overruns all pragmatic and policy-based considerations in all cases. As even many constitutional scholars forget much of the time, rights and remedies do not exist in a one-to-one correlation. In one well-known example, the prevailing plaintiffs in *Brown* v. *Board of Education*[20] got no immediate remedy, only a promise of school desegregation "with all deliberate speed."[21] Some had graduated from segregated schools before desegregation occurred. Similarly, people whose rights were violated in the past and who seek damages relief often discover that the violation of their rights will go unremedied. The doctrine of sovereign immunity will preclude suits for damages against the government. And if an aggrieved party sues the governmental official who violated her rights – say, by subjecting her to an unconstitutional search and seizure – she will often run afoul of a less known but hugely important doctrine of "official immunity." Interest-balancing explains the often complex relationship between constitutional rights and constitutional remedies. It also explains the mystifying rules that determine

[18] *Bendix Autolite Corp.* v. *Midwesco Enters., Inc.*, 486 U.S. 888, 897 (1988) (Scalia, J., concurring in the judgment).
[19] *See* Ronald Dworkin, A MATTER OF PRINCIPLE 69–71 (1985).
[20] 347 U.S. 483 (1954).
[21] *See Brown* v. *Bd. of Educ.* (*Brown II*), 349 U.S. 294, 301 (1955).

when courts will deem statutes unconstitutional "on their faces" versus only "as applied" – among other examples that the book will explore.

But what, the reader will demand to know, is an *interest*? And where do interests come from? This book offers answers to these and many other crucial questions about the nature of constitutional rights within American constitutional practice. Among the issues to be addressed are these:

The Role of the Constitution's Text and History in Creating Constitutional Rights. The status of strict judicial scrutiny as a judicial creation both raises important questions and teaches important lessons about the limited role of text and history as determinants of constitutional rights. The Constitution's text and original history matter in multiple ways to the Supreme Court's application of the strict scrutiny test. But careful analysis of strict scrutiny cases illustrates the large, creative role the Court plays, not only in weighing the rights that trigger strict scrutiny against purportedly compelling governmental interests, but also in identifying triggering rights in the first instance.

Constitutional Originalism. Constitutional "originalists" maintain that the Constitution's meaning was fixed at the time of its ratification and that contemporary constitutional interpretation should reflect the original meaning of constitutional language.[22] Nevertheless, leading originalist judges and Justices have embraced, rather than renounced, the strict judicial scrutiny test, even though that test is a twentieth-century judicial invention wholly unforeseen by the Founding generation. Originalists' embrace of strict scrutiny does not necessarily reveal them as hypocrites or falsify the main claims on which nearly all originalists unite. Nonetheless, the endorsement of strict judicial scrutiny as a measure of constitutional validity imposes limits on the kind of originalism that anyone could plausibly defend as "our law,"[23] or a theory that captures the animating assumptions of most current constitutional doctrine, rather than a proposal for radical reform.

Rights as Trumps. By calling for rights sometimes to yield to compelling governmental interests, strict scrutiny problematizes Professor Dworkin's famous characterization of rights as "trumps" that prevail categorically over all competing considerations of prudence, convenience, and expediency. To try to rescue Dworkin's claim, we can immediately distinguish the ultimate rights that emerge from the strict scrutiny test from those that trigger strict scrutiny in the first place. Having drawn that distinction, we can insist that the former are trumps even if the latter are not. But in order for the claim that the former are "trumps" to be more than

---

[22]   *See* Lawrence B. Solum, *Originalism and Constitutional Construction*, 82 FORDHAM L. REV. 453, 459–62 (2013) (identifying the "Fixation Thesis" and "Constraint Principle" as the "core of contemporary originalism"); Lawrence B. Solum, *The Fixation Thesis: The Role of Historical Fact in Original Meaning*, 91 NOTRE DAME L. REV. 1 (2015).

[23]   *See* William Baude, Essay, *Is Originalism Our Law?*, 115 COLUM. L. REV. 2349 (2015).

tautological, we will need to extract some non-obvious insights about what interests are and how rights relate to interests.

The Nature of "Interests." As used in constitutional law, the term "interests" functions as a placeholder for goods, benefits, and opportunities that reasonable and rational people would want for themselves and their prosperity. John Rawls's famous ideas of an "original position" and a "veil of ignorance" provide a useful analogy: Parties behind the veil would seek to promote or realize interests.[24] So, presumably, would the authors and ratifiers of a constitution. Interests matter in constitutional adjudication because the courts, to adjudicate cases under the Free Speech or Equal Protection Clause, for example, must imagine those provisions as protections for interests that the Supreme Court must identify. Looking at the Free Speech Clause in *Texas* v. *Johnson*, the Court imputed an interest in protecting "expressive conduct" such as flag-burning, even though it is not "speech" in the literal sense. Conversely, the Court assumes that there is no protected First Amendment interest in falsely crying fire in a crowded theater, even though such a cry would literally constitute speech.[25] Under the Equal Protection Clause, the Court identifies a protected interest in freedom from discrimination on the basis of gender, despite the absence of evidence that the Fourteenth Amendment was originally understood this way. Yet the Court has not (so far) identified a significantly protected constitutional interest in freedom from discrimination based on IQ or educational attainment.

Crucially, the Constitution's strategy for protecting interests is two-pronged. On the one hand, it confers judicially enforceable rights (that courts must identify on the basis of an interest-based analysis). On the other hand, it vests powers in the government to protect citizen interests that do not give rise to judicially enforceable constitutional rights. For example, we all have interests in personal security that justify the attribution of a "governmental interest," sometimes compelling in character, in national security.[26] We have interests in empowerment and health that underlie claims of governmental interests in enacting laws related to education and medical care. How to compare and accommodate diverse kinds of interests that sometimes compete with one another is perhaps the most fundamental challenge of practical reasoning. Constitutional law must struggle with that challenge without the aid of any algorithm. It should be no surprise that constitutional law incorporates, without having produced an elegant solution to, the most fundamental challenge of moral and political thought.

---

[24] *See* John Rawls, A THEORY OF JUSTICE, at xii (rev. ed. 1999); John Rawls, POLITICAL LIBERALISM 19, 304–24 (1993).
[25] *See Schenck* v. *United States*, 249 U.S. 47, 52 (1919).
[26] *See, e.g., Holder* v. *Humanitarian Law Project*, 561 U.S. 1, 38–40 (2010) (upholding a prohibition against speech used to train terrorist organizations in light of "real dangers" to national security).

Categorical Alternatives to Interest-Balancing in the Identification of Constitutional Rights. For a variety of reasons, characterization of the judicial function in constitutional cases as involving interest-balancing occasions anxiety, not only about the contingent character of constitutional rights, but also about the capacity of courts to weigh competing interests. Critics often call for a more categorical approach, such as one in which the courts confine themselves to invalidating legislation that reflects constitutionally forbidden intentions or purposes.[27] In examining the role of constitutionally forbidden intentions in constitutional law, I argue that courts cannot escape from the obligation of interest-balancing. Forbidden legislative intentions should matter as a trigger for interest-balancing pursuant to the strict judicial scrutiny formula. Nevertheless, the ultimately determinative consideration should be whether challenged legislation is narrowly tailored to a compelling governmental interest.

Rights as Constraints Rather than Privileges. On one familiar view, to have a right is to have a privilege (which might be broader or narrower) to do or say what one wants, regardless of social costs or harm to others. If the right to burn the flag as an act of political protest were a privilege in this sense, I could burn a flag whenever or wherever I wanted, regardless of the hazards I created or the government's reasons for wanting to stop me. But the strict scrutiny test is not framed to identify or protect privileges. Rather, in paradigmatic applications, it asks whether particular, challenged laws or statutes are narrowly tailored to compelling governmental interests. This focus of analysis reveals the rights that strict scrutiny protects not as privileges, but as constraints. As identified through the strict scrutiny test, constitutional rights constrain the government from enacting particular statutes or engaging in other actions without sufficiently good reasons for doing so. *Texas* v. *Johnson* exemplifies the distinction. The First Amendment constrained Texas from punishing flag-burning under a statute that barred the desecration of venerated objects. But the right to freedom of speech would not have constrained Texas from enforcing a law that forbade all lighting of fires on public property, justified by interests in protecting public safety, against someone who ignited a flag.

Rights and Remedies. The strict judicial scrutiny formula defines constitutional rights, but the practical significance of constitutional rights frequently depends on the remedies that are available to enforce them. Constitutional scholars sometimes portray the identification of constitutional rights as one exercise and the provision of remedies as another. Trumpeting the slogan "for every right, a remedy,"[28] they have

---

[27] See, e.g., Richard H. Pildes, *Avoiding Balancing: The Role of Exclusionary Reasons in Constitutional Law*, 45 HASTINGS L.J. 711 (1994); *see also* John Hart Ely, DEMOCRACY AND DISTRUST: A THEORY OF JUDICIAL REVIEW (1980).

[28] In the American constitutional tradition, the phrase evokes *Marbury* v. *Madison*, 5 U.S. (1 Cranch) 137 (1803), in which Chief Justice John Marshall stated: "The very essence of civil liberty certainly consists in the right of every individual to claim the protection of the laws, whenever he receives an injury . . . The government of the United States has been emphatically termed a government of laws, and not of

often expressed outrage whenever the Supreme Court betrays the promise that (they think) rights convey by denying an individually effective remedy, such as compensation in the form of money damages, to someone whose constitutional rights have been violated.

I take a contrary view. If constitutional rights properly reflect a comparison of competing interests, the Supreme Court should also take competing interests into account in crafting and awarding constitutional remedies. Even defenders of sovereign and especially official immunity doctrines frequently portray them as necessary evils, devised to protect public treasuries and to spare individual officials from personal liability simply for doing their jobs. In doing so, they assume that constitutional rights are constants and that remedies for rights violations are variables. But if rights are themselves defined through a process of interest-balancing, then rights are variables as much as remedies are. If there had to be a damages remedy for every violation of constitutional rights, the governmental interests that counsel against the recognition of rights in the first place would become more weighty, and the scope of judicially recognized ultimate rights might shrink. To take a historical example, if the social costs of the Supreme Court's decision to uphold a right to desegregated schooling in *Brown* v. *Board of Education*[29] had included the necessity of providing a damages remedy to every person who had suffered wrongful discrimination in the past, then the Supreme Court might have felt disabled from deciding *Brown* as it did.[30] The Justices, most of whom thought the case a very difficult one anyway, might have ruled that although maintaining segregated schools was morally troublesome, the Constitution did not forbid it, and waited for state legislatures or for Congress to abolish segregation. As that prospect should suggest, sometimes we are better off with relatively broader rights but restricted remedies than we would be with relatively narrower rights and more robust remedies.

Judicial Legitimacy and the Judicial Role. Insofar as courts applying strict scrutiny must make value-based and instrumental calculations about how best to promote competing interests, the question inevitably arises: How does the judicial role in doing so differ from the function of legislatures, which also should seek to balance and accommodate competing interests? And since the role that the courts play in administering strict scrutiny is one that they have defined for themselves, a deeper question is whether that role can be justified. This question is partly one of constitutional law, but it also implicates democratic theory. We should address it in those terms. A careful analysis of the conceptual foundations of strict scrutiny doctrine shows the need to rethink the justification for searching judicial review to protect inherently contestable, interest-based constitutional rights.

---

men. It will certainly cease to deserve this high appellation if the laws furnish no remedy for the violation of a vested legal right," *id.* at 163.

[29] 347 U.S. 483 (1954).

[30] *See* John C. Jeffries, Jr., *The Right-Remedy Gap in Constitutional Law*, 109 YALE L.J. 87, 99–101 (1999).

This book offers a fresh, nonstandard justification for judicial review. I argue that the best justification for aggressive judicial review is not that courts are inherently better than legislatures at defining constitutional rights and appraising competing governmental interests. It is, rather, that some of the interests that underlie constitutional rights are so important that they deserve a double safeguard: The government ought not be able to act in ways that either the legislature or a reviewing court believes incompatible with a commitment to ensuring and enforcing a robust scheme of rights against the government.

The book comprises seven chapters. Chapter 1 traces the historical emergence of strict judicial scrutiny during the 1960s and identifies the felt needs that the Supreme Court devised strict scrutiny to meet. Chapter 2 provides a close analytical examination of strict scrutiny's constituent elements, including those of fundamental rights, narrow tailoring, and compelling governmental interests. Chapter 3 explains how individual rights and governmental interests can be weighed against each other by arguing that fundamental rights themselves reflect interests. Chapter 3 also discusses in detail the kinds of contestable judgments that the Supreme Court must make to apply a strict scrutiny formula that was at its inception, and remains, incompletely theorized. Chapter 4 broadens the focus of inquiry beyond strict scrutiny to consider other tests that the Supreme Court has developed to define and enforce constitutional rights. As viewed through this broader lens, constitutional rights emerge as more diverse in their natures than an exclusive focus on strict judicial scrutiny would reveal. Nevertheless, Chapter 4's analysis generalizes the conclusions of Chapter 3 in two key respects: As examined through the windows furnished by judicial tests other than strict scrutiny, rights reflect interests that are subject to balancing, and they function as constraints on particular kinds of governmental action, not as encompassing privileges to say or do particular things regardless of legal or practical context. Chapter 5 examines the role of forbidden legislative intent in modern constitutional law and considers possible categorical alternatives to strict judicial scrutiny that purport to avoid interest-balancing. Chapter 6 delineates often unappreciated practical and conceptual interconnections between rights and remedies, including limitations that sometimes leave victims of rights violations with no judicial remedy whatsoever. Chapter 7 offers a justification for interest-balancing judicial review that does not depend either on original constitutional understandings or on the premise that courts possess greater moral and practical wisdom than do legislators.

1

The Historical Emergence of Strict Judicial Scrutiny

The modern judicial strict scrutiny test arose during the 1960s as a device to implement, or as the constitutional complement to, a related phenomenon of more primary significance. By the 1960s, a majority of the Justices of the Supreme Court had embraced a previously controversial jurisprudential distinction between ordinary rights and liberties, which the government could regulate upon the showing of any rational justification, and more fundamental or "preferred" liberties that deserved more stringent judicial protection.[1] That distinction had emerged in the aftermath of the *Lochner* era, which had seen the Court in entrenched opposition to progressive wages-and-hours and worker safety legislation and to federal efforts to revive a desperately depressed economy. The *Lochner* era came to a flaming demise in 1937 with the so-called "switch in time that saved the nine." With President Franklin Roosevelt having proposed a Court-packing scheme to salvage his legislative program, the Justices, by five to four votes, upheld major elements of the New Deal program in the spring of 1937. Shortly thereafter, one of the reviled "Four Horsemen," who had most consistently threatened to scuttle the New Deal, resigned from the Court and gave Roosevelt the first of a series of appointments. Within a few years, seven of the nine Justices owed their seats to Roosevelt. In what some political scientists have called the New Deal Settlement, the Age of Roosevelt extended from national politics into constitutional law.

First in opposing and then in remaking the Supreme Court, Roosevelt had a constitutional vision that – following his revamping of the Court's composition – remained substantially unchallenged through the 1940s, 1950s, 1960s, and 1970s. The core tenet of Roosevelt's philosophy viewed the Constitution as a flexible document that conferred broad federal regulatory, taxing, and spending powers adequate to tame the business cycle and create a social safety net. By contrast, the

---

[1]   *See* Roger K. Newman, Hugo Black: A Biography 295–96, 401–02 (2d ed. 1997); Martin Shapiro, FREEDOM OF SPEECH: THE SUPREME COURT AND JUDICIAL Review 58–59 (1966); Gerald Gunther, *The Supreme Court, 1971 Term – Foreword: In Search of Evolving Doctrine on a Changing Court: A Model for a Newer Equal Protection*, 86 HARV. L. REV. 1, 10 (1972) (describing education as a "preferred fundamental interest").

Court of the *Lochner* era had notoriously treated the Due Process Clause as a guarantee of economic liberties. Sometimes on due process and sometimes on Commerce Clause grounds, it had struck down both state and federal economic regulatory legislation in its effort to protect those economic liberties. In cases challenging federal regulatory and taxing authority and presenting claims of economic liberty, the Roosevelt vision called for courts to stand aside. "*Lochner*ism" was a constitutional sin and a fallacy.

The reconstituted, post-*Lochner* Court quickly and decisively established that challenges to economic regulatory legislation would henceforth trigger only all but meaningless rational basis scrutiny. As the Court pursued its anti-*Lochner* agenda, however, it quickly confronted the question of how far the taint of *Lochner*ism extended: In renouncing the protection of economic liberties, should the Court also abandon efforts to enforce rights to freedom of speech and religion, for example? To modern eyes, that question looks easy. To many of those living in 1937 and 1938, matters were more complicated. There was no ready-made model of differentiated constitutional review to apply. According to historians, the then-received tradition not only understood the institution of judicial review, but also the constitutional rights that judicial review enforces, within a conceptual framework that now has largely vanished. To put the point slightly differently, the rights revolution that began in the fight against *Lochner*ism, and from which strict scrutiny later emerged, was conceptual as well as substantive.

Before the collapse of the *Lochner* era in the late 1930s, the Supreme Court appears not to have understood constitutional adjudication as requiring standards of judicial review in the modern sense. Through most of constitutional history, the Court conceived its task as marking the conceptual boundaries that defined spheres of state and congressional power on the one hand and of private rights on the other.[2] Within "classical legal thought," as Duncan Kennedy has termed it, these spheres did not overlap.[3] Given that understanding, the Court did not view itself as weighing or accommodating competing public and private interests, but instead as applying boundary-defining techniques that rendered its analysis "an objective, quasi-scientific one."[4] Insofar as the Court was engaged in conceptual or quasi-scientific analysis for which the judiciary possessed a special competence, its assumptions afforded no justification for greater or lesser degrees of deference to other institutions' judgments concerning where the boundaries lay. To take just one

[2] *See* Duncan Kennedy, *Toward an Historical Understanding of Legal Consciousness: The Case of Classical Legal Thought in America*, 1850–1940, 3 RES. L. & SOC. 3, 6–8 (1980) (noting that the prevailing "legal consciousness" of the era from 1850 to 1940 presupposed the existence of institutional actors, each of which "had been delegated ... a power ... which was absolute within but void outside its sphere," with courts having the responsibility to prevent any institution from usurping power outside its proper sphere); G. Edward White, *Historicizing Judicial Scrutiny*, 57 S.C. L. REV. 1, 44–46 (2005) (describing the emergence of judicial boundary tracing).

[3] Kennedy, *supra* note 2, at 7.

[4] *Id.*

example, courts within the prevailing *Lochner*-era paradigm had no ground to be more or less deferential to claims of governmental authority to regulate economic activity than to regulate speech.[5]

By the beginning of the *Lochner* era, the conceptual presuppositions of classical thought were already under strain as a result of the Court's recognition that assertions of legislative authority must be "reasonable" to come within the boundaries of the states' "police power,"[6] which courts enforced through the Due Process Clause. From the perspective of the twenty-first century, inquiries into the reasonableness of legislation look like the application of a standard of review, but the Court still appears not to have understood its analysis in this way. Rather than viewing reasonableness as a standard of review that could be contrasted with other available standards, or as reflecting a judicially developed gloss on constitutional language, the Court apparently regarded it as a definitional requirement of valid exercises of the police power. Accordingly, although the *Lochner* era's most characteristic reasonableness inquiries involved economic regulatory legislation, the Court frequently framed its analysis in the same terms when assessing the constitutionality of legislation that restricted the exercise of speech[7] or religion[8] or that drew lines on the basis of race.[9] As appears obvious from a modern perspective, the demands of reasonableness can be – and were – understood more or less stringently, even by

---

[5] *See* White, *supra* note 2, at 3–4 ("[F]rom *Marbury* v. *Madison* to *United States* v. *Carolene Products Co.* [in 1938], the Court essentially subjected all challenged decisions of other branches to the same standard of review" (footnotes omitted)).

[6] *See Lochner* v. *New York*, 198 U.S. 45, 56 (1905) (asserting that "there is a limit to the valid exercise of the police power by the State," or else "the Fourteenth Amendment would have no efficacy," and that "the question necessarily arises" for the courts whether an exercise of the police power is "fair, reasonable, and appropriate").

[7] Although the Supreme Court articulated a "clear and present danger" test in *Schenck* v. *United States*, 249 U.S. 47, 52 (1919), it continued to apply a reasonableness test in other cases with First Amendment overtones, including *Meyer* v. *Nebraska*, 262 U.S. 390, 399–400 (1923), which struck down a state law that prohibited the teaching of foreign languages to young children, and *Pierce* v. *Society of Sisters*, 268 U.S. 510, 534–35 (1925), which invalidated a statute requiring parents to send their children to public schools. *See generally Thomas* v. *Collins*, 323 U.S. 516, 531 (1945) (citing *Meyer* and *Pierce* as establishing that "[t]he First Amendment gives freedom of mind the same security as freedom of conscience"). In *Whitney* v. *California*, 274 U.S. 357 (1927), overruled by *Brandenburg* v. *Ohio*, 395 U.S. 444 (1969), Justice Brandeis's concurring opinion appeared to assimilate the clear and present danger test at least partly to a reasonableness inquiry: "[T]here must be reasonable ground to fear that serious evil will result ... [And t]here must be reasonable ground to believe that the danger apprehended is imminent." *Id.* at 376 (Brandeis, J., concurring).

[8] Throughout the *Lochner* era, the Court adhered to the categorical approach of *Reynolds* v. *United States*, 98 U.S. 145, 166 (1879), which held that although the Free Exercise Clause protected belief, it did not protect conduct. Within this framework, the only possible protection against laws that impinged on the free exercise of religion came from the reasonableness test applied under the Due Process and Equal Protection Clauses.

[9] *See, e.g., Gong Lum* v. *Rice*, 275 U.S. 78, 85–86 (1927) (holding that school officials did not violate equal protection by requiring a child of Chinese ancestry to attend "a school which receives only colored children"); *Chiles* v. *Chesapeake & Ohio Ry. Co.*, 218 U.S. 71, 77 (1910) (permitting segregated railway cars and stating that "[r]egulations which are induced by the general sentiment of the community for whom they are made and upon whom they operate cannot be said to be

different judges or Justices in the same case.[10] Results were far from predictable. The Court upheld more legislation than it found invalid.[11] Seldom if ever, however, did either Court majorities or dissenting Justices suggest that whereas some exercises of the police power were within the boundaries of state authority as long as they were reasonable in the independent judgment of the courts, others should be subjected to more or less exacting judicial scrutiny.[12]

By 1937, *Lochner*-style reasonableness review of economic regulatory legislation had become practically and politically untenable, in part because the classical assumption that clear, apolitical boundaries separated the sphere of governmental powers from that of private rights had ceased to be credible.[13] In a series of decisions that would shape constitutional doctrine for decades to come, the Court, beginning in 1937, famously and emphatically abandoned its previous approach to economic regulatory legislation[14] in favor of a far more deferential rational basis review.[15] As the Court did so, however, two closely related questions loomed. First, would all claims of constitutional right henceforth trigger no more than an all but meaningless rational basis inquiry? Second, if not, would the otherwise discredited *Lochner* style of inquiry – premised on the notion that there are conceptual limits to legislative powers that courts have a distinctive capacity to ascertain through quasi-scientific legal reasoning – persist unaltered in pockets of constitutional law?

In response, the Court first tentatively and then more pointedly staked out the possibility that some constitutional rights might merit more judicial protection than economic liberties. In a celebrated footnote in the 1938 decision in *United States* v. *Carolene Products Co.*,[16] Justice Harlan Fiske Stone cited the rights listed in the Bill of Rights, rights crucial to the operation of the political process, and the rights of "discrete and insular minorities" to be free from discrimination as leading candidates to warrant "exacting judicial scrutiny."[17] Other cases shortly signaled the Court's developing position by insisting that a slightly narrower range of rights –

unreasonable"). According to Michael Klarman, *Korematsu* was almost entirely unprecedented in its declaration that race-based discriminations were categorically "suspect," and even in *Korematsu*, Klarman writes, "the Court actually applied its most deferential brand of rationality review." Michael J. Klarman, *An Interpretive History of Modern Equal Protection*, 90 MICH. L. REV. 213, 232 (1991).

[10] *See* Kennedy, *supra* note 2, at 12 (noting that, in *Lochner*, the majority opinion and Justice Harlan's dissent "employ[ed] exactly the same conceptual structure").

[11] *See* Laurence H. Tribe, AMERICAN CONSTITUTIONAL LAW §8–2, at 567 n.2 (2d ed. 1988).

[12] *See* White, *supra* note 2, at 3 (noting that it would be "misleading" to describe the Court's approach to judicial review as reflecting a particular level of scrutiny "because no other levels of scrutiny existed").

[13] *See id.* at 65 (reporting that, by the 1930s, "the increasingly refined doctrinal distinctions that the Court had fashioned ... appeared on the brink of collapse" and "provided additional evidence of their ideological character to the Court's critics").

[14] *See, e.g., United States* v. *Carolene Prods. Co.*, 304 U.S. 144, 152 (1938); *W. Coast Hotel Co.* v. *Parrish*, 300 U.S. 379, 397–99 (1937).

[15] *See, e.g., Olsen* v. *Nebraska ex rel. W. Reference & Bond Ass'n*, 313 U.S. 236, 246 (1941) ("We are not concerned ... with the wisdom, need, or appropriateness of the legislation.").

[16] 304 U.S. 144, 152 n.4 (1938).

[17] *Id.* at 152–53 n.4.

including the First Amendment rights of speech, association, and religion – enjoyed a "preferred position" and thus merited solicitous judicial protection.

As a historical matter, the Court's first reference to rights occupying a preferred position came in its 1942 decision in *Jones* v. *City of Opelika*[18] in an opinion by Chief Justice Stone, the author of the *Carolene Products* footnote.[19] "The First Amendment is not confined to safeguarding freedom of speech and freedom of religion against discriminatory attempts to wipe them out," the Chief Justice wrote.[20] "On the contrary the Constitution, by virtue of the First and the Fourteenth Amendments, has put those freedoms in a preferred position."[21] The Court echoed the language of "preferred position" in *Murdock* v. *Pennsylvania*[22] in 1943 and again in *Marsh* v. *Alabama*[23] in 1946: "When we balance the Constitutional rights of owners of property against those of the people to enjoy freedom of press and religion, as we must here, we remain mindful of the fact that the latter occupy a preferred position."[24] The Court also insisted that First Amendment rights merit stringent judicial protection in Justice Robert Jackson's iconic opinion in *West Virginia State Board of Education* v. *Barnette*:[25]

> The right of a State to regulate, for example, a public utility may well include, so far as the due process test is concerned, power to impose all of the restrictions which a legislature may have a "rational basis" for adopting. But freedoms of speech and of press, of assembly, and of worship may not be infringed on such slender grounds.[26]

Although decisions such as *Marsh* and *Barnette* reached famously speech-protective results, their methodology still bore little resemblance to that of modern courts applying strict judicial scrutiny. The Court's methodology involved a case-by-case balancing of free speech interests against competing governmental interests, as Justice Black explicitly stated in *Marsh*: "When we balance the Constitutional rights of owners of property against those of the people to enjoy freedom of press and religion, as we must here, we remain mindful of the fact that the latter occupy a preferred position."[27] Obviously, however, balancing – which can be very ad hoc, and need not involve any advance assignment of weights to either individual or competing governmental interests – could take more or less speech-protective forms. In deploying a

---

[18]   316 U.S. 584 (1942).
[19]   *See id.* at 608 (Stone, C.J., dissenting). The opinion was first published as a dissent but then adopted as the opinion of the Court following a rehearing. *See Jones* v. *City of Opelika*, 319 U.S. 103, 104 (1943) (per curiam).
[20]   *Jones*, 316 U.S. at 608.
[21]   *Id.*
[22]   319 U.S. 105 (1943).
[23]   326 U.S. 501 (1946).
[24]   *Id.* at 509.
[25]   319 U.S. 624 (1943).
[26]   *Id.* at 639.
[27]   326 U.S. at 509.

balancing methodology to protect speech rights during the 1940s, Justices disposed to protect speech in a relatively vigorous way held the upper hand.

Then in 1949 Justices Frank Murphy and Wiley Rutledge died, to be replaced by Tom Clark and Sherman Minton. With this change of personnel, the locus of power shifted. In a number of cases the Court began to balance more deferentially.[28] As the Court did so, its commitment to strong protection for fundamental rights came into question.

For a time, even the view that some constitutional rights were more preferred than economic liberties did not enjoy a secure position. In a concurring opinion in *Kovacs v. Cooper*[29] in 1949, Justice Felix Frankfurter attempted to debunk an appeal to the First Amendment's "preferred position" as relying on a "mischievous phrase."[30] Consistent with that view, he called for strong judicial deference to legislative judgments even in free speech cases.

Although destined not to prevail, Frankfurter's stance possessed a powerful internal logic, premised on the recognition that many if not most constitutional cases involve conflicts of or competition among values. The metaphor of balancing, which the Court had embraced in some of its early preferred-position cases, expresses that recognition. But the realist insight that courts must weigh competing values or interests poses a problem of justification for the judicial role in constitutional cases. If the Court was simply going to *balance* interests, much as the legislature presumably had balanced interests when it enacted a challenged statute, then why should the Court not defer to the legislative judgment about how the balance should be struck as much in free speech cases as in those involving economic liberties?

If any case epitomizes the problem that Justice Frankfurter framed – and to which the strict scrutiny test emerged as a partial response – that case might be *Dennis v. United States*.[31] *Dennis* was a free speech case, arising under the First Amendment, which says that "Congress shall make no law abridging the freedom of speech." At issue were the convictions of leaders of the Communist Party of the United States for various speech-related activities.

Although the First Amendment speaks in absolute terms, an eminently pedigreed line of reasoning had long held that it could not mean what it said. As Justice Holmes had written more than thirty years earlier, even the strongest partisan of free speech understands that it cannot protect false cries of fire in a crowded theater.[32]

Writing for a plurality but not a majority of the Justices in *Dennis*, Chief Justice Fred M. Vinson adapted the "clear and present danger" test that Holmes had

---

[28] See Stephen A. Siegel, *The Death and Rebirth of the Clear and Present Danger Test*, in Transformations in American Legal History 210, 217–20 (Daniel W. Hamilton & Alfred L. Brophy eds., 2009).

[29] 336 U.S. 77 (1949).

[30] *Id.* at 90 (Frankfurter, J., concurring).

[31] 341 U.S. 494 (1951).

[32] *Schenck v. United States*, 249 U.S. 47, 52 (1919).

developed for accommodating competing interests. Under it, interests supporting the protection of political speech should prevail over competing governmental interests absent "a clear and present danger that [speech] will bring about ... substantive evils that Congress has a right to prevent."[33] But Vinson's adaptation gutted the clear and present danger test of any substantial protective force. In his reformulation, the question became "whether the gravity of the 'evil,' discounted by its improbability, justifies such invasion of free speech as is necessary to avoid the danger."[34] In the fearful times of the Cold War, only two Justices resisted that conclusion that Communist Party leaders could be jailed for their speech and political organizing.

Justice Hugo Black stood with Justice William O. Douglas in dissent. Although Black had himself applied a "balancing" methodology in writing for the Court in *Marsh* v. *Alabama*, by the time of *Dennis* he had rethought his methodological position. Setting himself against the "free speech balancers" and the champions of a clear and present danger test, Black began to insist that the First Amendment conferred "absolute" protections. In *Dennis*, for example, he wrote that the Amendment's language did not "permit[] us to sustain laws suppressing freedom of speech and press on the basis of Congress' or our own notions of mere 'reasonableness.'"[35]

In making assertions about what the First Amendment permitted and forbade, Black was a proto-originalist, who often depicted himself as merely implementing decisions that the Founding generation had made through its adoption of the Free Speech Clause. As a purely historical matter, Black's claims of fidelity to original constitutional meaning seem dubious. Many historians contend that the Founders had a narrow view of the Free Speech Clause's protective ambit.[36] In 1798, congressional majorities and President John Adams viewed the First Amendment as no impediment to enactment of the Sedition Act, which made it a crime to criticize the President.[37] But the Sedition Act was controversial even in its time, viewed by many as partisan legislation directed against critics of the Federalist Party. History's verdict is that the Sedition Act was unconstitutional. But however one judges the history, Black had a contemporary worry. "Public opinion being what it now is," he wrote,

---

[33] *Id.*

[34] *Dennis*, 341 U.S. at 510 (quoting *United States* v. *Dennis*, 183 F.2d 201, 212 (2d Cir. 1950) (L. Hand, J.)).

[35] *Id.* at 580 (Black, J., dissenting).

[36] *See, e.g.,* Akhil Reed Amar, THE BILL OF RIGHTS: CREATION AND RECONSTRUCTION 23–24 (1998); Phillip I. Blumberg, REPRESSIVE JURISPRUDENCE IN THE EARLY AMERICAN REPUBLIC: THE FIRST AMENDMENT AND THE LEGACY OF ENGLISH LAW 4–6 (2010); Leonard W. Levy, EMERGENCE OF A FREE PRESS 204–05 (1985); Philip B. Kurland, *The Original Understanding of the Freedom of the Press Provision of the First Amendment*, 55 MISS. L.J. 225, 234–38 (1985). More recently, revisionist histories have depicted Founding era expectations that the Free Speech Clause would have a broader sweep but that it would not preclude regulations reasonably thought to protect the public interest. *See, e.g.,* Genevieve Lakier, *The Invention of Low-Value Speech*, 128 HARV. L. REV. 2167 (2015); Jud Campbell, *Natural Rights and the First Amendment*, 127 YALE L.J. 246 (2017).

[37] Alien and Sedition Acts of 1798, ch. 74, § 2, 1 Stat. 596 (expired 1801).

"few will protest the conviction of these Communist petitioners," and few might protest the suppression of speech by other critics of the prevailing political and cultural order. Short of free speech absolutism, Black worried that the Court would never ensure "First Amendment liberties ... the high preferred place where they belong in a free society."[38]

Although couched in partially instrumental terms in *Dennis*, Black's views about the First Amendment reflected his emerging jurisprudential philosophy or theory of the proper judicial role. In First Amendment and non-First Amendment cases alike, Black sought to carve out a judicial function that he thought posed no problems of justification or, as some would put it, of judicial legitimacy. In his view, the Court behaved legitimately when it enforced the judgments that the Constitution's Framers and ratifiers had made and that he thought the people of the United States had subsequently accepted. All agreed that the Constitution was law. And as Black saw it, upholding the Constitution as law required adhering to its literal meaning as read against the background of history.

Although Black had not worked out his proto-originalism in the same depth and detail as some current-day originalists, his judicial philosophy provided a two-edged discipline. In cases such as *Dennis*, it steeled courts to uphold constitutional rights. In others, however, it explained why courts should not, as he put it, "invent" them.[39] Black evidenced this view most stridently in "substantive due process" cases, in which some of his colleagues were prepared to hold that invasions of "unenumerated" but nevertheless fundamental rights were unconstitutional if conscience-shocking or severely unfair. The most reviled decisions of the *Lochner* era had employed a substantive due process methodology, which Black would have nothing to do with. Later in his career, he stuck to his guns by dissenting from a ruling that the government may not bar the use of contraceptives by married couples.[40]

Justice Frankfurter, who despised Black for personal reasons,[41] rejected Black's position on every point. Besides insisting that deferential balancing was appropriate in free speech disputes, Frankfurter seemed to feel secure that no serious issue of judicial legitimacy could arise even in substantive due process cases as long as courts were wise and restrained in their decisions about whether to invalidate legislation. Frankfurter gave a celebrated statement of his view in *Rochin* v. *California*, in which he held that police conduct that "shocks the conscience" – such as pumping the stomach of a criminal suspect in an effort to retrieve evidence – violates the Due Process Clause:

---

[38] *Dennis*, 341 U.S. at 581 (Black, J., dissenting).
[39] *See, e.g., Griswold* v. *Connecticut*, 381 U.S. 479, 507–27 (1965) (Black, J., dissenting).
[40] See *id.*
[41] *See, e.g.,* Noah Feldman, SCORPIONS: THE BATTLES AND TRIUMPHS OF FDR'S GREAT SUPREME COURT JUSTICES 384–85 (2010); Michael Kammen, A MACHINE THAT WOULD GO OF ITSELF: THE CONSTITUTION IN AMERICAN CULTURE 323 (2006).

The vague contours of the Due Process Clause do not leave judges at large. We may not draw on our merely personal and private notions and disregard the limits that bind judges in their judicial function ... To practice the requisite detachment and to achieve sufficient objectivity no doubt demands of judges the habit of self-discipline and self-criticism, incertitude that one's own views are incontestable and alert tolerance toward views not shared. But these are precisely the presuppositions of our judicial process. They are precisely the qualities society has a right to expect from those entrusted with ultimate judicial power.[42]

With Black and Frankfurter having staked out cleanly coherent polar positions, both about free speech cases and about the Supreme Court's role more generally, most of the other Justices offered no clear and consistent answers to either the methodological or the legitimacy issues that the dueling rivals framed. With the Court having no clear center of gravity, Justice Frankfurter wrote for Court majorities in *Beauharnais v. Illinois*,[43] which upheld a group libel statute, and *Kingsley Books, Inc. v. Brown*,[44] which sustained a state court's imposition of a prior restraint against the distribution of obscene materials. In neither case did the Court apply any exacting form of review.

Gradually, however, the preferred position view – which marked one of the divisions between Justices Black and Frankfurter, albeit not the only one – regained its ascendency. By the end of the 1950s and the early 1960s, academic commentators had no doubt that the Warren Court regarded some rights as more "preferred"[45] than others and applied a "double standard" depending on the nature of the right at stake.[46] But the Court still lacked sharply edged doctrinal formulae for protecting most preferred rights, even under the First Amendment. Moreover, in the domain of free speech, in particular, it was clear that balancing, in the end, was no more protective of speech than the Justices were prepared to make it in particular cases.[47]

---

[42] 342 U.S. 165, 170–72 (1952) (footnote omitted).

[43] 343 U.S. 250 (1952).

[44] 354 U.S. 436 (1957).

[45] *See, e.g.*, Robert B. McKay, *The Preference for Freedom*, 34 N.Y.U. L. REV. 1182, 1189–91, 1223–27 (1959) (describing the emergence of the primacy of First Amendment rights during the 1930s, 1940s, and 1950s).

[46] *See* Gunther, *supra* note 1, at 37; Robert G. McCloskey, *Economic Due Process and the Supreme Court: An Exhumation and Reburial*, SUP. CT. REV. 34, 40–41 (1962).

[47] Apart from free speech cases, the crystallizing commitment of the Warren Court to a substantially two-tiered scheme of constitutional rights – with some protected only by rational basis review, which scarcely amounted to any review at all, while others received more stringent protection – also rang through the Court's "incorporation" decisions, which sought to determine which provisions of the Bill of Rights were sufficiently "fundamental" to have been made applicable against the states by the Fourteenth Amendment. *Compare, e.g.*, Duncan v. Louisiana, 391 U.S. 145, 162–66, 166 n.1 (1968) (Black, J., concurring) (advocating incorporation), *with id.* at 171–73 (Harlan, J., dissenting) (disputing the notion that the Fourteenth Amendment incorporates the entire Bill of Rights). For further commentaries on the incorporation debates, *see* Charles Fairman, *Does the Fourteenth Amendment Incorporate the Bill of Rights? The Original Understanding*, 2 STAN. L. REV. 5 (1949); Louis Henkin, *"Selective Incorporation" in the Fourteenth Amendment*, 73 YALE L.J. 74 (1963); Stanley Morrison, *Does the Fourteenth Amendment Incorporate the Bill of Rights? The Judicial*

As the Warren Court struggled internally about how best to protect preferred rights, it also faced external challenges. Powerful voices from both the legal establishment – centrally including the eminent federal judge Learned Hand – and the academic community prominently accused the Court of lacking methodological discipline and, more fundamentally, of overstepping the defensible bounds of judicial authority in a constitutional democracy.[48] Much of the criticism undoubtedly reflected unease about the Court's decision in *Brown* v. *Board of Education*,[49] which upset nearly a century of settled southern expectations surrounding the permissibility of school segregation. But indictments of the Warren Court for judicial activism, among other sins, ran both broader and deeper.[50] Some of those raising their concerns most vocally were disciples of Justice Frankfurter – his former students in some cases, his former law clerks in others. At least some of the criticism stung. After receiving a frosty reception at a 1957 meeting in London of the American Bar Association, Chief Justice Earl Warren resigned his membership.[51]

THE EMERGENCE OF STRICT SCRUTINY

It was in this context that strict scrutiny emerged during the 1960s as the Supreme Court's most characteristic test for defining and enforcing preferred or fundamental constitutional rights. The now canonical strict scrutiny formula – defined by paired requirements that the government defend infringements on fundamental rights by showing a "compelling" governmental interest to which an infringement is "narrowly tailored" – emerged gradually, indeed almost imperceptibly. Its specific origins are impossible to pinpoint, the pattern of its proliferation difficult to trace. Justice Anthony Kennedy has spoken of the migration of the strict scrutiny formula from equal protection to first amendment cases.[52] By contrast, Justice John Harlan, in the 1964 case of *McLaughlin* v. *Florida*,[53] sought to explain why "[t]he necessity test," which he thought "developed to protect free speech against state infringement[,] should be equally applicable in a case

Interpretation, 2 STAN. L. REV. 140 (1949). Specifically at stake in the incorporation debates was whether some rights deserved more judicial protection against possible infringement by the states than did others. *See* White, *supra* note 2, 65–68 (2005) (noting the importance of incorporation cases to the Supreme Court's development of tiers of judicial scrutiny).

[48]   *See* Barry Friedman, THE WILL OF THE PEOPLE 256–57 (2009).
[49]   347 U.S. 483 (1954).
[50]   *See* Friedman, *supra* note 48, at 254–58.
[51]   *Id.* at 256.
[52]   *See Simon & Schuster, Inc.* v. *Members of the N.Y. State Crime Victims Bd.*, 502 U.S. 105, 124–28 (1991) (Kennedy, J., concurring in the judgment); *see also* Peter J. Rubin, *Reconnecting Doctrine and Purpose: A Comprehensive Approach to Strict Scrutiny after Adarand and Shaw*, 149 U. PA. L. REV. 1, 3 n.1 (2000) (asserting that "the formal concept of strict scrutiny developed in the area of equal protection").
[53]   379 U.S. 184 (1964).

involving state racial discrimination."[54] A case could also be made that the modern strict scrutiny test has proximate origins in other doctrines as well. All that can be said with unequivocal confidence is that the modern formula evolved simultaneously in a number of doctrinal areas – and, intriguingly, did so within less than a decade. Whereas before the 1960s, there was no strict scrutiny as we know it today, by the end of the decade it dominated numerous fields of constitutional law.

Doctrine Involving Race-Based Classifications

Among the strands of doctrine forming the early history of strict judicial scrutiny, one involved race-based classifications under the Equal Protection Clause and, in cases challenging actions by the federal government, under the Due Process Clause of the Fifth Amendment. For nearly 100 years after the ratification of the Equal Protection Clause, the Supreme Court tolerated a regime of "separate but equal." In 1954, *Brown v. Board of Education*[55] held that "in the field of public education the doctrine of 'separate but equal' has no place."[56] But in framing its conclusion in this way, *Brown* stopped short of articulating any general standard of review of race-based classifications. Indeed, a reader of *Brown* – which heavily emphasized the distinctive features of public education in explaining why segregation was impermissible – could easily have concluded that "separate but equal" accommodations could continue "with respect to common carrier and public recreational facilities."[57]

Bolling v. Sharpe,[58] a companion case to *Brown* that invalidated segregation by the federal government in its operation of the District of Columbia schools, hinted at broader implications. In language that can be seen in retrospect as anticipating the modern approach, the Court said that "[c]lassifications based solely upon race must be scrutinized with particular care, since they are contrary to our traditions"[59] and thus, the Court added, are "constitutionally suspect."[60] As authority for this broader proposition, the Court cited the 1944 decision in *Korematsu v. United States*,[61] which also included language that can be seen as anticipating what we now call strict scrutiny. In reviewing a World War II military order excluding all persons of Japanese descent from designated areas of the West Coast, Justice Hugo Black began the Court's opinion by declaring –

[54] *Id.* at 197 (Harlan, J., concurring); Stephen A. Siegel, *The Origin of the Compelling State Interest Test and Strict Scrutiny*, 48 AM. J. LEGAL HIST. 355, 356 (2006) (largely agreeing with Justice Harlan that strict scrutiny originated in the First Amendment context).
[55] 347 U.S. 483 (1954).
[56] *Id.* at 495.
[57] Paul G. Kauper, *Segregation in Public Education: The Decline of* Plessy v. Ferguson, 52 MICH. L. REV. 1137, 1154 (1954).
[58] 347 U.S. 497 (1954).
[59] *Id.* at 499.
[60] *Id.*
[61] 323 U.S. 214 (1944).

without citation of precedent – that "all legal restrictions which curtail the civil rights of a single racial group are immediately suspect" and that "courts must subject them to the most rigid scrutiny."[62] But Black's analysis belied his words. Having promised searching judicial review, he upheld the exclusion order on the basis of no evidence besides what Justice Jackson, writing in dissent, termed the "unsworn, self-serving statement, untested by any cross-examination," of the general who had ordered the exclusion.[63]

In the evolution of constitutional doctrine, perhaps the biggest step toward the modern test in race-discrimination cases came in *McLaughlin v. Florida*[64] in 1964. *McLaughlin* involved a challenge under the Equal Protection Clause to a Florida statute that forbade the habitual occupation of a room at night by "[a]ny negro man and white woman, or any white man and negro woman," who were not married to each other.[65] *McLaughlin* pronounced all race-based classifications "constitutionally suspect," quoting *Bolling*,[66] and "subject to the 'most rigid scrutiny,'" citing *Korematsu*.[67] Laws embodying race-based classifications could be upheld, the Court said, "only if ... necessary, and not merely rationally related, to the accomplishment of a permissible state policy."[68] This language approaches the modern formulation, but omits the demand for a "compelling" state interest – a requirement that a Supreme Court majority first formally articulated in a race discrimination case, *Palmore v. Sidoti*,[69] in 1984.

Intervening between *McLaughlin* and *Palmore*, however, was *Regents of the University of California v. Bakke*,[70] in which Justice Lewis Powell's controlling opinion, much of which was joined by no other Justice, expressly applied what he called "strict"[71] or "the most exacting scrutiny"[72] to gauge the permissibility of an affirmative action program. A case could thus be made that the first application of strict scrutiny in a race case involved affirmative action.

Bakke aside, Justice Kennedy presumably had *McLaughlin v. Florida* in mind, and possibly also *Bolling* and *Korematsu*, when he claimed that the modern version of strict scrutiny had emerged in cases involving race discrimination and had migrated to First Amendment doctrine. But that claim obviously cannot be judged without looking at developments in other areas.

---

[62] *Id.* at 215.
[63] *Id.* at 245 (Jackson, J., dissenting).
[64] 379 U.S. 184 (1964).
[65] *Id.* at 184 (quoting Fla. Stat. § 798.05 (repealed 1969)).
[66] *Id.* at 192 (quoting *Bolling v. Sharpe*, 347 U.S. 497, 499 (1954)).
[67] *Id.* (quoting *Korematsu v. United States*, 323 U.S. 214, 216 (1944)).
[68] *Id.* at 196.
[69] 466 U.S. 429 (1984).
[70] 438 U.S. 265 (1978).
[71] *Id.* at 290 (opinion of Powell, J.).
[72] *Id.* at 300.

Free Speech Cases

As noted already, Justice Harlan's concurring opinion in *McLaughlin* defended the Court's application of a test – which he termed "[t]he necessity test" – that he described as having emerged in prior cases "to protect free speech."[73] In fact, free speech cases in the years before *McLaughlin* could helpfully have been divided into two categories, of which Justice Harlan drew attention only to one. The cases cited by Justice Harlan had made clear that speech is a right of special importance and had ruled, accordingly, that broad restrictions would not be permitted when narrower restrictions would adequately protect the government's underlying interests.[74] In these cases the Court seldom if ever made a formal demand that a regulation be "necessary" to promote a valid state interest, as Justice Harlan appeared to imply. Nonetheless, he offered a fair summary of the cases' import: Free speech decisions prior to *McLaughlin* had required that restrictions of speech satisfy what would today be regarded as the "necessity" or "narrow tailoring" prong of the strict scrutiny test.[75] But those decisions said nothing about "compelling" government interests.

In another subcategory of free speech cases that Justice Harlan did not cite, the Supreme Court had begun before *McLaughlin* to articulate a position that would eventually evolve into the "compelling interest" prong of strict scrutiny. In the 1958 case of *Speiser* v. *Randall*,[76] the Court had pointed expressly to the absence of any "compelling" state interest to justify its ruling that the state of California could not maintain a scheme for the assignment of tax exemptions "which must inevitably result in suppressing protected speech."[77] The Court again applied a compelling interest test in *NAACP* v. *Button*,[78] decided in 1963, in which it held that a Virginia statute barring the solicitation of legal business could not constitutionally be applied

---

[73] 379 U.S. at 197 (Harlan, J., concurring).

[74] *See id.* (citing *NAACP* v. *Alabama*, 377 U.S. 288, 307 (1964) (remarking that "a governmental purpose to control or prevent activities constitutionally subject to state regulation may not be achieved by means which sweep unnecessarily broadly"); *Saia* v. *New York*, 334 U.S. 558, 562 (1948) (requiring that instrumentalities of public speech "be controlled by narrowly drawn statutes"); *Martin* v. *City of Struthers*, 319 U.S. 141, 147 (1943) (stating that the distribution of information "can so easily be controlled by traditional legal methods . . . that stringent prohibition can serve no purpose but that forbidden by the Constitution, the naked restriction of the dissemination of ideas"); *Thornhill* v. *Alabama*, 310 U.S. 88, 96 (1940) (directing courts to "'weigh the circumstances' and 'appraise the substantiality of the reason advanced' in support of" regulations that abridge First Amendment freedoms (quoting *Schneider* v. *New Jersey*, 308 U.S. 147, 161, 162 (1939))); *Schneider*, 308 U.S. at 161, 162, 164 (same); *McGowan* v. *Maryland*, 366 U.S. 420, 466–67 (1961) (Frankfurter, J., concurring) (stating that a statute that "furthers both secular and religious ends," but does so by means that unnecessarily promote religion, should be declared unconstitutional)). On the history of the narrow tailoring and related requirements in First Amendment jurisprudence, see Note, *Less Drastic Means and the First Amendment*, 78 YALE L.J. 464 (1969), and Siegel, *supra* note 54.

[75] *See McLaughlin*, 397 U.S. at 197 (Harlan, J., concurring) (arguing that the "statute has not been shown to be necessary to the integrity of the [relevant] law, assumed arguendo to be valid, and that necessity, not mere reasonable relationship, is the proper test").

[76] 357 U.S. 513 (1958).

[77] *Id.* at 529.

[78] 371 U.S. 415 (1963).

to the NAACP's activities in promoting equal-rights litigation on the ground that "only a compelling state interest ... can justify limiting First Amendment freedoms."[79] Indeed, *Button* also prefigured the modern narrow tailoring requirement when it stated: "Broad prophylactic rules in the area of free expression are suspect. Precision of regulation must be the touchstone in an area so closely touching our most precious freedoms."[80]

When the various strands of free speech doctrine are seen in conjunction, it is certainly fair to say that before the 1964 *McLaughlin* decision, First Amendment free speech cases had begun to develop both a vocabulary and a related set of doctrinal ideas that would shortly coalesce into the modern strict scrutiny test. There were free speech cases anticipating the "necessity" or "narrow tailoring" prong, and other cases anticipating the "compelling interest" requirement. In *NAACP* v. *Button*, the Supreme Court had even begun to bring the two together, though still without employing all of the vocabulary by which modern strict scrutiny is defined.

Freedom of Association Cases

Although Justice Harlan spoke indiscriminately in *McLaughlin* of "free speech cases" that had established the "necessity" test, one of the cases that he cited, the 1958 decision in *NAACP* v. *Alabama ex rel. Patterson*,[81] involved freedom of association. In that case, the Court invalidated a judicial order requiring the NAACP to disclose the names and addresses of its Alabama members. If anything, by the time of *McLaughlin* in 1964, the Court had come closer to the modern strict scrutiny formulation in freedom of association cases than in cases involving direct restraints on speech. In several decisions during the 1950s, majority opinions insisted that only a "compelling" interest could justify infringements on constitutional rights to freedom of association, albeit in cases in which the Court actually applied a relatively deferential balancing test and found no constitutional violation.[82] But the Court gave a more robust interpretation of the compelling interest requirement in 1960 decisions in *Bates* v. *City of Little Rock*,[83] which held unconstitutional a demand that an Arkansas branch of the NAACP divulge its membership list, and in *Shelton* v. *Tucker*,[84] which similarly invalidated an Arkansas statute requiring teachers to file annual reports listing all organizations to which they belonged.[85] *Bates* further

---

79 *Id.* at 438.
80 *Id.* (citations omitted). *Button* also involved freedom of association claims. *See id.* at 438–39.
81 357 U.S. 449 (1958).
82 *See, e.g., Barenblatt* v. *United States*, 360 U.S. 109, 127 (1959) (citing *Sweezy* v. *New Hampshire*, 354 U.S. 234, 255, 265 (1957) (Frankfurter, J., concurring in the result)); *Uphaus* v. *Wyman*, 360 U.S. 72, 81 (1959).
83 361 U.S. 516 (1960).
84 364 U.S. 479 (1960).
85 Among the points of interest about *Shelton* is that the petitioners' brief in the case included language that anticipates the modern strict scrutiny test: "[T]he statute does not meet the constitutional test of

anticipated the modern strict scrutiny formulation by saying that even if a compelling government interest existed, the Court would need to examine whether there was a "reasonable relationship" between the statute's burdens on free association and the compelling interest that those burdens were purportedly designed to promote.[86]

The Supreme Court echoed *Bates*'s language and approach in several subsequent cases, including *Gibson* v. *Florida Legislative Investigation Committee*,[87] decided in 1963. As had *Bates*, *Gibson* found no constitutionally sufficient justification for a requirement – imposed in *Gibson* by a committee of the Florida legislature – that the NAACP disclose its membership list.[88] Again echoing *Bates*, *Gibson* also probed the connection between the state's ends, whether compelling or not, and the means that it had chosen to promote those ends.[89] In order to justify its demand for information, *Gibson* said, the state must "convincingly show a substantial relation between the information sought and a subject of overriding and compelling state interest."[90]

Free Exercise Doctrine

If the Court came close to applying the modern requirements of strict scrutiny in *Gibson*, it achieved comparable proximity in *Sherbert* v. *Verner*,[91] a 1963 case under the Free Exercise Clause. Sherbert lost her job when she refused to work on Saturday, the Sabbath day of her Seventh Day Adventist faith. When she applied for unemployment compensation, the South Carolina Employment Security Commission denied her claim on the ground that her unemployment was voluntary, occasioned not by the absence of any suitable job but by her refusal to work on Saturday.[92] In response, Sherbert claimed that by denying her unemployment benefits because she engaged in conduct mandated by her religious faith, the state violated the Free Exercise Clause. In an opinion by Justice William Brennan, the Supreme Court agreed with Sherbert. By denying unemployment benefits, Brennan reasoned, the state imposed a "substantial infringement" on Sherbert's free exercise

---

imposing the narrowest restriction on individual freedom that is necessary to meet the supposed evil." Brief for Petitioners at 10, *Shelton*, 364 U.S. 479 (1960) (Nos. 14, 83), 1960 WL 98558, at *10. A Westlaw search of briefs for Supreme Court cases before 1970 that contained "compelling" in the same sentence as "interest" and also contained a variation of the words "narrow" or "necessary" produced 287 hits, but of these only the brief in *Shelton* proposed a test close to the modern strict scrutiny formula.

[86] *Bates*, 361 U.S. at 525.

[87] 372 U.S. 539 (1963).

[88] *Id.* at 540 (describing the order for the NAACP to produce its membership list); *id.* at 557 (finding no compelling governmental interest).

[89] *See id.* at 546–50.

[90] *Id.* at 546.

[91] 374 U.S. 398 (1963).

[92] *See id.* at 399–402.

of her religion.[93] Such an infringement, he wrote, could be justified only by "some compelling state interest" and a demonstration that "no alternative forms of regulation would combat" the evils that the state sought to prevent "without infringing First Amendment rights."[94] This formulation does not employ the precise language now associated with strict scrutiny, but it includes the modern test's central conceptual elements: It insists that the government cannot infringe on First Amendment rights without demonstrating an unusually powerful justifying interest and without further showing that its restriction is necessary or narrowly tailored to promote that interest.

Infringements on "Fundamental" Rights under the Equal Protection Clause

The Supreme Court has held that strict scrutiny can be triggered under the Equal Protection Clause on either of two bases: when a statute employs a suspect classification such as race or, alternatively, when a statute employs an otherwise non-suspect classification to limit the exercise of a "fundamental" right. The Court's first use of the term "strict scrutiny" in anything like the modern sense came in a case in the second, fundamental rights category: *Skinner v. Oklahoma*.[95] *Skinner*, which was decided in 1942, arose from a state statute providing for the mandatory sterilization of some, but not other, three-time felons. Writing for the Court, Justice William O. Douglas appeared to assume that the statute could survive the highly deferential "rational basis review" normally applied under the Equal Protection Clause. If the state had drawn its lines among offenses and offenders solely to impose longer prison terms on some than on others, the Court would presumably have ruled that the state's distinctions could not be adjudged wholly irrational and would have upheld them. But mere rational basis review was inappropriate, the Court suggested, because the challenged statute infringed upon the right to procreate – "one of the basic civil rights of man" that was "fundamental to the very existence and survival of the race."[96] As seen through the lens of subsequent developments, *Skinner*'s crucial innovation was to identify a "fundamental" right – in this case, that of procreation – that was not traceable to any specifically "enumerated" constitutional guarantee, such as the First Amendment. In place of rational basis review, "strict scrutiny of the classification which a State makes in a sterilization law is essential," the Court said, "lest unwittingly, or otherwise, invidious discriminations are made against groups or types of individuals in violation of the constitutional guaranty of just and equal laws."[97]

Although *Skinner* was a potentially path-breaking decision, opening the way for strict scrutiny of statutory classifications distributing and withdrawing other

---

[93]   *Id.* at 406.
[94]   *Id.* at 406–07.
[95]   *Skinner v. Oklahoma ex rel. Williamson*, 316 U.S. 535 (1942).
[96]   *Id.* at 541.
[97]   *Id.*

"fundamental" but non-enumerated rights, *Skinner* did not pause to specify what "strict scrutiny" entailed. Nor did the Supreme Court give sustained attention to the criteria for identifying fundamental rights that might trigger strict scrutiny under the Equal Protection Clause for another two decades.[98] During the mid-1960s, however, the Supreme Court began to emphasize the fundamental character of the right to vote.[99] Then, as Justice Harlan wrote in dissent, it first explicitly formulated the position that all classifications bearing on the distribution of fundamental rights trigger strict scrutiny under the Equal Protection Clause in its 1969 decision in *Shapiro v. Thompson*.[100] *Shapiro* is the case in which the modern version of the strict scrutiny test made its first unambiguous appearance in a Supreme Court majority opinion.

At issue in *Shapiro* was the constitutionality of state laws establishing a one-year waiting period before new residents could collect welfare benefits. Writing for the Court, Justice Brennan held that the challenged statutes operated as penalties on the "fundamental" right to travel and that "any classification which serves to penalize the exercise of [a fundamental constitutional] right, unless shown to be necessary to promote a compelling governmental interest, is unconstitutional."[101] In support of this proposition, Justice Brennan referred to the Court's earlier holdings in *Skinner v. Oklahoma, Korematsu v. United States, Bates v. Little Rock*, and *Sherbert v. Verner*.[102]

Less than two months after *Shapiro v. Thompson*, the Court substantially repeated its formulation of the strict scrutiny test in *Kramer v. Union Free School District No. 15*,[103] a case involving the distribution of voting rights under the Equal Protection Clause. Because the right to vote was fundamental, the Court said, it "must determine whether the exclusions [of some from the opportunity to vote] are necessary to promote a compelling state interest."[104] With the decisions of *Shapiro* and *Kramer* in 1969, if not before, strict scrutiny had assumed its modern doctrinal form.

Strict Scrutiny under the Due Process Clause

Not until 1973, in *Roe v. Wade*,[105] did the Supreme Court apply the narrowly-tailored-to-a-compelling-interest formula in a case involving a right deemed

---

98   The Court relied in part on the importance of the right to appeal a criminal conviction in requiring the state to furnish a free trial transcript to indigent defendants in *Griffin v. Illinois*, 351 U.S. 12 (1956), and in holding that the state must appoint counsel for indigent defendants pursuing a first appeal granted as a matter of statutory right in *Douglas v. California*, 372 U.S. 353 (1963). But neither the plurality opinion in *Griffin* nor the majority opinion in *Douglas* characterized the right in issue as "fundamental" nor described its analysis as the application of "strict scrutiny."

99   *See, e.g., Kramer v. Union Free Sch. Dist. No. 15*, 395 U.S. 621, 626 (1969); *Harper v. Va. State Bd. of Elections*, 383 U.S. 663, 667 (1966) (citing *Yick Wo v. Hopkins*, 118 U.S. 356, 370 (1886)).

100   394 U.S. 618 (1969).

101   *Id.* at 634.

102   *Id.*

103   395 U.S. 621 (1969).

104   *Id.* at 627.

105   410 U.S. 113 (1973).

fundamental under the Due Process Clause. By 1973, however, the elements of the compelling interest test were established in other areas. *Roe* simply imported it into the domain of substantive due process.

Although *Roe* was the first Supreme Court majority opinion to apply strict scrutiny in a substantive due process case, an earlier concurring opinion at least arguably played a more pioneering role in formulating strict scrutiny's now-canonical requirements. So far as I can tell, the first articulation of the strict scrutiny test that is wholly consonant with formulations that have survived into the twenty-first century came in 1965 in a concurring opinion in *Griswold v. Connecticut*,[106] which held that a Connecticut statute forbidding the use of contraceptives could not be enforced against married couples in the privacy of their bedrooms. In a convoluted majority opinion, Justice Douglas held that the statute violated a right of privacy contained in the "penumbras" of multiple provisions of the Bill of Rights.[107] For Douglas, the idea that the Due Process Clause protected substantive liberties remained tainted beyond redemption by the judicial practices of the *Lochner* era.[108] Given a choice between *Lochner* and penumbras, Douglas chose penumbras.[109]

Justice Goldberg's concurring opinion took a different tack. Breaking with Douglas on the due process issue, Goldberg argued that the Due Process Clause, as interpreted in light of the Ninth Amendment,[110] protected certain "fundamental" rights, that "marital privacy" numbered among them, and that the states may not abridge "fundamental" liberties without making a showing now associated with strict judicial scrutiny: "Where there is a significant encroachment upon personal liberty, the State may prevail only upon showing a subordinating interest which is compelling." The law must be shown "necessary, and not merely rationally related to, the accomplishment of a permissible state policy."[111]

A Historical Summing Up

Overall, if one asks when, where, or in which case the modern strict scrutiny test first emerged, the question has no obvious answer. But a general conclusion presents itself with crystal clarity. To seek the precise origins of the formula that today defines strict scrutiny is almost surely to pursue the wrong question. Before 1960, what we would now call strict judicial scrutiny did not exist. There were precursors, but the

[106] 381 U.S. 479 (1965).
[107] *See id.* at 484–86.
[108] *See Lochner v. New York*, 198 U.S. 45 (1905).
[109] *See Griswold*, 381 U.S. at 481–82 ("Overtones of some arguments suggest that *Lochner v. State of New York* should be our guide. But we decline that invitation." (citation omitted)). For an analysis of both Justice Douglas's penumbra approach and the principal criticisms directed at it, see David Luban, *The Warren Court and the Concept of a Right*, 34 HARV. C.R-C.L. L. REV. 7, 27–37 (1999).
[110] The Ninth Amendment provides that "The enumeration in the Constitution, of certain rights, shall not be construed to deny or disparage others retained by the people." U.S. CONST. amend. IX.
[111] *Griswold*, 381 U.S. at 497 (Goldberg, J., concurring) (citation omitted) (first quoting *Bates v. City of Little Rock*, 361 U.S. 516, 524 (1960); then quoting *McLaughlin v. Florida*, 379 U.S. 184, 196 (1964)).

precursors employed varied linguistic formulae as the Court worked out the demands that strict scrutiny today expresses. By the end of the 1960s, by contrast, the narrowly-tailored-to-a-compelling-interest formula had not only become sharply defined, but also had assumed a position of dominant importance in otherwise diverse fields of constitutional law. When the pattern is seen as a whole, the striking phenomenon is that the Supreme Court, which had not used compelling interest tests before, began during the 1960s to develop tests in diverse doctrinal areas that foreshadowed the modern strict judicial scrutiny standard and that would be replaced by that single formula before the decade's end.

EXPLAINING THE RISE OF STRICT JUDICIAL SCRUTINY

The rise of strict judicial scrutiny is partly attributable to the changing composition of the Supreme Court and the Justices' relatively idiosyncratic personalities and concerns. But the strict scrutiny formula also reflected, by responding to, a distinctive, identifiable, and continuing set of methodological concerns involving judicial self-discipline and anxieties about judicial legitimacy.

Though it is customary to speak of "the Warren Court" as a unitary phenomenon, there was no clearly dominant liberal bloc through the 1950s and into the early 1960s.[112] The most readily identifiable liberals – Chief Justice Warren and Justices Black, Douglas, and Brennan – lacked a consistent fifth vote. That situation changed in 1962 when Justice Frankfurter retired, to be replaced first by Arthur Goldberg, then by Abe Fortas.[113] With the advent of Justice Goldberg, doubts no longer persisted about whether the Court was committed to the robust protection of "preferred rights" pursuant to a "double standard." It was. The remaining questions were: Which rights occupy the preferred category, and by what standard or standards of review should those preferred rights be protected?

In response to the second of these questions, the Warren Court's empowered liberal majority initially proceeded on a largely ad hoc basis, with the protection of preferred rights frequently varying from right to right. In First Amendment cases, for example, the Court's approach was eclectic. To take one notable example, *New York Times Co.* v. *Sullivan*[114] held that false and defamatory speech about public officials enjoys First Amendment protection unless uttered with knowledge that the speech was false or with reckless disregard for the truth.[115] Similarly, *Brandenburg* v. *Ohio*[116] laid down a test of constitutional permissibility that was unique to the specific problem with which it dealt: "[T]he constitutional guarantees of free speech and free press do not permit a State to forbid or proscribe advocacy of the use of force or

---

[112] *See* Morton J. Horwitz, THE WARREN COURT AND THE PURSUIT OF JUSTICE 10–12 (1998).
[113] *See id.*; Lucas A. Powe, Jr., THE WARREN COURT AND AMERICAN Politics 211–12 (2000).
[114] 376 U.S. 254 (1964).
[115] *Id.* at 279–80.
[116] 395 U.S. 444 (1969) (per curiam).

of law violation except where such advocacy is directed to inciting or producing imminent lawless action and is likely to incite or produce such action."[117] The Warren Court's famously path-breaking decisions involving the constitutional rights of criminal suspects were also typically ad hoc in their approach, not governed by any recurrent formula, and frequently laid down categorical rules that required no further assessment of competing interests.[118]

Over time, however, the Justices began to grasp, subconsciously if not consciously, that strict scrutiny furnished a generically available response to a generic problem – or, perhaps more precisely, to a nested congeries of generic problems. The most obvious problem to which strict scrutiny responds arose whenever the Court's majority wished to define presumptively protected rights relatively broadly – as it could not easily have done in many cases if it were to lay down a flatly categorical prohibition – and in which it wished to give more protection to those rights than rational basis review or even mere "balancing" would ensure. In other words, in contrast with most of the other doctrinal tests that the Warren Court developed, strict scrutiny was capable of adaptation on an almost generic basis to protect rights that the Court thought merited strong but less than absolute protection. As the earlier face-off between free speech absolutists and balancers had helped to demonstrate, the view that all properly "preferred" rights are wholly unyielding seemed unduly rigid, while an unstructured balancing methodology threatened to subvert the premise that fundamental rights truly occupy a preferred status at all. As between these two positions, the strict scrutiny formula – forbidding infringements of fundamental rights unless those infringements are necessary to promote a compelling governmental interest – bore the hallmarks of an inspired compromise, pushed most strongly within the Supreme Court by the Warren Court's greater compromiser, Justice William Brennan.[119]

On the one hand, strict scrutiny avoided unworkably high-minded rigidity: When truly compelling interests were involved, the government could do what necessity dictated. What is more, in invalidating statutes pursuant to the strict scrutiny formula, the Court could appear accommodating by holding out the possibility that if the government's interest were truly urgent, the government could protect it

---

[117] *Id.* at 447.

[118] *See, e.g., Miranda v. Arizona*, 384 U.S. 436 (1966) (enforcing a right to be free from compelled self-incrimination); *Douglas v. Alabama*, 380 U.S. 415 (1965) (upholding a right to confrontation of adverse witnesses); *Gideon v. Wainwright*, 372 U.S. 335 (1963) (holding that all felony defendants have a right to appointed counsel if they cannot afford a lawyer). For a general discussion of categorical requirements in constitutional law, see Jeffrey L. Fisher, *Categorical Requirements in Constitutional Criminal Procedure*, 94 GEO. L.J. 1493 (2006).

[119] *See* Powe, *supra* note 113, at 303 (observing that "[w]hen the liberals came to dominate, Brennan's time arrived" and identifying "[s]trict scrutiny" and "compelling interests," *inter alia*, as "the vocabulary of unconstitutionality in Brennan's jurisprudence"); *id.* at 221, 371, 453–54 (discussing Brennan's application of the strict scrutiny formula in particular cases); Siegel, *supra* note 54 (discussing Justice Brennan's role in the development of the compelling state interest standard).

by writing a more precisely tailored statute.[120] On the other hand, the compelling interest formula gave content to the notion that preferred rights were indeed preferred and that strict scrutiny was truly strict, at least in the minds of those Justices committed to robust judicial protection.[121] Invocation of strict scrutiny signaled a categorical shift from rational basis review that was notoriously toothless from the 1940s through the 1960s, when the Court would uphold statutes based on any imaginable governmental purpose. When the strict scrutiny formula appeared to solve the standard-of-review problem in one context, it was natural for the Court to adapt it for application to others – and to engage in further refinements of the test as it did so.

The strict scrutiny formula also represented at least a partial response to a second generic problem, involving the preservation or establishment of judicial legitimacy in identifying and enforcing controversial rights.[122] The term "legitimacy" is an elusive one, with multiple meanings. In one usage, the concern is with justification. It involves the principles of political morality, if any, that would justify the Court in claiming authority to displace the judgments of politically accountable officials based on morally and frequently legally contestable judgments of its own. In 1962, Professor Alexander Bickel memorably characterized the problem of moral legitimacy as involving "the counter-majoritarian difficulty."[123] Political institutions purport to represent political majorities. At least on the surface, the Supreme Court lacks a democratic pedigree. I shall return to issues involving the moral or political legitimacy of robust judicial review, especially in Chapter 7.

A related sense of "legitimacy" focuses on sociological concerns, involving the capacity of the Supreme Court to inspire respect from the public and obedience from political officials. In the 1960s, obedience to Court decisions could not simply be taken for granted. The Supreme Court's school segregation mandate in *Brown* v. *Board of Education*[124] provoked "massive resistance."[125] As late as 1964, only 1 percent of African American school children in the South attended an integrated school.[126] The Court's 1962 decision mandating an end to school prayer was also widely defied in some regions of the country.[127] With public resistance to some of the Warren Court's signature decisions matched by expressions of concern from elite cohorts of

---

[120] See Powe, *supra* note 113, at 117.
[121] See *id.* ("The technique of approving ends, but finding fault with the means, suited Brennan well, for it allowed everyone – save the absolutists – to take some consolation from the opinion, and in Brennan's hands this technique served his increasingly liberal and egalitarian objectives.").
[122] For discussion of the concept of legitimacy and its application to issues of the judicial role, see Richard H. Fallon, Jr., Law and Legitimacy in the Supreme Court (2018).
[123] Alexander M. Bickel, The Least Dangerous Branch 16 (1962).
[124] 347 U.S. 483 (1954).
[125] Michael J. Klarman, From Jim Crow to Civil Rights: The Supreme Court and the Struggle for Racial Equality 344–408 (2004).
[126] *Id.* at 362–63.
[127] Frank J. Sorauf, The Wall of Separation: The Constitutional Politics of Church and State 294–300 (2d ed. 2015).

the legal profession and legal academy, Professor Martin Shapiro perceptively summarized the Court's problem of sociological legitimacy: If the Court were to maintain public support in carrying out an agenda that required pervasive interest-balancing and other, related judgments of political morality and prudence, it would have to wrap itself tightly in the trappings of legal norms, methods, and determinacy or quasi-determinacy.[128] In other words, the Court confronted a political challenge – and its best response to that political challenge, simply as an instrumental matter, was to insist that its function involved law, not politics, and was governed by distinctively legal norms.

As compared with balancing and ad hoc judgments, the strict scrutiny test promised disciplined legal inquiries pursuant to a recurring, legally-pedigreed formula. As the recurrently applicable formula applied to a broad range of preferred or fundamental rights cases, strict scrutiny performed the welcome function of binding the Court to a standard that the legal profession, and even the public, could recognize as fit for judicial administration.

The third of the nested problems to which strict scrutiny responded was closely related to the second. It involved the challenge of judicial self-discipline as the Supreme Court assumed an expanding role in protecting individual rights in the post-*Lochner* era. As brought out in *Griswold* v. *Connecticut,* in which Justice Douglas's majority opinion firmly rejected any reliance on *Lochner*-like methodological premises,[129] the ghost of *Lochner* overhung constitutional law during the period in which strict scrutiny developed. Against that background, the Warren Court's recurring juxtapositions of preferred or fundamental rights, frequently protected by strict judicial scrutiny, with ordinary liberties, protected only by rational basis review, appears to have embodied a self-conscious commitment to judicial self-discipline in cabining the reach of the judicial role. Whereas *Lochner*-era jurisprudence knew no tiers of judicial inquiry, and maps awkwardly onto either strict scrutiny or rational basis review, the Warren Court followed the path marked by the earliest "preferred position" decisions in assuming that the basic architecture of constitutional doctrine should be broadly two-tiered. There were then and continue today to be a number of exceptions to the largely two-tiered framework, some of which I shall discuss at the end of this chapter and others of which I shall consider in Chapter 4. To take just one example, criminal procedural doctrines include a number of categorical prohibitions. But even after diversity is acknowledged and due allowance for exceptions is made, the two-tiered structure to which the Court had gestured as early as the *Carolene Products* case in 1938 has remained largely intact, and the prevailing distinction between preferred rights and ordinary liberties has mostly been implemented with two judicial tests. One pillar of the doctrinal edifice, rational basis review, was designed to eliminate what post-New Deal Justices

[128] Martin Shapiro, *The Supreme Court and Constitutional Adjudication: Of Politics and Neutral Principles,* 31 GEO. WASH. L. REV. 587, 605–06 (1963).
[129] *Griswold* v. *Connecticut,* 381 U.S. 479, 481–82 (1965).

predominantly viewed as the relatively untethered, case-by-case fairness review that marked the *Lochner* era (even if the *Lochner*-era Justices would have rejected that characterization).[130] In cases involving ordinary liberties, the Court should not repeat its past errors of judicial overreaching.

The other architectural pillar, consisting of preferred or fundamental rights protected either by strict judicial scrutiny or some comparably stringent test, also served disciplining functions. On the one hand, recognition of a category of highly preferred or fundamental rights promised to restrain the impulse to "balance" away important civil liberties during times of crisis, as some of the Justices believed had happened in the McCarthy era,[131] and as might plausibly be thought to have happened with respect to rights to freedom from race-based discrimination in *Korematsu*. (In a considered dictum in *Trump* v. *Hawaii* (2018), Chief Justice Roberts wrote: "*Korematsu* was gravely wrong the day it was decided, has been overruled in the court of history, and – to be clear – 'has no place in law under the Constitution.'"[132]) On the other hand, a design that afforded very stringent protection to fundamental rights, and allowed the judiciary no easy escape from enforcing the rights that it so denominated, operated as a discipline against elevating too many rights to the preferred category. Strict judicial scrutiny thus helped to ensure that the strictures against judicial overreaching that had emerged from the *Lochner* period could retain vitality.[133]

In speaking of self-disciplining devices and their allure, I do not wish to stake out too rigid a position. In particular, I do not mean to challenge the conclusion of Professor Lucas Powe that none of the Warren Court Justices "seemed to care about theory" during the 1960s, and that most were more concerned with results than with doctrine.[134] Self-discipline comes in degrees, and different Justices may have had more or less self-discipline in mind. In addition, it is in the nature of *self*-disciplining mechanisms that they can be applied consistently or inconsistently and that they can be strengthened or weakened through interpretation. Nevertheless, we cannot understand the emergence of strict judicial scrutiny as a generic constitutional test

---

[130]   *See* David E. Bernstein, Lochner v. New York: *A Centennial Retrospective*, 83 WASH. U. L.Q. 1469, 1473 (2005) (noting how, beginning in the 1960s, *Lochner* "became a leading case in the 'anti-canon,' the group of wrongly decided cases that help frame what the proper principles of constitutional interpretation should be").

[131]   *See, e.g., Konigsberg* v. *State Bar*, 366 U.S. 36, 61 (1961) (Black, J., dissenting) (stating that the Framers "did all the 'balancing' that was to be done" with respect to the Bill of Rights); *Hannah* v. *Larche*, 363 U.S. 420, 494 (1960) (Douglas, J., dissenting) (remarking, in a voting rights case, that as "important as these civil rights are, it will not do to sacrifice other civil rights in order to protect them").

[132]   118 S. Ct. 2392, 2424 (2018) (quoting *Korematsu*, 323 U.S. at 248 (Jackson, J., dissenting)).

[133]   *See* Jack M. Balkin, *"Wrong the Day It Was Decided": Lochner and Constitutional Historicism*, 85 B. U. L. REV. 677, 686 (2005) ("The *Lochner* narrative that we have inherited from the New Deal projects on to the Supreme Court between 1897 and 1937 a series of undesirable traits – the very opposite of those characteristics that supporters of the New Deal settlement wanted to believe about themselves.").

[134]   Powe, *supra* note 113, at 303.

without viewing it as a response to equally generic challenges. And a recurring, generic challenge was to provide assurances that the Supreme Court had not become too big for its britches and would remain confined within a properly judicial role.

One further feature of the strict scrutiny formula deserves mention. The Justices could, and did, agree that infringements on preferred rights could be upheld only if necessary to promote a compelling government interest without agreeing on a number of contentious issues, the full importance of which would become evident only when the formula had to be applied. To put the point perhaps more straight-forwardly, the decisions initially propounding the strict scrutiny test failed to specify what its central terms meant – a key omission to which I shall return in the next chapter.

STRICT SCRUTINY'S LATER LIFE: A THUMBNAIL SKETCH

Unlike many other innovations of the Warren Court, the strict scrutiny test has continued unchanged, and its sweep has remained large (though perhaps slightly diminished), under the Burger, Rehnquist, and Roberts Courts. Numerous factors have converged to produce this result. Among these is stare decisis: The Supreme Court does not lightly overrule its precedents.[135] Even apart from stare decisis, most of the considerations that recommended the compelling interest test to the Warren Court – as responses to a nested set of generic challenges – would have made it equally attractive to subsequent Courts.

To say that the Burger, Rehnquist, and Roberts Courts have continued to apply the strict scrutiny formula developed by the Warren Court is not to say that they have maintained all elements of the predominantly two-tiered jurisprudential regime in which that formula once was located. Nor, to repeat, have I meant to claim that the entire universe of constitutional law could ever have been divided exclusively into categories of strict scrutiny on the one hand and rational basis review on the other. Constitutional law has always included some categorical rules, especially in the domain of criminal procedure. Nearly without exception, those accused of crimes punishable by imprisonment have a right to trial by jury. As the familiar *Miranda* rule makes clear, criminal suspects who have been taken into police custody have nearly categorical rights not to have any confessions that they may make introduced against them unless they have been apprised of their right to remain silent and have been offered a lawyer. Other tests dot other areas of constitutional law as well.

---

[135] *See Dickerson v. United States*, 530 U.S. 428, 443 (2000) (noting that a departure from precedent requires "some 'special justification'" (quoting *United States v. Int'l Bus. Machs. Corp.*, 517 U.S. 843, 856 (1996))); Henry Paul Monaghan, *Stare Decisis and Constitutional Adjudication*, 88 COLUM. L. REV. 723, 757 (1988) ("[P]recedent binds absent a showing of substantial countervailing considerations.").

Even if we focus for now just on the central conceptual territory that the juxtaposition of strict judicial scrutiny with highly relaxed rational basis review once defined, two consequential developments have occurred since strict scrutiny developed in the 1960s. The first has involved the introduction of several varieties of "intermediate scrutiny," differentiated both from rational basis review and from the compelling interest test. During the early 1970s, the Supreme Court divided over whether to apply strict scrutiny or rational basis review in challenges to gender-based classifications.[136] A 1976 decision in *Craig* v. *Boren*[137] split the difference by introducing a test under which gender-based discriminations will survive challenge only if "substantially related" to "important" governmental interests.[138] In *Craig*, a dissenting opinion protested that "we have had enough difficulty with the two standards of review which our cases have recognized ... so as to counsel weightily against the insertion of still another 'standard' between those two."[139] Nonetheless, the innovation has apparently proved happy in the eyes of the Justices. The Court now applies intermediate scrutiny not only to statutes that discriminate on the basis of gender, but also to governmental discriminations against children born out of wedlock.[140]

In the kind of doctrinal migration that characterized the development of strict scrutiny, a close analogue of the test developed in *Craig* has assumed a role under the First Amendment. In *FCC* v. *League of Women Voters*,[141] the Court invalidated a restriction on political editorializing by public broadcasting stations on the ground that "that the specific interests sought to be advanced ... are either not sufficiently substantial or are not served in a sufficiently limited manner to justify the substantial abridgment of important journalistic freedoms which the First Amendment jealously protects."[142] Comparable but differently formulated tests of mid-level stringency have developed to address other issues under the First Amendment, including those arising from the regulation of commercial speech and the zoning of businesses predominantly featuring sexually explicit or "adult" speech. A form of intermediate scrutiny – though one with a distinctive structure – has also emerged in abortion cases. Whereas *Roe* v. *Wade*[143] held that infringements on the "fundamental" right to abortion could be upheld only if necessary to promote a compelling governmental interest,[144] *Planned Parenthood*

---

[136] Compare *Frontiero* v. *Richardson*, 411 U.S. 677, 682 (1973) (plurality opinion) (stating that "classifications based upon sex, like classifications based upon race, alienage, and national origin, are inherently suspect and must therefore be subjected to close judicial scrutiny" (footnotes omitted)), with *id.* at 691–92 (Powell, J., concurring in the judgment) (arguing that classifications based upon gender should not be subjected to strict scrutiny).

[137] 429 U.S. 190 (1976).

[138] *Id.* at 197.

[139] *Id.* at 220–21 (Rehnquist, J., dissenting).

[140] See *Clark* v. *Jeter*, 486 U.S. 456, 461 (1988).

[141] 468 U.S. 364 (1984).

[142] See *id.* at 402.

[143] 410 U.S. 113 (1973).

[144] *Id.* at 152–55.

of Southeastern Pennsylvania v. *Casey*[145] substituted a formula under which courts now assess whether abortion regulations place an "undue burden" on a woman's right to terminate an unwanted pregnancy up to the point of fetal viability.[146]

Beyond introducing an intermediate scrutiny test that diminishes strict scrutiny's architecturally disciplining significance, the Court, in recent years, has further muddied the once-clear line between strict scrutiny and rational basis review by occasionally imbuing rational basis review with a bite that its protestations in other cases wholly disavow.[147] The Court has especially notably blurred the lines between its traditional tiers of review in cases involving gay rights, in which it has skeptically scrutinized the constitutionality of legislation but without formally signaling that more than rational basis review applies.[148]

Under these circumstances, some commentators depict the tiered regime of judicial review as decayed and crumbling.[149] Others see the creeping return of *Lochner*-like inquiries into the overall reasonableness of challenged legislation as

---

[145]   505 U.S. 833 (1992).

[146]   *Id.* at 874 (joint opinion of O'Connor, Kennedy, and Souter, JJ.).

[147]   In cases decided over a number of years but accelerating during the 1970s, the Court has made it clear that rational basis view is not invariably "toothless," *Mathews* v. *Lucas*, 427 U.S. 495, 510 (1976), but permits more or less deferential application in different kinds of cases. *See* Robert C. Farrell, *Successful Rational Basis Claims in the Supreme Court from the 1971 Term through Romer v. Evans*, 32 IND. L. REV. 357, 357 (1999) (identifying ten rational basis claims upheld by the Supreme Court); Suzanne B. Goldberg, *Equality without Tiers*, 77 S. CAL. L. REV. 481, 512–13 (2004) (noting that the Supreme Court has applied rational basis review to invalidate nearly a dozen classifications since 1973); Gunther, *supra* note 1, at 30 (describing cases in which the Court based a decision "centrally on interventionist use of equal protection without explicit invocation of strict scrutiny"). Over the past three decades, the Court has thus invoked a seemingly heightened form of rational basis review to invalidate statutes disadvantaging the intellectually disabled, *see City of Cleburne* v. *Cleburne Living Ctr.*, 473 U.S. 432, 446–50 (1985), and gays, *see Romer* v. *Evans*, 517 U.S. 620, 631–35 (1996), among others, but without tying its hands in future cases by mandating the application of strict judicial scrutiny. In *Lawrence* v. *Texas*, 539 U.S. 558 (2003), Justice Kennedy's substantive due process opinion invalidated a prohibition against sodomy without invoking strict judicial scrutiny.

[148]   *See, e.g., United States* v. *Windsor*, 570 U.S. 744, 775 (2013) (holding that the Defense of Marriage Act violated the Fifth Amendment without specifying the level of scrutiny applied); *Lawrence*, 539 U.S. at 578 (invalidating an anti-sodomy ordinance under the Due Process Clause without invoking strict scrutiny); *Romer*, 517 U.S. at 632 (holding that a Colorado constitutional amendment that barred anti-discrimination protections for gays and lesbians failed to meet even the rational basis test).

[149]   *See, e.g.*, Jeffrey M. Shaman, CONSTITUTIONAL INTERPRETATION: ILLUSION AND REALITY 74 (2001) ("In the last five decades, the Supreme Court has engaged in a continuous reworking of the multi-tier system [of judicial scrutiny] ... Through this ongoing exercise, the system has become highly rarefied to the point where it threatens to collapse of its own complexity."); Goldberg, *supra* note 147, at 485 ("The long-standing stasis of the set of classifications deemed suspect or quasi-suspect initially suggests the need to reconsider the tiers ... While lack of expansion does not necessarily mean the screening system is flawed, it does suggest possible ossification of the governing framework that warrants careful examination." (footnote omitted)); Andrew Koppelman, *Beyond Levels of Scrutiny:* Windsor *and "Bare Desire to Harm,"* 64 CASE W. RES. L. REV. 1045 (2014); White, *supra* note 2, 1, 3 ("Recently, several commentators suggested that the Court's established scrutiny levels typology ... is on the verge of degeneration.").

gauged from a judicial vantage point.[150] Although containing kernels of truth, these positions are overstated. In claiming continuing significance for the strict judicial scrutiny formula as administered by the Supreme Court, I would not know precisely how to calibrate the force that it or any other doctrinal test exerts, though I would maintain confidently that the effect is by no means negligible. One can be a bit of a realist, as one ought to be, while also taking doctrinal formulas such as the narrowly-tailored-to-a-compelling-interest test seriously. If so, anyone who wishes to understand Supreme Court decision-making needs to delve into the structure and elements of strict judicial scrutiny. The practice of strict scrutiny, in turn, provides a window into the nature of constitutional rights that emerges when we ask, what would constitutional rights need to be like in order to be identifiable and enforceable in this particular way?

---

[150] *See* David D. Meyer, Lochner *Redeemed: Family Privacy after* Troxel *and* Carhart, 48 UCLA L. REV. 1125, 1128 (2001) (arguing that the Supreme Court's family privacy cases "signal that the polestar of the Court's emerging approach is 'reasonableness,' the very standard that the Court is supposed to have safely entombed along with *Lochner* itself").

2

Strict Scrutiny as an Incompletely Theorized Agreement

As embraced by the Warren Court in the 1960s, strict judicial scrutiny represented an indeterminate or incompletely theorized compromise.[1] The Justices could, and did, agree that infringements on preferred rights should be upheld only if necessary to promote a compelling government interest. But they did so without working out responses to a number of contentious issues, the full importance of which would become evident only when the formula had to be applied to unforeseen cases. It is little exaggeration to say that there are two versions of the strict scrutiny test, between which the Supreme Court has never chosen decisively. According to one interpretation, strict scrutiny closely approximates, as it should closely approximate, the "absolutism" in the protection of preferred rights that Justice Black championed. On a second interpretation, strict scrutiny is more nearly an all-things-considered balancing test,[2] distinguished from other balancing tests by its premise that the stakes on the rights side of the scale are extremely high and that the government's interests must therefore be unusually weighty to overcome them.

STRICT SCRUTINY AS A NEARLY CATEGORICAL PROHIBITION

If understood as enforcing a nearly categorical prohibition against the infringement of fundamental rights, strict scrutiny marks a genuine alternative to the kind of balancing that would, in Justice Black's terms, allow First Amendment and other similarly fundamental rights to be "balanced away." We can see the contrast by considering an analogous position in moral philosophy known as "threshold deontology." Among moral philosophers, it is widely believed that some rights have a moral or ontological status, rooted in respect for persons, that forbids their violation

---

[1]   *Cf.* Cass R. Sunstein, *Commentary, Incompletely Theorized Agreements*, 108 HARV. L. REV. 1733, 1735–36 (1995) (arguing that "[p]articipants in legal controversies try to produce incompletely theorized agreements on particular outcomes" rather than "agree[ing] on fundamental principle" (emphasis omitted)).

[2]   Justice Scalia referred to strict scrutiny as a "balancing test" in *Employment Division* v. *Smith*, 494 U.S. 872, 883 (1990).

merely to promote overall utility or to achieve good consequences or avoid bad ones.[3] In ordinary cases, neither balancing nor any close analogue should be permitted. Only in extreme cases – when the costs of enforcing rights absolutely reach the "threshold" of being catastrophic or otherwise practically intolerable – is the violation of rights morally acceptable.[4]

Professor Charles Black once interpreted the approach of Justice Hugo Black in these terms. Taking the right not to be tortured as an example, Professor Black argued that although "[t]he right not to be tortured cannot, literally, be an 'absolute' . . . the right not to be tortured is entirely unsuitable for 'balancing' against competing considerations of convenience, comfort, and safety, as we 'balance' . . . the ordinary affairs of life, with a view to setting the course of prudence."[5] As applied to constitutional law, an interpretation of strict judicial scrutiny that is modeled on this approach would not only provide a check against the balancing away of fundamental rights. It would also anchor strict judicial scrutiny in a conception of the judicial role that the public ought to respect and recognize the need for. On this interpretation of strict judicial scrutiny, the Court's job is not to redo the legislature's balancing, but to confirm or disconfirm the legislative judgment that a peculiarly urgent practical necessity makes it permissible for the government to contravene a fundamental principle of continuing validity – such as, for example, the principle that the government should never single someone out for adverse treatment based on race or religion.

The attraction of viewing strict scrutiny as enforcing a nearly categorical prohibition depends partly on a conception of the appropriate judicial role in enforcing rights, but it may also depend partly on the nature of the right that one has in view. Hanging in the background of the Court's initial embrace of the strict scrutiny formula was *Korematsu v. United States*,[6] in which the Court, in pre-strict scrutiny days, upheld the de facto internment of US citizens of Japanese descent during World War II. With cases such as *Korematsu* in mind, some of the Justices have frequently written as if strict scrutiny, in the resonant phrase of Professor Gerald Gunther, should be "'strict' in theory and fatal in fact."[7]

---

3   *See, e.g.,* Robert Nozick, ANARCHY, STATE, AND UTOPIA 30–33 (1974).
4   *See, e.g.,* Charles Fried, RIGHT AND WRONG 9–13 (1978); Ronald Dworkin, *The Rights of Myron Farber,* N.Y. R. BOOKS, Oct. 26, 1978, at 34, 34; *see also* Sanford H. Kadish, *Torture, the State and the Individual,* 23 ISR. L. REV. 345, 346 (1989) ("The use of torture is so profound a violation of a human right that almost nothing can redeem it – almost, because one can not rule out a case in which the lives of many innocent persons will surely be saved by its use against a single person . . .").
5   Charles L. Black, Jr., *Mr. Justice Black, The Supreme Court, and the Bill of Rights,* HARPER'S MAG., Feb. 1961, at 63, 67.
6   323 U.S. 214 (1944).
7   Gerald Gunther, *The Supreme Court, 1971 Term – Foreword: In Search of Evolving Doctrine on a Changing Court: A Model for a Newer Equal Protection,* 86 HARV. L. REV. 1, 8 (1972); see also Peter J. Rubin, *Reconnecting Doctrine and Purpose: A Comprehensive Approach to Strict Scrutiny after Adarand and Shaw,* 149 U. PA. L. REV. 1, 4 (2000) (asserting that "most have concluded that a judicial

To cite just one example, the Supreme Court has frequently described the free-dom of speech in terms that make its claims sound almost categorically unyielding.[8] An especially striking instance of nearly absolutist rhetoric comes from *American Booksellers Ass'n v. Hudnut,*[9] in which Judge Frank Easterbrook, in a decision subsequently affirmed by the Supreme Court, assumed for the sake of argument that the "pornography" that a municipality sought to prohibit – defined as "the graphic sexually explicit subordination of women"[10] – would "tend to perpetuate subordination" of women and "leads to affront and lower pay at work, insult and injury at home, [and] battery and rape on the streets."[11] Even crediting these assumptions, Judge Easterbrook thought the Constitution could not tolerate a city's enforcing "an approved point of view."[12]

Concurring in the judgment in *City of Richmond v. J.A. Croson Co.,*[13] Justice Scalia spoke in similar terms: "At least where state or local action is at issue, only a social emergency rising to the level of imminent danger to life and limb – for example, a prison race riot, requiring temporary segregation of inmates – can justify an exception to the principle embodied in the Fourteenth Amendment that '[o]ur Constitution is color-blind.'"[14] So did Justice Thomas in *Grutter v. Bollinger:*[15] "[O]nly those measures the State must take to provide a bulwark against anarchy, or to prevent violence, will constitute 'a pressing public necessity'"[16] capable of satisfy-ing strict scrutiny.

In *Croson,* however, Justice Scalia spoke in a concurring rather than a majority opinion, and in *Grutter,* Justice Thomas wrote in dissent. Both of those cases

determination to apply 'strict scrutiny' is little more than a way to describe the conclusion that a particular governmental action is invalid").
8   *See, e.g., United States v. Playboy Entm't Grp.,* 529 U.S. 803, 817 (2000) (asserting that "[e]rror in marking [the] line" between protected and unprotected speech "exacts an extraordinary cost" because "[i]t is through speech that our convictions and beliefs are influenced, expressed, and tested").
9   771 F.2d 323 (7th Cir. 1985), *aff'd,* 475 U.S. 1001 (1986).
10 INDIANAPOLIS, IND., CODE § 16–3(q).
11 *Hudnut,* 771 F.2d at 329.
12 *Id.* at 332. *See also United States v. Alvarez,* 567 U.S. 709, 724–26 (2012) (striking down the Stolen Valor Act, which criminalized falsely claiming receipt of military medals, under the "most exacting scrutiny" because the government did "satisfy [its] heavy burden when it seeks to regulate protected speech," even though the Court declared that the "interest in protecting the integrity of the Medal of Honor is beyond question").
13 488 U.S. 469 (1989).
14 *Id.* at 521 (Scalia, J., concurring in the judgment) (alteration in original) (citation omitted) (quoting *Plessy v. Ferguson,* 163 U.S. 537, 559 (1896) (Harlan, J., dissenting)).
15 539 U.S. 306 (2003).
16 *Id.* at 353 (Thomas, J., concurring in part and dissenting in part); *see also id.* ("The Constitution abhors classifications based on race, not only because those classifications can harm favored races or are based on illegitimate motives, but also because every time the government places citizens on racial registers and makes race relevant to the provision of burdens or benefits, it demeans us all."); *Gratz v. Bollinger,* 539 U.S. 244, 270 (2003) (describing the application of strict scrutiny as being necessary because "[r]acial classifications are simply too pernicious to permit any but the most exact connection between justification and classification" (alteration in original) (quoting *Fullilove v. Klutznick,* 448 U.S. 448, 537 (1980) (Stevens, J., dissenting))).

involved challenges to race-based affirmative action. Although a majority of the Justices has thought that race-based classifications should trigger strict scrutiny even when they are used to promote racial inclusion rather than exclusion, a majority, so far, has shrunk from insisting on a nearly categorical prohibition. In *Adarand Constructors, Inc.* v. *Peña*,[17] a case involving a challenge to race-based affirmative action, a Court majority called for the application of strict judicial scrutiny but expressly rejected "the notion that strict scrutiny is 'strict in theory, but fatal in fact.'"[18] A majority of the Justices subsequently followed up on that dictum by upholding affirmative action programs in *Grutter* v. *Bollinger*[19] and *Fisher* v. *University of Texas*[20] based on compelling interests in educational diversity.[21]

Nor do these affirmative action cases stand alone. According to a study by law professor Adam Winkler, United States courts of appeals uphold laws that are subjected to strict judicial scrutiny nearly one third of the time, typically without reversal by the Supreme Court.[22] Within the High Court itself, the Justices did not treat strict scrutiny as a nearly categorical prohibition in *Nixon* v. *Administrator of General Services*,[23] which deemed the government to have a compelling interest in recovering the presidential papers of Richard Nixon that were of general historical interest,[24] even though all previous presidents had been permitted to provide unilaterally for the disposition of their papers. The Court took a similarly flexible, balancing-type approach in *Storer* v. *Brown*,[25] which upheld a state statute that denied ballot access to independent candidates who had voted in party primaries or been registered as a party member during the preceding year.

STRICT SCRUTINY AS WEIGHTED BALANCING

If or when strict scrutiny does not embody a nearly categorical prohibition against suspect governmental actions, we might think of it as a weighted balancing test, signaling a constitutional presumption against permitting the infringement of pre-ferred rights, but no more. Justice Thurgood Marshall argued repeatedly that strict scrutiny should be understood in these terms. According to him, the requirement

---

[17] 515 U.S. 200 (1995).
[18] *Id.* at 237 (quoting *Fullilove*, 448 U.S. at 519 (Marshall, J., concurring in the judgment)).
[19] 539 U.S. 306 (2003).
[20] 136 S. Ct. 2198 (2016).
[21] For further discussion of diversity as a compelling governmental interest and on more general uncertainty surrounding the strict scrutiny formula, see Ozan O. Varol, *Strict in Theory, but Accommodating in Fact?*, 75 Mo. L. Rev. 1243 (2010).
[22] *See* Adam Winkler, *Fatal in Theory and Strict in Fact: An Empirical Analysis of Strict Scrutiny in the Federal Courts*, 59 Vand. L. Rev. 793, 796 (2006) ("Overall, 30 percent of all applications of strict scrutiny – nearly one in three – result in the challenged law being upheld.").
[23] 433 U.S. 425 (1977).
[24] *See id.* at 467–68.
[25] 415 U.S. 724 (1974).

that infringements on certain rights be justified by a "'[c]ompelling state interest' is merely a shorthand description of the difficult process of balancing individual and state interests that the Court must embark upon when faced with a classification touching on fundamental rights."[26] More recently, Justice Stephen Breyer has adopted a similar perspective. He has referred pointedly to "the version of strict scrutiny" that the Supreme Court's affirmative action "cases embody" as one that "diversity" should easily satisfy in efforts to enhance racial mixing in grade schools and high schools.[27] Similarly, he has argued that "any attempt *in theory* to apply strict scrutiny to gun regulations will *in practice* turn into an interest-balancing inquiry, with the interests protected by the Second Amendment on one side and the governmental public-safety concerns on the other, the only question being whether the regulation at issue impermissibly burdens the former in the course of advancing the latter."[28]

Like the near absolutist interpretation of strict scrutiny, the balancing approach possesses arguable virtues that an analogy brings out. In their efforts to protect fundamental rights, most western liberal democracies have adopted a "proportionality" test that takes account of multiple factors that possess at least prima facie moral relevance. As applied in Germany, Canada,[29] and Israel[30] and by the European Court of Justice,[31] the proportionality test encompasses three doctrinal sub-tests, all of which must be satisfied for legislation to survive judicial review.[32] The first asks whether a measure restricting basic rights is rationally related to a desired end.[33] The second, called "the principle of

---

[26] *Richardson v. Ramirez*, 418 U.S. 24, 78 (1974) (Marshall, J., dissenting); *see also San Antonio Indep. Sch. Dist. v. Rodriguez*, 411 U.S. 1, 98–99 (1973) (Marshall, J., dissenting) (arguing that the Court's equal protection cases have "applied a spectrum of standards" and that "the degree of care with which the Court will scrutinize particular classifications [depends] ... on the constitutional and societal importance of the interest adversely affected and the recognized invidiousness of the basis upon which the particular classification is drawn").

[27] *Parents Involved in Cmty. Sch. v. Seattle Sch. Dist. No. 1*, 551 U.S. 701, 837 (2007).

[28] *District of Columbia v. Heller*, 554 U.S. 570, 689 (2008) (Breyer, J., dissenting).

[29] *See R. v. Oakes*, [1986] 1 S.C.R. 103, para. 70 (Can.); *Canada v. Bedford*, [2013] 3 S.C.R. 1101.

[30] *See HCJ 2065/04 Beit Sourik Vill. Council v. Gov't of Isr.* 58(5) PD 807 (2004) (Isr.) (interpreting Article 8 of Israel's Basic Law to reflect a principle of proportionality).

[31] The principle of proportionality has long been treated as a general principle of European Community law. *See* Nicholas Emiliou, THE PRINCIPLE OF PROPORTIONALITY IN EUROPEAN LAW: A COMPARATIVE STUDY 134–70 (1996).

[32] The Canadians apply an additional sub-test, which is the rough equivalent of the American demand for a compelling or substantial government interest, before they reach questions relating to proportionality: "the objective, which the measures responsible for a limit on a *Charter* right or freedom are designed to serve, must be 'of sufficient importance to warrant overriding a constitutionally protected right or freedom.'" *Oakes*, 1 S.C.R. 103, para. 69 (quoting *R. v. Big M Drug Mart Ltd.*, [1985] 1 S.C.R. 295, para. 163); *see also Mounted Police Ass'n of Ontario v. Canada* (A.G.), 2015 S.C.C. 1, para. 145 (holding that "the creation of a separate labour relations regime, free from collective bargaining and unionism" is not "rationally connected to the goal of ensuring a stable, reliable and neutral police force").

[33] In *Oakes*, the Canadian Supreme Court explained that the measures "must not be arbitrary, unfair or based on irrational considerations. In short, they must be rationally connected to the objective." *Id.*

necessity" in Germany[34] and "the least injurious means test" in Israel,[35] holds that the means, "even if rationally connected to the objective ... should impair 'as little as possible' the right or freedom in question."[36] The third, called "the principle of proportionality *stricto sensu*" in Germany[37] and the "proportionate means test" in Israel,[38] invites the court to balance societal interests against individual rights by asking whether an infringement of rights is proportionate to the desired objective.[39]

Just as judges and constitution-writers in other liberal democracies have thought that proportionality tests permit an appropriately nuanced appraisal of competing interests, Justices of pragmatic sensibility have sometimes interpreted strict scrutiny as contemplating relatively flexible inquiries, not as designed to prove "fatal" in nearly all cases. Consistent with this philosophy, the Supreme Court has often appeared to engage in a relatively ad hoc, weighted balancing of public and private interests in freedom of association cases in which it has strictly scrutinized governmental demands for information.[40] After crediting the government's purpose as a permissible one, the Court goes on in such cases to ask whether the government's interests are sufficiently weighty to justify the actual, sometimes disparate effects on

---

para. 70. Germany, however, merely demands a "legitimate purpose." *See* David Bilchitz, *Socio-Economic Rights, Economic Crisis, and Legal Doctrine*, 14 INT'L J. CONST. L. 710, 735 (2014).

[34] Emiliou, *supra* note 31, at 29–30; Rosalind Dixon, *The Core Case for Weak-Form Judicial Review*, 38 CARDOZO L. REV. 2193, 2199–200 (2017); Vicki C. Jackson, *Thayer, Holmes, Brandeis: Conceptions of Judicial Review, Factfinding, and Proportionality*, 130 HARV. L. REV. 2348, 2363–64 (2017); Vicki C. Jackson, *Constitutional Law in an Age of Proportionality*, 124 YALE L.J. 3094, 3113 (2015).

[35] *Beit Sourik*, HCJ 2065/04, para. 41.

[36] *Oakes*, 1 S.C.R. 103, para. 70 (quoting *Big M Drug Mart*, 1 S.C.R. 295, para. 139). In Canada, the Court has taken a "flexible approach" to this second sub-test, giving greater judicial deference to legislative judgment in socio-economic cases. Mary C. Hurley, *Charter Equality Rights: Interpretation of Section 15 in Supreme Court of Canada Decisions* 13 (Parliamentary Info. & Research Serv., Background Paper BP-402E, 2005); *see also* Jackson, *supra* note 34, at 3114 (explaining that "the minimal impairment test does *not* necessarily imply that if any less restrictive approach can be imagined, the law is invalid," "Canadian courts will look to see whether there is an obvious and workable alternative").

[37] *See* Emiliou, *supra* note 31, at 23–66, 134–70 (describing German jurisprudence).

[38] *Beit Sourik*, HCJ 2065/04, para. 41. *See also* Aharon Barak, *Proportional Effect: The Israeli Experience*, 57 U. TORONTO L.J. 369, 374 (2007) ("This test examines the proper correlation between the benefit stemming from attainment of the proper object and the extent of its effect upon the constitutional right. It focuses upon the results of the statute. It examines the proper ratio between the benefit stemming from attainment of the object and the deleterious effect upon the human right ... It is a principle of balancing. It requires placing colliding values and interests side by side and balancing them according to their weight." (footnote omitted)).

[39] See *Oakes*, 1 S.C.R. 103, para. 71 ("Even if an objective is of sufficient importance, and the first two elements of the proportionality test are satisfied, it is still possible that, because of the severity of the deleterious effects of a measure on individuals or groups, the measure will not be justified by the purposes it is intended to serve. The more severe the deleterious effects of a measure, the more important the objective must be if the measure is to be reasonable and demonstrably justified in a free and democratic society.").

[40] *See, e.g.*, *Brown v. Socialist Workers '74 Campaign Comm.*, 459 U.S. 87, 92–98 (1982); *Nixon v. Administrator of General Services*, 433 U.S. 425, 467–68 (1977).

different groups' associational interests, but it has done so without suggesting that regulation could be justified only if it was necessary to avert a cataclysm.[41] Other examples of the deployment of strict scrutiny as little more than a balancing test come from cases under the Free Exercise Clause during the period in which all substantial burdens on the exercise of religion triggered strict scrutiny.[42] A leading example is *United States* v. *Lee*, in which the Court held that the government had a compelling interest in collecting Social Security taxes from the Old Order Amish, despite their strong religious objections to making the required payments.[43] In *Lee*, the Court treated interests in administrative convenience as compelling, without any evidence of remotely catastrophic consequences if the Amish – who also had religious objections to collecting Social Security benefits – failed to make payments into the system. Not without reason did Justice Scalia's majority opinion in *Employment Division* v. *Smith*,[44] which rejected strict scrutiny of most facially neutral statutes that do not specifically single out religious exercise for prohibition, describe the test that the Court had previously employed as a "balancing test."[45] As we have seen already, moreover, dissenting Justices have protested vehemently that the Court, wrongly, reduced strict scrutiny to the status of a mere balancing test in cases rejecting constitutional challenges to race-based affirmative action programs.

Partly in light of unhappy historical experience in the United States, Justices who resist treating strict scrutiny as a form of weighted balancing would find the analogy to other nations' proportionality tests more troubling than alluring. The worry is that a form of strict scrutiny modeled on proportionality inquiries might tend to deprive rights of any "special force as trumps."[46] To root the objection in distinctive aspects of American constitutional experience, interpretation of strict scrutiny as no more than a weighted balancing test may raise alarms associated with *Lochner* on the one hand and with cases such as *Dennis* v. *United States*,[47] in which some Justices protested that the Court wrongly balanced away First Amendment rights,[48] on the other.

---

[41]   *See Nixon*, 433 U.S. at 467–68 (upholding a statute giving the government custody of former President Nixon's presidential records, without any showing of cataclysmic harm).

[42]   In *Sherbert* v. *Verner*, 374 U.S. 398 (1963), the Court held that strict scrutiny applied in free exercise cases – a rule that stood until *Employment Division* v. *Smith*, 494 U.S. 872 (1990), in which the Court held that neutral, generally applicable laws incidentally burdening the exercise of religion are permissible. In *Smith*, the Court distinguished free exercise cases that employed strict scrutiny to strike down government action as either complicated by other constitutional protections, *id.* at 881, or confined to unemployment compensation, an area of law already replete with individual exemptions, *id.* at 883–84.

[43]   *United States* v. *Lee*, 455 U.S. 252, 256–60 (1982).

[44]   *Smith*, 494 U.S. at 883–84 (collecting other cases).

[45]   *Id.* at 883.

[46]   *See* David M. Beatty, THE ULTIMATE RULE OF LAW 171 (2004).

[47]   341 U.S. 494 (1951).

[48]   *See id.* at 580 (Black, J., dissenting); *id.* at 584–86 (Douglas, J., dissenting).

STRICT SCRUTINY AS A MOTIVE- OR PURPOSE-BASED INQUIRY

Although most of the Supreme Court's strict scrutiny cases invite interpretation as involving either nearly categorical or weighted-balancing interpretations, it is a further indication of the incompletely theorized nature of strict scrutiny that some Justices and commentators have advanced a third interpretation. According to them,[49] strict scrutiny is or ought to be an "illicit motive" test, aimed at "smoking out" forbidden governmental purposes. In this view, strict scrutiny does not determine when the infringement of a right can be *justified* by competing governmental interests, as both the catastrophe and weighted balancing versions of the test do. Instead, it defines constitutional rights as rights not to be harmed by governmental acts taken for forbidden purposes, such as promoting white privilege at the expense of racial minorities or suppressing speech based on disagreement with its message. On this interpretation, otherwise "suspect" statutes that fail strict scrutiny should be presumed to reflect forbidden legislative purposes. In my judgment, this is not a plausible interpretation of strict judicial scrutiny as the Court nearly always applies it, but more nearly an alternative. I shall discuss motive- or purpose-based tests as a possible approach to the protection of constitutional rights in Chapter 5.

For now, the important conclusion is the one stated at the outset: Even after more than fifty years, the Supreme Court's commitment to strict judicial scrutiny is undertheorized and indeterminate. It is little exaggeration to say that there are two compelling interest tests – or, on one view, three. Not surprisingly, uncertainty and confusion have arisen about which version the Court will apply in cases in which the differences among the tests would result in different outcomes. Indeed, the coexistence of rival versions of strict scrutiny has not infrequently occasioned confusion among the Justices themselves.

THE ELEMENTS OF STRICT JUDICIAL SCRUTINY

Just as the Justices who formulated the strict scrutiny test never came together on how strict strict scrutiny ought to be, they never thought through or reached agreement on how to give content to several crucial but vague concepts that the formula presupposes. However the purposes of strict scrutiny are characterized, there are three steps in applying the test: (1) identifying the preferred or fundamental rights the infringement of which triggers strict scrutiny, (2) determining which governmental interests count as "compelling," and (3) giving content to the requirement of necessity or narrow tailoring. Perhaps unsurprisingly in light of the unsettled purposes of strict scrutiny, the natures of these inquiries are less well understood and

---

[49] *See, e.g.*, John Hart Ely, Democracy and Distrust: A Theory of Judicial Review 145–48 (1980); Charles Fried, *Types*, 14 Const. Comment. 55, 62–63 (1997); Elena Kagan, *Private Speech, Public Purpose: The Role of Governmental Motive in First Amendment Doctrine*, 63 U. Chi. L. Rev. 413, 414 (1996); Jed Rubenfeld, *Affirmative Action*, 107 Yale L.J. 427, 428–29 (1997).

less clearly defined than one might otherwise have expected after decades of application. Performance of each of these steps requires the Supreme Court to make critical value judgments.

Triggering Rights

In order to apply strict scrutiny, courts must determine at the outset whether a sufficiently important individual right or constitutionally protected interest has been infringed to call that test into play. As I emphasized in the Introduction, this threshold inquiry immediately points up the need for distinctions among types or categories of constitutional rights. An *ultimate right* is a right that emerges from, or survives the application of, strict scrutiny or some other applicable constitutional test. But prior to decisions about the existence or non-existence of an ultimate right come determinations about whether parties claiming rights violations have *triggering rights* to the application of some test of constitutional validity under a particular constitutional provision and, if so, exactly what *scrutiny right* is triggered – a right to strict scrutiny or to something less (such as rational basis review). In many contexts, however, it will be simply taken for granted that if the requisite type or degree of infringement of an abstract right has occurred, strict scrutiny must be applied. With that situation in mind, I shall frequently refer in this chapter to triggering rights *to* strict scrutiny, even though triggering rights can sometimes incorporate, and thus be partially defined by, other tests of ultimate constitutional validity.

I shall say a good deal about the nature and sources of triggering rights to strict scrutiny (and, in some instances, to other tests of constitutional validity) in the next chapter. For now, two points will suffice to bring the relationships among triggering rights to strict scrutiny, compelling governmental interests, and narrow tailoring preliminarily into focus. First, although the strict scrutiny formula requires the identification of triggering rights, the Justices of the Supreme Court, in embracing strict scrutiny, did not to agree to, and have not subsequently converged on, a methodology for identifying triggering rights to strict judicial scrutiny.

The issue of methodology in defining triggering rights to strict scrutiny implicates many of the central debates about constitutional law. Among these are debates that pit originalists against living constitutionalists. Without getting into details at this point, I would venture a preliminary observation about the assumptions and implications of the strict scrutiny formula. By requiring courts to weigh individual rights against potentially compelling governmental interests, the strict scrutiny formula makes it impossible to insist – as Justice Black often did[50] – that the authors of constitutional provisions such as the First Amendment made all of the balancing judgments that courts need to make in applying those provisions. Almost inevitably, moreover, courts that must take consequences into account in determining whether

---

[50]   *See, e.g., Dennis v. United States,* 341 U.S. 494, 580–81 (1951) (Black, J., dissenting).

rights must yield to compelling governmental interests will feel a pull to take consequences into account in defining and identifying triggering rights in the first place.

Although extended discussion must await Chapter 3, a single example may furnish a helpful foreshadowing. Intuitively, we may think that strict scrutiny should apply to protect free speech rights in all cases in which the government prohibits "speech" that comes within "the freedom of speech." But the Supreme Court has quite sensibly taken a different approach. To see the point, consider a statute – such as I imagined in the Introduction – that prohibits the lighting of fires on public property. Now imagine that a protestor at a political rally sets fire to an American flag as a symbolic protest against governmental policies that the protestor thinks reprehensible. In *Texas* v. *Johnson*,[51] the Supreme Court invalidated a statute that made flag-burning, along with the desecration of other venerated objects, a crime. In a familiar rendition, *Texas* v. *Johnson* recognized a right to burn the flag as an act of political protest. But if we ask whether that purported right would apply against a statute that bans the lighting of fires on public property for substantial governmental reasons that are unrelated to the suppression of speech – such as protecting public property and those using it from conflagration – the answer would be no.

The triggering right to strict judicial scrutiny that the Court recognized in *Johnson* defines a constraint, not a general privilege to engage in speech or expressive activity, and that constraint is triggered only by some kinds of governmental regulations. It does not apply to restrictions that affect speech or expressive activities only incidentally. A general prohibition against outdoor fires would fall into the latter category, even as applied to an act of flag-burning, and therefore would not provoke strict judicial scrutiny.[52] (It would, instead, lead to the application of a different constitutional test that an even-handed regulation aimed at all outdoor fire-lighting would almost certainly satisfy with ease.[53]) We could generalize from this example: The Supreme Court frequently holds that the effects of government regulations in making the exercise of constitutional liberties more difficult or even illegal do not trigger strict judicial scrutiny in the absence of a singling out of the exercise of a fundamental right for regulation or a governmental aim or purpose of burdening constitutional rights.

---

[51] 491 U.S. 397 (1989).

[52] *See id.* at 403.

[53] *See, e.g., United States* v. *O'Brien*, 391 U.S. 367, 377 (1968) (formulating a test under which "a government regulation is sufficiently justified if it is within the constitutional power of the Government; if it furthers an important or substantial governmental interest; if the governmental interest is unrelated to the suppression of free expression; and if the incidental restriction on alleged First Amendment freedoms is no greater than is essential to the furtherance of that interest"). *See generally* John Hart Ely, DEMOCRACY AND DISTRUST: A THEORY OF JUDICIAL REVIEW 105–16 (1980) (discussing the need for differential judicial review of statutes that target speech based on the message that it communicates and those that seek to prohibit harms unrelated to the message being asserted).

And if we ask why not, there are two plausible answers. The first involves forbidden legislative intentions: When a statute singles out speech of expressive conduct for regulation in an anti-flag-burning statute, the Court suspects that the legislature has acted with a constitutionally forbidden intention or motive of suppressing expression that it dislikes. I shall say a good deal more about forbidden legislative intentions and their role within strict scrutiny inquiries in Chapter 5. For now, suffice it to say that while forbidden intentions frequently lead a court to apply strict scrutiny, and ought to, the ensuing judicial analysis aims at determining whether a legislative infringement on expressive liberty is objectively justified. In other words the "narrow tailoring" and "compelling interest" analyses are not well designed to determine what the legislature's motives or intentions really were. Taken as a totality, the strict scrutiny formula asks courts to determine whether statutes are so necessary to promote compelling governmental interests that they ought to be upheld, regardless of governmental motivations. What is more, strict scrutiny is often triggered, and ought to be, even in cases in which the legislature's motivations should not reasonably be suspect.

The second plausible explanation for the Court's ruling that strict scrutiny applied in *Texas* v. *Johnson*, even though it would not apply in the case of a general prohibition against outdoor fires, is that the framing of applicable triggering and scrutiny rights required controversial judgments about desirable or undesirable consequences. If every statute that incidentally made the communication of ideas or the practice of religion more difficult elicited strict judicial scrutiny, the Court would be overwhelmed with strict scrutiny cases that would require difficult judgments and would likely result in the invalidation of many sensible statutes. For example, every statute imposing a tax may leave taxpayers with less money to engage in expressive activity or religious observance. Shrinking from the challenge that a broad extension of triggering rights to strict scrutiny would pose, the Court has defined the First Amendment triggering rights that produce strict scrutiny in a way that accords central significance to statutory language and legislative purposes, not incidental effects in burdening speech or religion, in most cases. Understandably enough, the Justices do not want strict scrutiny to apply to tax statutes that may incidentally burden speech or religion by making it more difficult to afford a microphone or the costs of a religious pilgrimage. To echo now-familiar vocabulary, constitutional rights are constraints, partly defined by specific triggers, and not more general privileges to engage in speech or conduct without governmental interference of any kind.

The second crucial point about triggering and scrutiny rights that deserves mention here also follows from *Texas* v. *Johnson*, which arose under the Free Speech Clause of the First Amendment. The Supreme Court's most famous debates about which constitutional rights or interests should be protected by strict judicial scrutiny have occurred in substantive due process cases. For example, the Justices have recurrently debated whether there is a fundamental abortion right protected by strict judicial scrutiny[54] and, more generally, whether fundamental rights under the Due Process Clause must be narrowly defined and firmly rooted in the nation's history and traditions.[55] Conservative Justices have frequently embraced the latter formulation. Liberals have more frequently rejected it.

But fixation on issues involving triggering rights in substantive due process cases should not create the impression that courts can identify triggering rights under other constitutional provisions without making difficult, sometimes controversial judgments. The methodological and substantive problems that attend the identification of triggering rights are ubiquitous, as the Court's First Amendment jurisprudence illustrates. The First Amendment protects "the freedom of speech," not all speech in all contexts. Justice Holmes's famous example of false cries of fire in a crowded theater exemplifies "speech" the prohibition of which ought not to trigger searching judicial review.[56] Other examples to which nearly everyone agrees that strict scrutiny need not apply include threats ("Your money or your life"), offers of bribes, and speech used to solicit crimes or fix prices.[57] In cases that reached the Supreme Court, the Justices have ruled that obscenity, fighting words, and child pornography lie outside the Free Speech Clause, too.[58]

---

[54] Compare *Planned Parenthood of Se. Pa.* v. *Casey*, 505 U.S. 833, 869 (1992) (joint opinion of O'Connor, Kennedy, and Souter, JJ.) (concluding that "it is a constitutional liberty of the woman to have some freedom to terminate her pregnancy"), *and Roe* v. *Wade*, 410 U.S. 113, 153 (1973) (stating that the "right of privacy, whether it be founded in the Fourteenth Amendment's concept of personal liberty . . . or . . . in the Ninth Amendment's reservation of rights to the people, is broad enough to encompass a woman's decision whether or not to terminate her pregnancy"), *with Whole Woman's Health* v. *Hellerstedt*, 136 S. Ct. 2292, 2329 (2016) (Thomas, J., dissenting) ("The Court has simultaneously transformed judicially created rights like the right to abortion into preferred constitutional rights, while disfavoring many of the rights actually enumerated in the Constitution. But our Constitution renounces the notion that some constitutional rights are more equal than others."); *Casey*, 505 U.S. at 953 (Rehnquist, C.J., concurring in the judgment in part and dissenting in part) (arguing that "the Court was mistaken in *Roe* when it classified a woman's decision to terminate her pregnancy as a 'fundamental right'"), *and Roe*, 410 U.S. at 172–77 (Rehnquist, J., dissenting) (disputing the conclusion that a due process right protects a woman's decision whether to terminate her pregnancy).

[55] Compare *Washington* v. *Glucksberg*, 521 U.S. 702, 719–22 (1997) (holding that to be protected under the Due Process Clause, rights must be narrowly defined and deeply rooted in the nation's history and traditions), *and Michael H.* v. *Gerald D.*, 491 U.S. 110, 122–23 (1989) (plurality opinion) (arguing that rights must be both "fundamental" and "traditionally protected by our society" to be protected under the Due Process Clause), *with Glucksberg*, 521 U.S. at 752 (Souter, J., concurring in the judgment) (arguing that the Court can strike down "arbitrary impositions" or "purposeless restraints" under the Due Process Clause (quoting *Poe* v. *Ullman*, 367 U.S. 497, 543 (1961) (Harlan, J., dissenting)), *and Michael H.*, 491 U.S. at 139–40 (Brennan, J., dissenting) (arguing that rights need not have been traditionally protected to be protected under the Due Process Clause).

[56] *Schenck* v. *United States*, 249 U.S. 47, 52 (1919).

[57] See Frederick Schauer, *Categories and the First Amendment: A Play in Three Acts*, 34 VAND. L. REV. 265, 268–71 (1981); Frederick Schauer, *The Boundaries of the First Amendment: A Preliminary Exploration of Constitutional Salience*, 117 HARV. L. REV. 1765, 1770–71 (2004) [hereinafter Schauer, Boundaries].

[58] See *New York* v. *Ferber*, 458 U.S. 747, 764 (1982) (child pornography); *Miller* v. *California*, 413 U.S. 15, 23 (1973) (obscenity); *Chaplinsky* v. *New Hampshire*, 315 U.S. 568, 571–72 (1942) (fighting words). *But see R.A.V.* v. *City of St. Paul*, 505 U.S. 377, 383–85 (1992) (remarking that "these areas of speech can,

Sometimes the Justices of the Supreme Court agree unanimously about whether a regulation of expression triggers strict scrutiny under the First Amendment, but sometimes, as in *Texas* v. *Johnson*, they disagree. Apart from dividing about whether flag-burning was a protected form of expression, the Justices have disagreed about whether restrictions on corporate expenditures aimed at influencing the outcome of political campaigns should elicit searching review. Many theorists and some Justices have argued that corporate expenditures on political campaigns lie outside the historical understanding of First Amendment protections and have little or no normative claim to constitutional protection.[59] The opposing position has prevailed, at least temporarily. Significantly, however, almost no one seems to think that inquiries into the original historical meaning of the First Amendment can decisively resolve the issues presented by either *Texas* v. *Johnson* or cases involving corporate expenditures on political campaigns. Those issues are too multidimensional, calling for judgments about when First Amendment interests are implicated at all, which specific test of constitutional validity to apply (if any), and whether governmental interests deserve to prevail over individual rights or interests under the applicable test.

In *United States* v. *Stevens*,[60] the Supreme Court firmly rejected the view that "[w]hether a given category of speech enjoys First Amendment protection depends upon a categorical balancing of the value of the speech against its societal costs."[61] Instead, Chief Justice Roberts wrote, restrictions on speech can be deemed not to trigger exacting scrutiny only if they fall within "historic and traditional categories long familiar to the bar,"[62] within which "the prevention and punishment of [speech] have never been thought to raise any Constitutional problem.'"[63] Significantly, however, this stance does not appear to be originalist. Some historians have concluded that the Founding generation understood "the freedom of speech" as narrowly delimited, possibly encompassing only a prohibition against prior restraints and a bar against prosecutions for seditious libel.[64] Others maintain that the free speech guarantee was originally thought to extend much more broadly, but not to confer protections against reasonable restrictions aimed at protecting public

---

consistently with the First Amendment, be regulated because of their constitutionally proscribable content . . . [but] that they are [not] categories of speech entirely invisible to the Constitution, so that they may be made the vehicles for content discrimination unrelated to their distinctively proscribable content" (emphasis omitted)).

[59] *See, e.g., Citizens United* v. *FEC*, 558 U.S. 310, 425–32 (2010) (Stevens, J., concurring in part and dissenting in part).

[60] 559 U.S. 460 (2010).

[61] *Id.* at 470 (quoting Brief for the United States at 8, *Stevens*, 559 U.S. 460 (No. 08-769)).

[62] *Id.* at 468 (quoting *Simon & Schuster, Inc.* v. *Members of N.Y. State Crime Victims Bd.*, 502 U.S. 105, 127 (1991) (Kennedy, J., concurring in the judgment)).

[63] *Id.* at 469 (quoting *Chaplinsky*, 315 U.S. at 571–72 (1942)).

[64] *See, e.g.,* Leonard W. Levy, Emergence of a Free Press xii–xv (1985); David A. Strauss, The Living Constitution 59–61, 75–76 (2010).

interests.[65] No historian, so far as I am aware, has ever suggested that the modern regime of strict scrutiny for all content-based restrictions, subject only to historically-based exceptions, approximates Founding-era beliefs in any way. Nor could the Chief Justice claim that his newly minted formula for identifying free speech triggering rights echoed prior cases.[66] Even his argument that prior cases were consistent with his conclusion required disputable distinctions.[67]

If Chief Justice Roberts possibly thought that he had a methodological approach that would substantially eradicate disputes about First Amendment triggering rights, events swiftly dashed his hopes. Two years later, in *United States* v. *Alvarez*,[68] the Court ruled by 6–3 that the Stolen Valor Act, which made it a crime falsely to claim to have won military medals, violated the First Amendment. But there was no majority opinion. Two concurring Justices rejected the premise that speech enjoys elevated First Amendment protection unless it occupies a historically prohibited category.[69] Justice Alito's dissenting opinion, which two other Justices joined, demonstrated the difficulty of identifying categories of speech traditionally excluded from the First Amendment. According to the dissenters, history and judicial precedent established that although some lies are protected, "a long line of cases" had recognized "that the right to free speech does not protect false factual statements that inflict real harm and serve no legitimate interest."[70] In their view, determining whether the lies prohibited by the Stolen Valor Act lay outside the First Amendment required a partly instrumental rather than purely historical investigation, framed to discern whether the Act's enforcement "would chill other expression that falls within the Amendment's scope."[71]

In the more recent case of *Janus* v. *American Federation of State, County, and Municipal Employees*,[72] which held that it violates the First Amendment for states to require public employees who are not union members to pay an "agency fee" to support collective bargaining, five Justices seemed to thrust the burden of proving that the First Amendment did not apply onto those resisting a challenge under the

---

[65] See, e.g., Jud Campbell, *Natural Rights and the First Amendment*, 127 YALE L.J. 246 (2017); Genevieve Lakier, *The Invention of Law-Value Speech*, 128 HARV. L. REV. 2167 (2015).

[66] *See Stevens*, 559 U.S. at 470 (acknowledging that the Government derived its proposed categorical balancing methodology from "descriptions in our precedents").

[67] *See id.* at 470–71 (distinguishing *New York* v. *Ferber*, 458 U.S. 747 (1982), which recognized an unprotected category of child pornography, on the ground that "*Ferber* presented a special case: The market for child pornography was 'intrinsically related' to the underlying abuse [of children], and . . . '[i]t rarely has been suggested that the constitutional freedom for speech and press extends its immunity to speech or writing used as an integral part of conduct in violation of a valid criminal statute.'" (quoting *id.* at 759, 761–62)).

[68] 567 U.S. 709 (2012).

[69] *Id.* at 730 (Breyer, J., concurring in the judgment) (rejecting "a strict categorical analysis").

[70] *Id.* at 739 (Alito, J., dissenting).

[71] *Id.* at 750.

[72] 138 S. Ct. 2448 (2018).

Free Speech Clause: "The Union offers no persuasive founding-era evidence that public employees were understood to lack free speech protections."[73] But four Justices dissented. Arguably, too, the relevant question was not whether public employees lacked First Amendment protections, but whether the right to free speech encompassed a right not to be made to pay agency fees.

Comparable difficulties in identifying triggering rights to strict scrutiny arise under the Equal Protection Clause. All now agree – though, as we have seen, most once did not – that race-based classifications that harm racial minorities should be strictly scrutinized. But the Justices have divided closely and repeatedly in determining that affirmative action programs that seek to promote racial inclusion, not exclusion, deserve to be treated as similarly suspect. They have disagreed, too, about whether a state ballot provision that effectively barred race-based affirmative action by state governmental institutions, including colleges and universities, should trigger strict judicial scrutiny.[74]

Compelling Governmental Interests

Application of strict scrutiny also obviously requires the identification of compelling governmental interests. Equally plainly, what will count as a compelling interest depends on the version of the test that a court applies. An interest that suffices as compelling under the balancing version would not necessarily pass muster under the test that permits infringements of protected rights only to avert catastrophes – as is brought out in debates about whether interests in "diversity" in elite educational institutions are compelling or not.[75] Regardless of the version of strict scrutiny, the generative cases that launched the strict scrutiny test said nothing about how courts should identify compelling interests. In subsequent cases, too, the Supreme Court has frequently adopted an astonishingly casual approach in labeling asserted governmental interests as either compelling or not compelling.[76]

---

[73]   *Id.* at 2470.

[74]   *See Schuette* v. *Coal. to Defend Affirmative Action, Integration & Immigrant Rights & Fight for Equality by Any Means Necessary (BAMN)*, 134 S. Ct. 1623, 1634 (2014) (finding that strict scrutiny did not apply); *id.* at 1663 (Sotomayor, J. dissenting) ("Where, as here, the majority alters the political process to the detriment of a racial minority, the governmental action is subject to strict scrutiny.").

[75]   *Compare Grutter* v. *Bollinger*, 539 U.S. 306, 327–33 (2003) (holding student body diversity to be a compelling interest), *with id.* at 353 (Thomas, J., concurring in part and dissenting in part) (arguing that "only those measures the State must take to provide a bulwark against anarchy, or to prevent violence," suffice as compelling interests to justify race discrimination).

[76]   *See, e.g.*, *New York* v. *Ferber*, 458 U.S. 747, 756–57 (1982) ("It is evident beyond the need for elaboration that a State's interest in 'safeguarding the physical and psychological well-being of a minor' is 'compelling.'" (quoting *Globe Newspaper Co.* v. *Superior Court*, 457 U.S. 596, 607 (1982))); *United States* v. *Playboy Entm't Grp., Inc.*, 529 U.S. 803, 825 (2000) (noting that "[e]ven upon the assumption that the Government has an interest in substituting itself for informed and empowered parents, its interest is not sufficiently compelling"); *see also* Timothy M. Bagshaw, *The Phantom Standard: Compelling State Interest Analysis and Political Ideology in the Affirmative*

Courts and commentators have sometimes suggested that compelling interests are rooted in and can be derived from the Constitution itself.[77] They have argued, for example, that values underlying the Equal Protection Clause give the states a compelling interest in eradicating private discrimination on the basis of race and gender.[78] Courts and commentators have also suggested that the Constitution presupposes fairly conducted elections and thus can generate compelling interests in limiting rights to the extent necessary to preserve electoral fairness.[79]

Sometimes, however, the Supreme Court labels interests as compelling on the basis of little or no textual inquiry. Examples include cases in which the Court has found a compelling interest in protecting children from one or another purported injury[80] and in preserving the lives of viable fetuses and the health of pregnant women.[81] Controversy seldom emerges when a consensus exists about the overriding importance of a governmental interest on the facts of a particular case. But as much discord sometimes erupts about the importance of a state interest as about whether strict scrutiny ought to apply. To take just two prominent examples, dissenting Justices have argued vehemently that there is no compelling interest in diversity in public education, even though a majority of the Justices have held otherwise.[82] By contrast, dissenting Justices sometimes see compelling interests where a majority

---

Action Context, 2013 UTAH L. REV. 409, 427 ("[B]ecause of the lack of any explicit standard governing whether an asserted state interest is compelling for purposes of strict scrutiny analysis, justices may craft strict scrutiny's ends analysis in such a way as to privilege particular ideological understandings in their jurisprudence."); Stephen E. Gottlieb, *Tears for Tiers on the Rehnquist Court*, 4 U. PA. J. CONST. L. 350, 366–67 (2002); Stephen E. Gottlieb, *Compelling Governmental Interests: An Essential but Unanalyzed Term in Constitutional Adjudication*, 68 B.U. L. REV. 917, 932–37 (1998).

[77] See, e.g., *Regents of the Univ. of Cal. v. Bakke*, 438 U.S. 265, 311–13 (1978) (opinion of Powell, J.) (asserting that a public university has a compelling interest in being able to select a diverse student body that arises from its First Amendment right to academic freedom); David L. Faigman, *Measuring Constitutionality Transactionally*, 45 HASTINGS L.J. 753, 755–64 (1994) (describing an approach to interest balancing that "fully incorporates the foundational premises of the Constitution and offers precise guidelines to judges who must maneuver through the rocky shoals of constitutional adjudication," *id.* at 755).

[78] See *Roberts v. U.S. Jaycees*, 468 U.S. 609, 623–26 (1984) (gender).

[79] See Stephen Breyer, ACTIVE LIBERTY: INTERPRETING OUR DEMOCRATIC CONSTITUTION 43–50 (2005); *Tashjian v. Republican Party of Connecticut*, 479 U.S. 208, 217 (1986) (noting that the Constitution grants states "broad power to prescribe the 'Time, Places and Manner of holding Elections for Senators and Representatives'" and that this power "is matched by state control over the election process for state offices" (quoting U.S. CONST. art. I, § 4, cl. 1)); see also *Burson v. Freeman*, 504 U.S. 191, 198–99 (1992) (plurality opinion) (upholding a restriction on otherwise protected campaign speech within 100 feet of a polling place as justified by the "obviously" compelling government interests of protecting citizens' right to vote free from intimidation and "to vote in an election conducted with integrity and reliability").

[80] See *Denver Area Educ. Telecomms. Consortium, Inc. v. FCC*, 518 U.S. 727, 755 (1996) ("We agree with the Government that protection of children is a 'compelling interest.'").

[81] See, e.g., *Roe v. Wade*, 410 U.S. 113, 162–63 (1973).

[82] See *Fisher v. Univ. of Texas at Austin*, 570 U.S. 297, 327 (2013) (Thomas, J., concurring) ("Educational benefits are a far cry from the truly compelling state interests that we previously required to justify use of racial classifications."); *Grutter v. Bollinger*, 539 U.S. 306, 356–61 (2003) (Thomas, J., concurring in part and dissenting in part).

of their colleagues do not. For instance, dissenting justices have protested to no avail that the government has a compelling interest in avoiding the influence of corporate expenditures in political campaigns.[83]

Professor Bruce Ackerman once argued that judicial conservatives are more willing to find compelling interests implicit in or presupposed by the Constitution than to conclude that the Constitution implicitly creates or recognizes fundamental rights.[84] There are undoubtedly examples that would support his thesis. For example, in *Planned Parenthood of Southeastern Pennsylvania v. Casey*,[85] Justice Scalia found that the Constitution recognized a compelling interest in preserving fetal life,[86] even as he denied that women had a fundamental right to abortion.[87] Similarly, in *Cruzan v. Director, Missouri Department of Health*,[88] Justice Scalia found that states have a compelling interest in preventing suicide,[89] even as he denied that people have a fundamental right to choose to end their lives.[90] In other contexts, however, liberals, too, have proved quick to find compelling governmental interests. To repeat examples given already, liberal Justices have held over conservative dissents that states have a compelling interest in maintaining diverse student bodies in public universities,[91] and they have insisted loudly that there is a compelling interest in avoiding corporate influence on electoral politics.[92]

Given the complexities in the Justices' patterns of decision, we should consider the thesis that the elements of the strict scrutiny formula are likely to be symbiotically interactive: Whether consciously or subconsciously, the Justices may vary their calibration of the strength of an asserted governmental interest as either compelling or not compelling depending on their assessment of the importance of a triggering right. For example, liberal skepticism about whether affirmative action programs ought to elicit strict scrutiny may explain the readiness with which liberals label educational diversity a compelling interest.[93] And conservatives' belief that the

---

[83] See *Citizens United* v. FEC, 558 U.S. 310, 466 (2010) (Stevens, J., concurring in part and dissenting in part).

[84] See Bruce Ackerman, *Liberating Abstraction*, 59 U. CHI. L. REV. 317, 317–18 (1992).

[85] 505 U.S. 833 (1992).

[86] See *id.* at 982 (Scalia, J., concurring in the judgment in part and dissenting in part) (citing *Roe v. Wade*, 410 U.S. 113, 162 (1973)).

[87] See *id.* at 980.

[88] 497 U.S. 261 (1990).

[89] See *id.* at 298–300 (Scalia, J., concurring).

[90] See *id.*

[91] See *Grutter* v. *Bollinger*, 539 U.S. 306, 328 (2003).

[92] See *Austin* v. *Mich. Chamber of Commerce*, 494 U.S. 652, 666 (1990).

[93] Judicial liberals have sometimes argued explicitly that strict judicial scrutiny should not apply in cases presenting challenges to race-based affirmative action programs. *See, e.g.*, *Regents of Univ. of Cal. v. Bakke*, 438 U.S. 265, 356–63 (1978) (joint opinion of Brennan, White, Marshall, and Blackmun, JJ.); *City of Richmond* v. *J.A. Croson Co.*, 488 U.S. 469, 535 (1989) (Marshall, J., dissenting). In fact, four of the five justices in the *Grutter* majority – Stevens, Souter, Ginsburg, and Breyer – likely would have held that race-based affirmative action should be reviewed pursuant to a less exacting standard than that applied to other forms of race-based decision-making. *See Gratz* v. *Bollinger*, 539 U.S. 244, 301

Constitution strongly condemns all race-based decision-making may affect their judgments that there is no compelling interest in the kind of diversity that affirmative action programs seek to promote.[94] Reciprocally, conservatives seem more likely to find compelling state interests in cases in which they take a skeptical view of the asserted underlying triggering right. To take a relatively plain example, in cases involving regulation of sexually explicit cable television programming, Justice Scalia once affirmed that the government has a compelling interest in protecting children from exposure to sexually explicit broadcasts.[95] But he also expressed deep skepticism that sexual "pandering," as he called it, should trigger elevated scrutiny in the first place.[96]

Sympathies involving underlying rights aside, perhaps the most important point about compelling governmental interests within the strict scrutiny formula is that it will frequently matter crucially how the government's interest is defined.[97] In other words, there will often be an important "level of generality" question involving purportedly compelling governmental interests, just as there is in identifying triggering and scrutiny rights.

Affirmative action cases again exemplify the point. To appraise whether the government has a compelling interest in diversity that would justify affirmative action programs for public institutions of higher education,[98] we need to consider how the government's interest should be described: Is it an interest in *racial* diversity or, instead, an interest in diversity of perspectives for which racial background may

(Ginsburg, J., dissenting) ("Actions designed to burden groups long denied full citizenship stature are not sensibly ranked with measures taken to hasten the day when entrenched discrimination and its aftereffects have been extirpated."); *Wygant* v. *Jackson Bd. of Educ.*, 476 U.S. 267, 316 (1986) (Stevens, J., dissenting) ("There is ... a critical difference between a decision to *exclude* a member of a minority race because of his or her skin color and a decision to *include* more members of the minority in a school faculty for that reason.").

[94] *See Fisher* v. *Univ. of Texas at Austin*, 136 S. Ct. 2198, 2215 (2016) (Thomas, J., dissenting); *Fisher* v. *Univ. of Texas at Austin*, 570 U.S. 297, 2421, 2424 (2013) (Thomas, J., concurring) (writing that the "Constitution abhors classifications based on race" (quoting *Grutter*, 539 U.S. at 353 (Thomas, J., concurring in part and dissenting in part)) and then arguing that because "there is nothing 'pressing' or 'necessary' about obtaining whatever educational benefits may flow from racial diversity," it does not suffice as a compelling interest); *Grutter*, 539 U.S. at 353, (2003) (Thomas, J., concurring in part and dissenting in part) (stating that "every time the government places citizens on racial registers and makes race relevant to the provision of burdens or benefits, it demeans us all," and then rejecting educational diversity as a compelling interest).

[95] *See United States* v. *Playboy Entm't Group, Inc.*, 529 U.S. 803, 842–43 (2000) (Breyer, J., dissenting). Justice Scalia joined Justice Breyer's dissent.

[96] *See Ashcroft* v. *ACLU*, 542 U.S. 656, 676 (2004) (Scalia, J., dissenting) ("[C]ommercial entities which engage in 'the sordid business of pandering' by 'deliberately emphasiz[ing] the sexually provocative aspects of [their non-obscene products], in order to catch the salaciously disposed,' engage in constitutionally unprotected behavior." (alterations in original) (quoting *Playboy Entm't*, 529 U.S. at 831 (Scalia, J., dissenting))).

[97] *See* Charles Fried, *Two Concepts of Interests: Some Reflections on the Supreme Court's Balancing Test*, 76 HARV. L. REV. 755, 757–59 (1963) (demonstrating the diversity of ways in which competing interests can be formulated and noting the implications of this choice for the judicial role).

[98] *See, e.g., Grutter* v. *Bollinger*, 539 U.S. 306 (2003).

function as evidence, but evidence of only limited weight? A further complication arises if it would be possible for a university to achieve diversity without
affirmative action if, for example, it reduced its reliance on grades and test
scores as admissions criteria. Is the government's compelling interest one that
embraces both retaining high academic distinction and achieving diversity?[99]
Finally, because diversity is inherently a matter of degree, the question emerges
whether the government's interest should be defined as one in achieving
diversity per se, or whether, instead, it should be regarded as one in attaining
particular levels or *increments* of diversity?[100] In other words, is there
a compelling interest in moving from one level of diversity (that is more than
zero) to another, higher level that is still less than the government would ideally
like to reach, all else equal?

The analytic importance of level-of-generality questions such as these is by no
means peculiar to affirmative action cases. Consider, for example, a case in which
the government attempts to regulate the transmission of sexually explicit television
programming (whether over the public airwaves or via cable) and claims
a compelling interest in protecting children.[101] Surely there is a compelling interest
in protecting children, at least from serious harm, if the interest is stated wholly
abstractly, but this much generality may not prove helpful for anyone who takes the
"compelling interest" question seriously.[102] Perhaps it would be better to ask what

[99]   *Compare id.* at 339 (asserting that a university need not "choose between maintaining a reputation for
      excellence or fulfilling a commitment to provide educational opportunities to members of all racial
      groups"), *with id.* at 357 (Thomas, J., dissenting) ("[T]here is no pressing public necessity in
      maintaining ... an elite law school.").

[100] In *Grutter*, the University argued, and the Court appeared to accept, that the compelling interest was
      in achieving a critical mass of students from particular disadvantaged groups. *See id.* at 333 (majority
      opinion). As Chief Justice Rehnquist argued in dissent, however, this argument seemed to be belied
      by the University's practice of setting the necessary threshold for a critical mass much lower for some
      groups, such as Native Americans, than for others, most notably blacks. *See id.* at 380–86 (Rehnquist,
      C.J., dissenting). In *Fisher v. University of Texas at Austin*, 136 S. Ct. 2198 (2016), the Court appeared
      to confirm that the compelling interest was in achieving a critical mass. *Id.* at 2212. By contrast, Justice
      Alito argued in dissent that "[t]his intentionally imprecise interest is designed to insulate UT's
      program from meaningful judicial review." *Id.* at 2222. (Alito, J., dissenting). Justice Alito continued
      by describing confusion over whether the critical mass concept is tied to demographic numbers or
      some other method of calculation. *Id.* at 2225.

[101] *See, e.g., Ashcroft v. ACLU*, 542 U.S. 656, 683 (2004) (Breyer, J., dissenting) (finding that protecting
      children from commercial pornography is a compelling government interest); *Denver Area Educ.
      Telecomms. Consortium, Inc. v. FCC*, 518 U.S. 727, 755 (1996) (plurality opinion) ("We agree with the
      Government that protection of children is a 'compelling interest.'"); *Sable Commc'ns of Cal., Inc.
      v. FCC*, 492 U.S. 115, 126 (1989) ("We have recognized that there is a compelling interest in protecting
      the physical and psychological well-being of minors.").

[102] For example, in *United States v. Playboy Entertainment Group, Inc.*, 529 U.S. 803 (2000), Justice
      Kennedy's majority opinion expressed some doubt about whether the government had a compelling
      "independent" interest in shielding children from sexually explicit material or only a compelling
      interest in aiding the efforts of those parents who wanted their children to be shielded. *See id.* at 825.
      Writing in dissent, Justice Breyer maintained that the government's interest was compelling regard-
      less of the parents' views. *See id.* at 842 (Breyer, J., dissenting). *See also Reno v. ACLU*, 521 U.S. 844,

exactly is the harm that sexually explicit programming causes and whether there is a compelling interest in prohibiting that particular harm – perhaps a specified psychological dislocation, whether short-term or long-term. But even this formulation might seem too simple. If sexually explicit programming causes harm, it seems likely that it will damage some children but not others. Is it better, then, to inquire whether the government has a compelling interest in achieving a specific quantum of reduction in the risk or incidence of harm (since some children will presumably suffer the harm, and others will not, regardless of whether the government is permitted to impose a particular regulation)?[103]

To put the question this way might seem to collapse the "narrow tailoring" prong of strict scrutiny into the compelling interest element of the test. As reformulated, the question essentially becomes whether there is a compelling governmental interest in achieving as much reduction in the risk or incidence of harm as a challenged regulation is likely to achieve. But the risk on the other side is that the narrow tailoring inquiry will be left untethered if there is too little attention to exactly what the government's purportedly compelling interest is. Imagine that psychologists could establish conclusively that prolonged exposure to sexually explicit programming would cause severe psychological damage to one child in every 100,000, and that a prohibition against the transmission of such images during the hours between 6 a.m. and 10 p.m. would reduce by exactly half the likelihood that the vulnerable children would sustain the harm that otherwise would befall them. Should a court proceed on the flat assumption that the government (always) has a compelling interest in protecting children from serious harm, or possibly in protecting children from the particular kind of psychological harm in issue, or should it ask instead whether there is a compelling governmental interest in achieving the limited quantum of reduction in harm (or risk thereof) that the government could reasonably hope to achieve? Perhaps remarkably, Supreme Court cases yield no clear answer to this question.

864–65 (1997) (distinguishing between independent state interests in children's well-being and in aiding parents in shielding children from potentially harmful speech).

[103] The Supreme Court confronted a closely analogous question in *Brown v. Entertainment Merchants Association*, 564 U.S. 786, (2011). There, the Court employed strict scrutiny in striking down California's restrictions on the sale and rental of violent video games to minors. *Id.* at 805. California claimed an interest in supporting "parental authority" because the state only allowed adults to purchase violent video games. *Id.* at 802. The Court rejected this interest by first observing that parents may already exercise control based on video-game ratings that disclose whether games contain mature content. *Id.* at 803. Therefore, the Court argued the marginal change produced by the law at issue was not compelling: "Filling the remaining modest gap in concerned-parents' control can hardly be a compelling state interest." *Id.* California also asserted an interest in preventing "harmful effects on children," but the Court dismissed the harms in question as "small and indistinguishable from effects produced by other media." *Id.* at 800–01.

Narrow Tailoring

The "necessity" or "narrow tailoring" prong of the strict scrutiny test has sparked little systematic investigation.[104] A careful parsing of the cases reveals that this requirement encompasses at least three elements and may sometimes include a fourth. When the components of the Supreme Court's narrow tailoring inquiries are teased apart, it becomes clear that the test contains significant, unresolved ambiguities of which the Court appears startlingly unaware.

Proof of Necessity of Infringement on a Triggering Right. The first element of the narrow tailoring requirement insists that infringements of protected rights must be "necessary" in order to be justified.[105] The Supreme Court sometimes expresses essentially the same demand when it says that the government's chosen means must be "the least restrictive alternative" that would achieve its goals.[106] A law would not be "necessary" to achieve its compelling ends if the government could accomplish the same result through means that inflicted lesser burdens on protected rights.[107]

Underinclusiveness Inquiry. In identifying the requirements of narrow tailoring, the Supreme Court often says that governmental infringements on fundamental rights must not be "underinclusive":[108] A statute will not survive strict scrutiny if it fails to regulate activities that pose substantially the same threats to the government's

---

[104]   The most thorough treatments of which I am aware are Ian Ayres, *Narrow Tailoring*, 43 UCLA L. REV. 1781 (1996), and Eugene Volokh, *Freedom of Speech, Permissible Tailoring and Transcending Strict Scrutiny*, 144 U. PA. L. REV. 2417 (1996).

[105]   *See, e.g.*, Republican Party of Minn. v. White, 536 U.S. 765, 775 (2002) ("[T]o show that the [statute] is narrowly tailored, [the government] must demonstrate that it does not 'unnecessarily circumscrib[e] protected expression.'" (alteration in original) (quoting *Brown* v. *Hartlage*, 456 U.S. 45, 54 (1982))); *Kramer* v. *Union Free Sch. Dist. No. 15*, 395 U.S. 621, 632 (1969) ("[T]he classifications must be tailored so that the exclusion of appellant and members of his class is necessary to achieve the articulated state goal.").

[106]   *Ashcroft*, 542 U.S. at 666; *Playboy*, 529 U.S. at 815; *Sable Commc'ns*, 492 U.S. at 126; *see Fla. Star* v. *B.J.F.*, 491 U.S. 524, 538 (1989) (striking down a government action in part because less speech-restrictive alternatives were available); Volokh, *supra* note 104, at 2422.

[107]   *See United States* v. *Alvarez*, 567 U.S. 709, 726 (2012) ("The Government has not shown, and cannot show, why counterspeech would not suffice to achieve its interest."). The necessity or narrow tailoring requirement may explain why the Supreme Court has sometimes demanded that a government body explore race-neutral alternatives before implementing an affirmative action plan. At least one prominent commentator has expressed puzzlement about this requirement. According to him, "[t]he Court's preference for 'race-neutral means to increase minority participation' is inconsistent with narrow tailoring" because "[e]xtending affirmative action subsidies to non-victim whites produces less-tailored, over-inclusive programs." Ayres, *supra* note 104, at 1784. If this criticism fails, it must be because the Court believes that a race-neutral program would not infringe any triggering right at all and, accordingly, that infringement is not "necessary" for the government to accomplish its compelling goal. This is of course a controversial conclusion in view of the Supreme Court's suggestion in *Washington* v. *Davis*, 426 U.S. 229 (1976), that a facially neutral statute that was adopted for racially discriminatory reasons would trigger strict judicial scrutiny. *See id.* at 241–42.

[108]   *See Church of the Lukumi Babalu Aye, Inc.* v. *City of Hialeah*, 508 U.S. 520, 547 (1993) ("It is established in our strict scrutiny jurisprudence that 'a law cannot be regarded as protecting an interest "of the highest order" … when it leaves appreciable damage to that supposedly vital interest

purportedly compelling interest as the conduct that the government prohibits. Underinclusive regulations "diminish the credibility of the government's rationale"[109] for infringing on constitutional rights and generate suspicion that the selective targeting betrays an impermissible motive. Even absent concern about governmental motives, the demand that restrictions on constitutional rights not be underinclusive reflects an insistence that the government not infringe on rights when its doing so will predictably prove futile in accomplishing purportedly justifying goals.

It is far from clear, however, that every underinclusive statute is therefore necessarily unconstitutional.[110] Under *Roe v. Wade*,[111] regulations of abortion designed to protect the health of pregnant women were never deemed invalid just because the states that enacted them did not attempt to avert other threats to maternal health such as those posed by smoking or drinking or riding on motorcycles without a helmet. Nor has the Court suggested that a state cannot forbid parents to withhold medical care from their children,[112] thereby trenching on parents' constitutional rights to control their children's upbringing,[113] unless it also regulates all other conduct that threatens children's health.[114] By contrast, a five-Justice majority in *National Institute of Family and Life Advocates v. Becerra* found an underinclusiveness problem with a state statute that required pro-life crisis pregnancy centers to provide their clients with information about the availability of abortion.[115] Even if the state had a substantial or compelling interest in notifying pregnant women of state-sponsored abortion services, the Court deemed the challenged statute "wildly underinclusive" because it did not impose notification

unprohibited.'" (omission in original) (quoting *Fla. Star*, 491 U.S. 524, 541–42 (1989) (Scalia, J., concurring in part and concurring in the judgment))); *Brown* v. *Entm't Merchants Ass'n*, 564 U.S. 786, 802 (2011) (concluding that a regulation's underinclusiveness "when judged against its asserted justification ... is alone enough to defeat it").

[109] *City of Ladue* v. *Gilleo*, 512 U.S. 43, 52 (1994); *see Republican Party of Minnesota* v. *White*, 536 U.S. 765, 780 (2002).

[110] *See, e.g., Williams-Yulee* v. *Fla. Bar*, 135 S. Ct. 1656, 1668–70 (2015) ("Although a law's underinclusivity raises a red flag, the First Amendment imposes no freestanding 'underinclusiveness limitation.'" (quoting *R.A.V.* v. *St. Paul*, 505 U.S. 377, 387 (1992))). In that case, the state might have restricted other speech that was damaging to judicial integrity, but the court said the "First Amendment does not put a State to that all-or-nothing choice." *Id.* at 1670. The Court saw "good reason" for the lines Florida drew, and did not want to "punish Florida for leaving open more, rather than fewer, avenues of expression, especially when there is no indication that the selective restriction of speech reflects a pretextual motive." *Id.*

[111] 410 U.S. 113 (1973).

[112] *See Parham* v. *J.R.*, 442 U.S. 584, 630 (1979) (Brennan, J., concurring in part and dissenting in part) (stating that parental rights are limited in our society, as reflected by statutes and court decisions "that, *inter alia*, curtail parental authority ... to withhold necessary medical treatment" from their children).

[113] *See Wisconsin* v. *Yoder*, 406 U.S. 205, 232–33 (1972) (recognizing parents' rights to control their children's upbringing).

[114] See James G. Dwyer, *Parents' Religion and Children's Welfare: Debunking the Doctrine of Parents' Rights*, 82 CALIF. L. REV. 1371 (1994).

[115] 138 S. Ct. 2361 (2018).

requirements on other clinics that serve low-income women, and because the state had not undertaken a public information campaign.[116]

Overinclusiveness Inquiry. Just as the Supreme Court says that the narrow tailoring requirement forbids or at least strongly disfavors underinclusive statutes, it insists symmetrically that "overinclusive" statutes also fail strict judicial scrutiny.[117] As most often applied, the prohibition against overinclusiveness probably only repeats, or serves as a synonym for, the demand that any permissible regulation of protected rights must be "necessary" or "the least restrictive alternative." There is a potentially important difference, however. Whereas the "least restrictive alternative" formulation invites the conclusion that a regulation that is necessary to promote a compelling governmental interest will therefore satisfy strict scrutiny as long as no narrower regulation would suffice, the prohibition against overinclusiveness suggests that a statute might be condemned for lack of narrow tailoring even if no less restrictive alternative existed.[118]

To see the importance of this distinction, consider a hypothetical variation on the facts of *Korematsu v. United States,*[119] which upheld the World War II exclusion of all persons of Japanese ancestry from the West Coast of the United States. The military order involved in *Korematsu* applied to roughly 120,000 people.[120] Military officials defended it as necessary to prevent sabotage.[121] If we suppose, quite possibly counterfactually, that at least one act of sabotage would have occurred if the military had not enforced the exclusion, and that no other practicable steps would have proved equally effective, then the exclusion order would pass muster as "necessary" to achieve its ends. On the same supposition, however, the order would have imposed constitutionally suspect, race-based disabilities on many thousands of blameless people and thus might have been deemed impermissibly "overinclusive." Would the statute have passed the modern strict scrutiny test?

Supreme Court decisions give no clear answer. The Court has sometimes invalidated statutes that it deemed overinclusive without pausing to assess whether less restrictive alternatives existed that would have effectively protected the government's

---

[116]   *Id.* at 2375–76.

[117]   *See, e.g., First Nat'l Bank of Bos. v. Bellotti,* 435 U.S. 765, 792–95 (1978); *Simon & Schuster, Inc. v. Members of N.Y. State Crime Victims Board,* 502 U.S. 105, 121–23 (1991); *Citizens United v. FEC,* 558 U.S. 310, 362 (2010) ("[T]he statute is overinclusive [as to shareholder-protection interest] because it covers all corporations, including nonprofit corporations and for-profit corporations with only single shareholders."); Volokh, *supra* note 104, at 2422.

[118]   *Cf.* Eugene Volokh, *Crime-Facilitating Speech,* 57 STAN. L. REV. 1095, 1136 (2005) (observing that Supreme Court explications of the narrow tailoring formula leave open whether a least restrictive means will satisfy the requirement even if it is substantially overinclusive).

[119]   323 U.S. 214 (1944).

[120]   *See id.* at 241–42 (Murphy, J., dissenting).

[121]   *See id.* at 218–19 (majority opinion).

asserted interests.[122] In addition, the Court stated in dictum in *Johnson* v. *California*,[123] quoting *Grutter* v. *Bollinger*,[124] that "[w]hen race-based action [subject to strict scrutiny] is necessary to further a compelling governmental interest, such action does not violate the constitutional guarantee of equal protection so long as the narrow-tailoring requirement is *also* satisfied."[125] Some indicators point the other way, however. The Court said in dictum in *Sable Communications* v. *FCC*[126] that "[t]he Government may . . . regulate the content of constitutionally protected speech in order to promote a compelling interest if it chooses the least restrictive means to further the articulated interest."[127] And under even the most stringent interpretation of strict judicial scrutiny, regulation would seemingly need to be allowed to avert true catastrophes, notwithstanding possible "overinclusiveness" in the reach of a challenged statutory regulation.

Perhaps the most that can be said with confidence is that the Supreme Court has sent ambiguous signals about how the "least restrictive alternative" and "no over-inclusiveness" elements of the narrow tailoring test relate to one another.

The Analogy of Proportionality. It is imaginable, if only barely, that even the smallest element of underinclusiveness or overinclusiveness would condemn a statute subject to strict scrutiny. But if any underinclusiveness and perhaps especially any overinclusiveness is permissible, the question inevitably arises: How much under- or overinclusiveness is tolerable, and how much is too much? Although the Supreme Court has seldom if ever said so expressly, answering this question would appear to require an inquiry analogous (not necessarily identical) to those that other countries' courts conduct in assessing "proportionality."[128]

---

[122] *See, e.g., Dunn* v. *Blumstein*, 405 U.S. 330, 359–60 (1972) (invalidating a state durational residency requirement as insufficiently tailored to the state's interest in having an informed electorate without considering whether other mechanisms were available to ensure an informed electorate).

[123] 543 U.S. 499 (2005). Justice Thomas has said explicitly that the fact that alternative measures "are not completely effective . . . is no justification for the conclusion that prophylactic controls . . . are narrowly tailored." *Colo. Republican Fed. Campaign Comm.* v. *FEC*, 518 U.S. 604, 643–44 (1996) (Thomas, J., concurring in the judgment and dissenting in part).

[124] 539 U.S. 306 (2003). Also pertinent may be *Ashcroft* v. *Free Speech Coalition*, 535 U.S. 234 (2002), in which the Court said that in the First Amendment context, "[t]he overbreadth doctrine prohibits the Government from banning unprotected speech if a substantial amount of protected speech is prohibited or chilled in the process." *Id.* at 255. In doing so, it made no mention of a possible exception for cases in which a sweeping prohibition was nonetheless the least restrictive alternative that would be effective in achieving its end.

Ashcroft invalidated a provision of the Child Pornography Prevention Act that barred the dissemination of "virtual" child pornography. Against arguments that it was impossible even for experts to distinguish real from virtual child pornography and that the government must therefore be able to bar the latter in order to address the harms occasioned by the production of the former, the Court replied that an analysis under which "protected speech may be banned as a means to ban unprotected speech . . . turns the First Amendment upside down." *Id.* at 255.

[125] *Johnson*, 543 U.S. at 514 (emphasis added) (quoting *Grutter*, 539 U.S. 327).

[126] 492 U.S. 115 (1989).

[127] *Id.* at 126.

[128] *See supra* notes 29–39 and accompanying text.

In determining whether a particular degree of statutory under- or overinclusiveness is tolerable, a court must judge whether the harm attending a governmental infringement on a protected right is constitutionally acceptable in light of the government's compelling aims, the probability that the challenged policy will achieve them, and available alternative means of pursuing the same goals.[129]

The necessity for courts to conduct inquiries of this kind can be brought out by reflection on many of the actual and hypothetical cases that I have discussed already, including those involving the use of admittedly overinclusive race-based regulations to address the (greater or lesser) risk of genuine catastrophe[130] and the overinclusive regulation of sexually explicit television programming that would likely harm only some children.[131] For purposes of illustration, consider a situation in which the government claims that it must infringe on rights to freedom from discrimination on the basis of race or religion – for example, by subjecting certain classes of people to special scrutiny before they can ride on airplanes or work in high-risk facilities – in order to avert a calamitous terrorist strike. If the question is whether there is a compelling interest in avoiding a terrorist cataclysm, the answer is obviously yes. The problem, of course, involves the difficulty of knowing in advance whether particular restrictions on protected rights would be either necessary or sufficient to forestall the threat. Instead, one must deal in probabilities by attempting to assess how great a risk currently exists and how much reduction in that risk particular measures would likely achieve. One could frame the question as whether there is a compelling interest in achieving a projected quantum of risk reduction. But even if it would be theoretically possible to answer that question as if it stood in isolation, it is hard to imagine actual human beings doing so – and far from obvious why they ought to do so – without taking simultaneous account of the seriousness and scope of the deprivations of protected (triggering) rights that particular risk-reducing measures would entail. However one might gauge the constitutional costs of allowing race to help trigger heightened airport screening procedures, those costs are surely less than those that would attend prolonged race-based detention.

Coming at the same question of constitutional permissibility from the narrow tailoring side, a judge could ask whether there is a less restrictive alternative that would equally advance the government's interest in reducing the risk of terrorism. Typically if not invariably, however, any alternative that is less restrictive in theory is likely also to be less effective in fact. In assessing whether this consideration should be controlling, it may therefore be important to take note of whether a less restrictive alternative exists that would achieve almost as much risk reduction while infringing less on protected rights. Once again, it thus seems impossible to think sensibly about

---

[129] For a partly parallel argument that the application of strict scrutiny in affirmative action cases should focus on marginal costs and benefits, see Ian Ayres & Sydney Foster, *Don't Tell, Don't Ask*: Narrow Tailoring after Grutter *and* Gratz, 85 TEX. L. REV. 517 (2007).

[130] *See Korematsu v. United States*, 323 U.S. 214 (1944).

[131] *See United States v. Playboy Entm't Group, Inc.*, 529 U.S. 803 (2000).

compelling governmental interests and the narrow tailoring requirement as if they were sequentially isolated components of a bifurcated two-step inquiry – or as if every compelling interest were equally compelling or every infringement of a triggering right equally morally or constitutionally disturbing. In a practical sense, the dispositive, proportionality-like question becomes whether a particular, incremental reduction in risk justifies a particular infringement of protected rights in light of other reasonably available, more or less costly and more or less effective, alternatives.[132]

A similar inquiry will frequently be called for when a governmental regulation aims to lower the incidence of a harm without wholly extirpating it. An illustration comes from *Ashcroft v. ACLU*,[133] involving the constitutionality of the Child Online Protection Act ("COPA"), which sought to protect minors from exposure to sexually explicit material on the internet by requiring those posting such material for commercial purposes to take costly steps to deny access to minors.[134] Writing for the Court, Justice Kennedy invalidated the COPA on the ground that it was not "the least restrictive means" of protecting children:[135] Filtering software, which would restrict harms to children without infringing adults' rights, might be even more effective if it were put more broadly into place.[136] As Justice Breyer pointed out in dissent, however, filtering technology was already a part of the status quo: It was available, but parents and others with child-supervision responsibilities failed, for whatever reason, to employ it on a broad scale.[137] Under these circumstances, the COPA would have had some effect in diminishing the incidence of children's exposure to sexually explicit material (even though it would not have reduced the level to zero). Postulating ex ante that the government either has or does not have a compelling interest in protecting children from exposure to sexually explicit speech, and then inquiring whether a restriction is narrowly tailored to that end (which could never be achieved completely), makes the issue excessively abstract. As a practical matter, the constitutional question required marginal analysis: Were the COPA's incremental benefits in protecting children constitutionally justified in light of its infringement of protected freedoms? Once again, the ultimate question for decision seems inescapably to be one of proportionality (even though the formal strictures of the proportionality analysis used in other legal systems do not apply).[138]

---

[132] *Cf.* Rubin, *supra* note 7, at 14 (asserting that one aspect of the narrow tailoring inquiry involves "comparing the marginal benefits and costs of the use of a particular classification with those of some alternative if there is one").

[133] 542 U.S. 656 (2004).

[134] *See id.* at 661–63.

[135] *See id.* at 666–67.

[136] *See id.* at 667–68.

[137] *See id.* at 684 (Breyer, J., dissenting).

[138] A similar issue divided the Court in *United States* v. *Playboy Entertainment Group, Inc.*, 529 U.S. 803 (2000), which involved the constitutionality of a governmental regulation designed to ensure that cable television signals for sexually explicit channels would not "bleed" into the homes of non-

But we should not leap to the conclusion that just because one application of strict judicial scrutiny appears to reflect weighted balancing, the same is true of all applications. As the beginning of this chapter emphasized, there are different versions of the strict scrutiny test. The analytical structure of narrow-tailing inquiries may well vary with the other elements of the cases in which they are conducted.

CONCLUDING THOUGHTS

Before concluding this chapter, I should draw together the threads of its lengthy analysis. Three main conclusions have emerged.

First, the strict scrutiny test was under-theorized at the time of its emergence and remains under-theorized and substantially indeterminate today. It is little exaggeration to say that there are at least two different versions of strict judicial scrutiny. In one version, strict scrutiny enforces nearly categorical prohibitions against the infringement of rights. It is and ought to be almost invariably fatal in fact. In an alternative version, however, strict scrutiny is little more than a weighted balancing test. It signals a presumption for upholding claims of fundamental or preferred rights. But the degree of protection can vary with the relative importance of the right and the relative importance of the governmental interests that are respectively at stake. In this second version, strict judicial scrutiny is substantially similar – though not identical – to the proportionality tests that other western liberal democracies employ to protect but also to limit fundamental rights.

Second, although the strict scrutiny formula appears to contemplate categorically separate judicial inquiries into whether a triggering right exists and whether a restriction is narrowly tailored to a compelling governmental interest, those elements are likely to be symbiotically interactive in application. The Supreme Court's appraisal of the nature and importance of an asserted right appears to influence the version of strict scrutiny that it applies and its application of the compelling interest and narrow tailoring elements of the test.

Third, partly as a result of the under-theorization of the strict scrutiny test and partly as a result of the symbiotic interactions among its elements, the strict scrutiny

subscribers to those channels. The majority held that the regulation was not narrowly tailored because a less restrictive alternative was available: advertising cable subscribers' rights to contact their cable company and request that specific channels be blocked. *See id.* at 816. As Justice Breyer argued in dissent, however, it will almost always be possible to imagine a restriction on speech that is narrower than any particular restriction that the government might impose, *id.* at 841 (Breyer, J., dissenting), and the real question is thus whether the governmentally imposed restriction, "viewed in light of the proposed alternative, is proportionate to [the] need," *id.* at 846. *See also Brown v. Entm't Merchants Ass'n*, 564 U.S. 786, 847 (2011) (Breyer, J., dissenting) ("[I]n applying [strict scrutiny], I would evaluate the degree to which the statute injures speech-related interests, the nature of the potentially-justifying 'compelling interests,' the degree to which the statute furthers that interest, the nature and effectiveness of possible alternatives, and, in light of this evaluation, whether, overall, 'the statute works speech-related harm ... out of proportion to the benefits that the statute seeks to provide.'" (omission in original) (quoting *Playboy Entm't*, 529 U.S. at 841 (Breyer, J., dissenting))).

test permits and even requires judges to engage recurrently in only minimally structured appraisals of the significance of competing values or interests in many cases. In addition to posing challenges involving judicial legitimacy and the justification of the judicial role in administering strict scrutiny, the need for courts to compare or weigh individual rights against competing governmental interests poses a conceptual puzzle. That conceptual puzzle, which frames the agenda for the next chapter, involves the nature or structure of constitutional rights: How should we understand what constitutional rights are (in any or all of their various forms) such that they can sensibly be compared with or balanced against competing governmental interests?

3

Rights and Interests

In all of their manifestations, constitutional rights function as constraints on the legitimate power of government.[1] But because rights are conditioned by governmental interests, as the strict scrutiny test makes manifest, we cannot understand the nature of constitutional rights without exploring what interests are and how, as a conceptual matter, rights and interests are related.

In response to the second of these questions, involving the relationship between rights and interests, my thesis can be summarized succinctly. In constitutional law as in moral theory, rights are constructs, designed to reflect and protect interests that are equally if not more fundamental.[2] Ultimate rights, which emerge from the strict scrutiny formula, clearly reflect an assessment of the weight of governmental interests as either compelling or not compelling. In ways that Chapter 2 traced, the scrutiny right that strict scrutiny defines also emerged from an all-things-considered assessment of multiple competing considerations in the historical context of the 1960s. Insofar as abstract and triggering rights are concerned, I propose to postpone extended discussion of their legal sources – involving whether, for example, either abstract rights, triggering rights, or both are necessarily linked tightly to the Constitution's text and originally understood meaning. Too much controversy attends that issue. But if we ask about the nature rather than the origins of abstract and triggering rights, we do best to conceptualize abstract constitutional rights, and triggering rights as well, as reflections of more fundamental, constitutionally cognizable interests that judges need to identify and sometimes weigh against one another.

[1] See T. M. Scanlon, THE DIFFICULTY OF TOLERANCE: ESSAYS IN POLITICAL PHILOSOPHY 151–52 (2003).
[2] See, e.g., Joseph Raz, THE MORALITY OF FREEDOM 166 (1986) (defining rights such that a person X has a right if and only if "an aspect of X's well-being (his interest) is a sufficient reason for holding some other person(s) to be under a duty"); Frank I. Michelman, *Liberties, Fair Values, and Constitutional Method*, 59 U. CHI. L. REV. 91, 94–95 (1992) (recognizing that constitutional liberties are recognized to protect corresponding interests); T. M. Scanlon, *Rights and Interests, in* 1 ARGUMENTS FOR A BETTER WORLD: ESSAYS IN HONOR OF AMARTYA SEN 68 (Kaushik Basu & Ravi Kanbur eds., 2009); T. M. Scanlon, Jr., *Freedom of Expression and Categories of Expression*, 40 U. PITT. L. REV. 519, 535–36 (1979) (noting that what rights are recognized depends on necessity and feasibility of protecting particular interests); Judith Jarvis Thomson, *Some Ruminations on Rights*, 19 ARIZ. L. REV. 45, 55–56 (1977) (recognizing that rights reflect interests).

Insofar as the moral bases of constitutional rights are concerned, the most foundational moral right is to have one's interests taken into account and weighed equally with those of others.[3]

THE NATURE OF INTERESTS

In the sense in which I shall use the term, the concept of "interests" is itself a vague one. It refers to goods, protections, and opportunities that we as citizens under the Constitution, like other reasonable and rational beings, have good reason to care about securing for ourselves, our families, and subsequent generations. When the term is used in this way, the parties to an imagined social contract, or behind Rawls's veil of ignorance, would have interests for which they would seek protection in the form of rights. Similarly, we would want and expect those who write constitutions and laws to perform their tasks with the importance of various goods, protections, and opportunities in mind. If the term interests is used accordingly, then interests furnish foundations for the identification of moral and political rights, and they would drive the decisions of constitution-writers about which rights to embody in constitutions. Interests would also furnish materials on the basis of which judges deciding previously underdetermined cases would identify abstract rights and define or construct triggering rights. But interests as thus defined are not necessarily rights themselves.

Nor need the interests that support the recognition of a right be exclusively those of the right-holder. In designing a system of rights, it may make sense to assign rights to some partly to protect the interests of others. We might confer rights on churches in order to protect the interests of their members, on the press to protect the interests of the public in the free flow of information, or on parents to protect the interests of their children. But within a scheme of this kind, in which constitutional rights function as constraints on the discretion of the government and its officials, the justification for recognizing a right involves the protection of interests.

As thus defined, the term "interests" acts as a place-holder pending further analysis and argument. It leaves open what we have good reason to value and which interests the Constitution protects. But my proposed analysis of rights in terms of interests deliberately achieves a kind of conceptual leveling. The interests that underlie the identification or construction of triggering rights, like those that are candidates to count as compelling governmental interests, can be arrayed within a decision-making apparatus that requires value-based assessments of normatively acceptable and unacceptable results and more or less desirable outcomes. Indeed, if interests

---

[3] *Cf., e.g.,* Ronald Dworkin, *Justice and Rights, in* TAKING RIGHTS SERIOUSLY 150, 179–83 (1977) (proposing that "Rawls's most basic assumption is . . . that [people] have a right to equal respect and concern in the design of political institutions," *id.* at 182); H. L. A. Hart, *Are There Any Natural Rights?*, 64 PHIL. REV. 175, 175 (1955) (defending the thesis that, if there are any moral rights, there is at least one natural right: "the equal right of all [people] to be free").

are stand-ins for goods, protections, and opportunities that reasonable and rational people would value, we can think of the governmental interests that sometimes compete with individual interests as representing goods, protections, and opportunities that reasonable and rational people would also care about, and would want their government to provide, or at least to be empowered to provide, for its citizens.[4]

Consider governmental interests in maintaining national security and in ensuring the availability of health care to as many citizens as possible. Although these governmental interests may compete with the individual interests of some citizens – for example, their liberty interests in being free from unwanted restrictions or obligations – governmental interests in another sense represent interests that reasonable and rational people would seek to protect by conferring governmental powers. Constitutional designers might think that they could best protect some interests by creating judicially enforceable constitutional rights but better secure others by empowering the government to enact appropriate legislation, including legislation that creates statutory rights. These might include, for example, statutory rights to educational benefits or payments under the Social Security system that would not exist by direct, judicially enforceable, constitutional mandate.

Accordingly, although constitutional rights are important, we should not think of them as our only or even necessarily our most practically important rights in a day-to-day sense. The New Deal constitutional revolution and the demise of *Lochner*-era constitutionalism embodied a recognition that the government has crucial yet politically discretionary functions in furnishing its citizens with goods and opportunities that make fulfilling lives possible. To understand constitutional rights in a post-New Deal world, we must view the Constitution's strategy for protecting the kinds of interests that sometimes undergird constitutional rights as being complex and multipartite. Designed to protect interests, the Constitution relies on government to promote the wellbeing and even the flourishing of its citizens, but subject to interest-based limitations that we denominate as constitutional rights.

In offering an interest-based account of rights, including constitutional rights, I should anticipate paired objections. One would insist that whatever might be true of moral rights, constitutional rights are a species of positive law: Their content depends on the historical decisions of the legal authorities who wrote and ratified the Constitution and possibly on subsequent decisions by judges and other interpreters. For the moment, I would reply only that in order to interpret rights-creating constitutional language that is even moderately abstract, and to understand abstract and triggering rights as subject to being outweighed by competing governmental interests, we most perspicuously conceptualize constitutional rights as reflecting interest-based calculations. This formulation does not preclude the possibility, which I discuss later, that history might define or limit the interests that properly

---

[4] *Cf.* Raz, *supra* note 2, at 5 ("[Government] does not have an interest independent of, one which is not a reflection of, the interests of its subjects.").

bear on constitutional interpretation. Nor, more strongly, does it deny that history might determine the interpretive conclusion that particular constitutional guarantees, such as the First Amendment and the Equal Protection Clause, reflect particular interests.

Resistance to an interest-based conceptualization of rights may also come from those committed to the view that rights are fundamental, not subject to the trade-offs or balancing that they associate with strongly consequentialist, possibly utilitarian, moral theories. Viewing rights as "side constraints" on permissible governmental action,[5] some theories posit that human agents are "ends in themselves" and thus bearers of rights that cannot be violated for the sake of any other end.[6] In practice, however, theories of this kind tend to work most plausibly to explain why people should have rights – or at least why everyone's interests should count equally in a moral or constitutional calculus – and much less successfully to explain which ultimate rights people do or ought to have.

Operating at a high level of abstraction, Rawls, for example, identifies personhood with a capacity for the exercise of "moral powers" and argues that rights necessary to the development of those moral powers should be recognized.[7] But the basic rights that he derives – including rights to freedom of speech and religious autonomy – are so abstract as to settle few practical questions. Does freedom of speech encompass hate speech directed at racial or religious minorities? Do corporations have speech rights? Does freedom of religion immunize religious observers from sanctions for engaging in otherwise prohibitable conduct under the criminal law? To answer questions such as these, a fuller set of considerations must be brought to bear.

The same analysis carries over into the constitutional domain. Justice Black liked to say that the First Amendment guarantee was "absolute," but it is plausibly absolute only after interests that compete with free speech interests have been taken into account, first in the identification of triggering and scrutiny rights and then in the application of a further test such as strict judicial scrutiny. Rawls, in contemplating the enshrinement of principles of justice in a written constitution, explicitly postulated that abstract rights should be rendered concrete through a succession of stages that extended beyond a constitution's ratification. Because it was important for a constitution "to be widely supported," Rawls thought it "best not to burden it with [too] many details and qualifications," even though details and qualifications would require subsequent specification.[8]

Writing with respect to moral rights, Professor T. M. Scanlon argues that claims of right are "generally backed" by (1) a "claim about how individuals would behave or

[5] *See* Robert Nozick, ANARCHY, STATE, AND UTOPIA 28–35 (1974).
[6] *See* Immanuel Kant, GROUNDWORK OF THE METAPHYSICS OF MORALS (Mary Gregor ed. & trans., 1998) (1785); Christine M. Korsgaard, CREATING THE KINGDOM OF ENDS (1996); *see also infra* note 11.
[7] John Rawls, A THEORY OF JUSTICE xiii (rev. ed. 1999); John Rawls, POLITICAL LIBERALISM 19, 304–24 (1993).
[8] Rawls, POLITICAL LIBERALISM, *supra* note 7, at 232.

how institutions would work in the absence of this particular assignment of rights,"
(2) a value-based claim that "this result would be unacceptable," and (3) a "further
empirical claim about how the envisaged assignment of rights will produce
a different" and normatively preferable outcome.[9] That framework also illuminates
constitutional analysis. Adapting it to constitutional law, we can say that rights reflect
interests and that which interests should be protected in which ways depends partly
on enduring values, often as reflected in constitutional language, but partly also on
historically contingent, instrumental reasoning. This is a very crude first formulation, about which I shall need to say a good deal more. More precise claims about
empirical consequences and their acceptability or unacceptability are likely to
emerge in the progression from abstract to triggering to scrutiny to ultimate rights.
Nevertheless, Scanlon's framework fits both the history and the analytical assumptions of strict judicial scrutiny. The Supreme Court developed the strict scrutiny test
through a process of partly instrumental reasoning as a means of protecting fundamental rights or interests. In addition, application of the test requires courts to assess
what is acceptable and unacceptable not only in light of the rights-generating
interests that underwrite abstract rights, but also in light of competing governmental
interests and contingently available alternative mechanisms for protecting those
governmental interests.

   To say that rights reflect interests is not necessarily to say that rights must
have utilitarian foundations. I have suggested conceptualizing the calculations
of the parties behind Rawls's veil of ignorance as being interest-based, yet Rawls
argued against, not for, utilitarianism.[10] We may have interests in avoiding
certain kinds of impositions and treatment, even if making ourselves vulnerable
to such impositions and treatment would maximize average wealth, utility, or
some other measure of collective well-being. Indeed, some such interests might
be weighty enough to generate rights that would indeed function as categorical
side-constraints, even if many abstract and triggering rights would yield to
competing governmental interests under at least some imaginable circumstances. Let us imagine, for sake of argument, that stifling expression that
many find disturbing – flag-burning, for example, or expressions of protest
during the national anthem – would be utility-maximizing in light of some
measure of utility. Even if so, we might think it unacceptable to stifle speech or
expression if the stifling imposed large burdens or frustrations on the would-be
speakers in order to avoid relatively small burdens on or disturbances to
a relatively large number of others.

---

9   T. M. Scanlon, *Rights, Goals, and Fairness*, 11 ERKENNTNIS 81, 89 (1977), *reprinted in* Scanlon, *supra*
     note 1, at 26, 35.
10 *See* Rawls, A THEORY OF JUSTICE, *supra* note 7, at 144–53, 160–68. *But see, e.g.*, John C. Harsanyi, *Can
     the Maximin Principle Serve as a Basis for Morality? A Critique of John Rawls's Theory*, 69 AM. POL.
     SCI. REV. 594, 598 (1975) (arguing that parties in the original position would choose the principle of
     average utility).

To view rights as reflecting interests in this way "solves" one problem about how it is possible to compare rights with interests and to weigh one against the other: Rights, as we know them, are interest-based, designed to protect some interests without doing too much damage to others. But conceptualizing rights as based on interests admittedly leaves another potential "incommensurability" problem untouched. The unresolved problem involves the diversity of interests that we have under the Constitution and as reasonable and rational beings. I have suggested that some of our interests involve the achievement of more rather than less favorable states of affairs, but that we also have interests in how we are treated by the law and by others, quite apart from the states of affairs to which particular forms of treatment might conduce. For example, in addition to having interests in not being stopped from communicating our views even if a particular regime of censorship might conduce to peace, tranquility, and prosperity, we may have interests in privacy that we regard as so important that we would think it unacceptable for the government to sacrifice them in order to achieve small increments in the security of millions or even hundreds of millions of people that, in the aggregate, might seem to assume large proportions. Philosophers refer to moral views that recognize rights that frustrate utility maximization or promotion of the public interest as "deontological," as distinguished from pervasively consequentialist frameworks that focus exclusively on the overall or average wellbeing, happiness, or utility within a community as a whole.[11]

As the free speech and privacy examples may illustrate, the problem is whether all of our various kinds of interests are sufficiently commensurable with one another to permit rational judgments about how to weigh, balance, or accommodate them when they compete. If we move from the constitutional to the moral realm, this may be the deepest problem of practical reasoning, at least for those who believe that morality has a deontological element.[12] Although I shall sometimes refer to interest-based moral reasoning as involving "balancing," my use of this metaphor does not imply that interests can be quantified for purposes of comparison. Appeals to weighing and balancing in the realm of rights and interests sensibly imply no more than that competing considerations can be seen in relation to one another and that we can say such things, for example, as that interests in free speech deserve to prevail over interests in sparing public officials from emotional distress when they are criticized for their official actions. Both in our moral lives and in the domain of

---

[11] *See, e.g.,* Dworkin, *supra* note 1, at xi (describing rights as "trumps" against certain collective goals); Rawls, A Theory of Justice, *supra* note 7, at 26–27; Samuel Scheffler, The Rejection of Consequentialism 2 (1982) (characterizing deontological views as those that "maintain that it is sometimes wrong to do what will produce the best available outcome overall"); *see also* Thomas Nagel, *The Fragmentation of Value, in* Mortal Questions 128 (1979).

[12] *See, e.g.,* Isaiah Berlin, Four Essays on Liberty (1969); Nagel, *supra* note 11; Bernard Williams, *Conflicts of Values, in* Moral Luck: Philosophical Papers 1973–1980, at 71 (1981); *see also* Incommensurability, Incomparability, and Practical Reason (Ruth Chang ed., 1997) (including chapters by Elizabeth Anderson, Ruth Chang, Cass R. Sunstein, and Joseph Raz, among others).

political morality, we characteristically assume that we can discern what we or other reasonable and rational beings ought to do in cases of conflict between one person's interests, which might be our own, and those of others.[13]

In modern moral philosophy, the leading method for addressing such issues and conflicts is the reflective equilibrium methodology that Rawls developed.[14] That method has many complexities, some of which I shall elaborate in due course. But a simplified model will suffice as a starting point. In addressing problems involving collisions of competing interests – for example, one in which allowing free expression by some will cause acute emotional distress to others – we are likely to begin with two relevant sets of moral views. One is a provisional set of principles that we think describe the relative priorities of free speech interests and interests in avoiding emotional trauma, even if the principles are not wholly determinate. Also relevant, however, are our case-specific provisional judgments about what should be deemed permissible, forbidden, or obligatory under particular circumstances.

The method of reflective equilibrium calls for us to work back and forth between our moral principles and our case-specific moral judgments and to try to bring them into rational alignment with one another. In the course of reflection, we do not accept either our principles or our case-by-case judgments as having a necessary priority over the other. Adjustment can come on either end, or on both, as we seek to bring our understanding of controlling principles and morally best outcomes into harmony with one another.

As Scanlon emphasizes, the ultimate point of reflective equilibrium analysis is not psychological consistency but moral reliability.[15] However much we might crave an Archimedean perspective, none exists. We start where we are, with moral intuitions and convictions. When engaging in moral thinking, we should not trust our case-by-case intuitions unless they are explicable in terms of principles that we can endorse more generally. But we need to test our principles too. Principles should be rejected or reformulated if they yield results that strike us as morally unacceptable, upon due reflection, in too many cases. Interests are of crucial importance on both sides of the equation. Interests underlie both our case-by-case judgments of what is fair and acceptable and our principles, which might include, for example, a robust commitment to freedom of speech because of the vital interests that free expression serves.

In introducing reflective equilibrium analysis as a model of interest balancing, I mean to elide, but only for the moment, a point that will strike many readers as fundamental. Rather obviously, there are large, important distinctions between moral and political reasoning, on the one hand, and constitutional decision-making, on the other. For now, I would only ask readers who are skeptical of the reflective equilibrium analogy to acknowledge three points to which common sense and everyday experience attest: First, nearly all of us assume in our moral lives that

---

[13]　*See, e.g.,* T. M. Scanlon, Being Realistic about Reasons 2–3 (2014).
[14]　*See* Rawls, A Theory of Justice, *supra* note 7, at 20–21, 48–53.
[15]　*See, e.g.,* Scanlon, *supra* note 13, at 77–78.

we can balance competing interests in rationally defensible ways. Accordingly, even if we are not self-conscious about it, we presuppose that we can rationally determine what to do in light of diverse, competing considerations or interests. Second, judges' and Justices' moral and political views have a deep influence on their decision-making in many morally controversial cases, just as our own moral views influence our constitutional judgments. It would be naïve to think that moral and political reasoning, or some analogue, has no role whatsoever in constitutional law. Third, the phenomenon of reasonable moral disagreement among morally conscientious people is a familiar and troubling one, but also one that is typically limited in scope. Nearly all reasonable people agree about the wrongness of murder and theft, the importance of free speech, and the need to respect zones of privacy. Even so, we know that reasonable and rational people will sometimes balance interests differently from the way that we do.

With these three points in mind, we can easily grasp why constitutional law is what Professor Dworkin called an "argumentative practice," with some of the arguments running deep.[16] If constitutional rights reflect interests in the way that I have suggested, we can understand why nearly everyone agrees that we should have abstract constitutional rights denominated as rights to freedom of speech, freedom of religion, due process, and the equal protection of the laws. At the same time, we can grasp how disagreement can erupt about the specific content of rights that reflect those interests. Although agreed at a high level of abstraction that some set of interests deserves the protection of a constitutional guarantee, we might differ about how exactly to define that set, especially in light of the potential for competition or even conflict among the diverse interests that reasonable and rational people would have. An interest-based theory of constitutional rights, which posits that decisions defining or recognizing constitutional rights reflect partly tactical or consequence-sensitive judgments about how best to protect and accommodate competing interests, thus has the virtue of being able to explain the central debates and divisions in constitutional law.

I should be equally clear, however, about what the very general account that I have offered does not accomplish. I have not provided, and will not attempt to advance, a determinate formula for resolving debates about competing interests of constitutional stature. My aim in offering a theory of constitutional rights as both reflecting interests and as sometimes capable of being outweighed by interests is more to explain what constitutional argument is about than to prescribe results in particular cases. My theory, in other words, is not a normative theory of which rights we ought to have but an analytical or interpretive theory about what constitutional rights are and about how we can have meaningful debates about them within our constitutional practice. Rights are constructs, devised to protect interests, that

---

[16] *See* Ronald Dworkin, Law's Empire 3–4, 13 (1986).

function as constraints on the discretion of the government and its officials, including their discretion to promote or protect other interests in particular ways.

SOURCES OF CONSTITUTIONALLY PROTECTED AND
COGNIZABLE INTERESTS

Given the potential for disagreement about how to identify and accommodate relevant constitutional interests, we need to confront the question – which I postponed earlier – of where the interests that bear on constitutional law come from. We might think that originalists would take one sharply etched view, non-originalists or living constitutionalists another. But matters turn out to be more tangled.

As Chapter 2 observed, the Supreme Court has seldom required that asserted governmental interests – including those denominated as "compelling" – have clearly identifiable links to particular constitutional provisions.[17] A plausible case might thus be made that governmental interests need not be traced to the Constitution's language or history.

This point deserves careful reflection. Parties to constitutional controversies frequently argue about the necessary foundation of triggering rights in textual or historical sources and insist that other modes of derivation overreach the proper limits of judicial power. But ultimate rights depend on judicial judgments about governmental interests fully as much as they do on triggering rights. Why, we might ask, should the courts be more constrained in identifying one input into the strict scrutiny test (triggering rights) than in identifying the other (governmental interests)?

When we come to the interests that undergird individual rights, the demand for grounding in the Constitution's text and history frequently grows insistent. Yet even a cursory survey of Supreme Court practice reveals that the Constitution's text and history, though informative and even decisive in some respects, frequently fall short of determining judicially cognizable triggering and scrutiny rights. The same might as readily be said about the role of text and history in delimiting the range of interests that constitutional provisions protect. Rather, the Court often proceeds by imputing to the Constitution the purpose of protecting interests that then justify the recognition of triggering rights that have only a tenuous relationship to the Constitution's text and history.

With regard to both text and history, there are myriad examples. We can start with the text of the Free Speech Clause of the First Amendment, the interpretation of

---

[17]   See, e.g., Stephen E. Gottlieb, *Compelling Governmental Interests: An Essential but Unanalyzed Term in Constitutional Adjudication*, 68 B.U. L. Rev. 917, 937–38 (1988); see also Bruce Ackerman, *Liberating Abstraction*, 59 U. Chi. L. Rev. 317, 317–19 (1992) (arguing that conservative Supreme Court Justices who seek narrow construction of rights typically join liberals in favoring broad interpretations of government's powers).

which has not typically spawned as much methodological controversy as the Due Process and Equal Protection Clauses, for example. Two clear cases of First Amendment doctrines that can be justified only by loose interpretation of the constitutional text, driven by imputed purposes and interests, are those governing restrictions on speech by institutions other than Congress and rights to expressive association. The First Amendment begins with the words "Congress shall make no law" abridging the freedom of speech. Nevertheless, the Supreme Court has held that the Speech Clause applies to restrictions on speech and expression by the executive and judicial branches as well as by Congress.[18] Obviously, the Court believes that the interests that underlie the Free Speech Clause could not be protected adequately if executive and judicial censorship were unrestrained. For similar reasons, the Court has recognized rights of expressive association, any infringement of which will trigger strict judicial scrutiny, even though the words "freedom of association" appear nowhere in the First Amendment's text.[19]

On the other side of the ledger, the Supreme Court has long assumed that some forms of speech and expression lie wholly outside the scope of the First Amendment, despite being speech in the literal sense. In doing so, the Court seems to have supposed, whether consciously or unconsciously, that certain kinds of speech or expression implicate few if any interests that the First Amendment should be construed to protect. Apart from such well-known examples as "obscenity"[20] and false cries of fire in a crowded theater,[21] the Court has not applied any level of elevated scrutiny in allowing restrictions on the advertising of securities, price-fixing, bribery, or the solicitation of crimes for private gain.[22]

In the domain of equal protection, all of the Justices seem committed to the idea that the Due Process Clause of the Fifth Amendment imposes equal protection norms on the federal government,[23] even though "due process" and "equal protection" would appear to be distinct concepts, and even though the Equal Protection Clause applies only to the states. (The relevant provision of the Fourteenth Amendment begins by asserting that "No State shall . . .") By finding an abstract right to non-discrimination by the federal government in the Due Process Clause, the Supreme Court provides a textual foundation for its conclusion that race- and

---

[18] See, e.g., N.Y. Times Co. v. United States, 403 U.S. 713 (1971). For general discussion of the extension of First Amendment principles to the executive and the judiciary, and of the more general relationship of linguistic meaning to constitutional meaning, see Curtis A. Bradley & Neil S. Siegel, *Constructed Constraint and the Constitutional Text*, 64 DUKE L.J. 1213, 1245–46 (2015); David A. Strauss, *The Supreme Court, 2014 Term – Foreword: Does the Constitution Mean What It Says?*, 129 HARV. L. REV. 1, 30–34 (2015).

[19] See, e.g., Boy Scouts of Am. v. Dale, 530 U.S. 640, 647–48 (2000).

[20] See, e.g., Miller v. California, 413 U.S. 15, 23 (1973).

[21] See Schenck v. United States, 249 U.S. 47, 52 (1919).

[22] Frederick Schauer, *The Boundaries of the First Amendment: A Preliminary Exploration of Constitutional Salience*, 117 HARV. L. REV. 1765, 1770 (2004).

[23] See, e.g., Adarand Constructors, Inc. v. Pena, 515 U.S. 200, 213–18 (1995); Bolling v. Sharpe, 347 U.S. 497, 498–99 (1954).

gender-based discrimination by the federal government infringe triggering rights, but the constitutional text surely does not drive, even if it may accommodate, the Court's conclusion. In both cases the Court has ascribed to the Due Process Clause the purpose of protecting interests that the Clause's language does not plainly encompass.

The absence of a clear textual mandate for Supreme Court decision-making is more controversial and even notorious in substantive due process cases upholding abortion rights[24] and rights to gay marriage.[25] There may be good reasons why there should be controversy concerning whether the Due Process Clause comprehends rights to abortion and gay marriage but not whether it encompasses a nearly universally acknowledged right to freedom from race discrimination. But if there are such good reasons, they involve factors other than the semantic meaning of the Constitution's text.

With the Constitution's text having only limited explanatory power, we can ask whether the original historical meaning of constitutional language has driven the Supreme Court's decisions about the abstract, triggering, and scrutiny rights that the Constitution creates and the underlying interests that support recognition of those rights. To begin with the First Amendment once again, most commentators agree that the Supreme Court has paid little attention to the specifics of constitutional history. According to a number of historians, many if not most members of the Founding generation understood the Free Speech Clause as having a narrowly truncated reach (by modern standards).[26] These historians believe that few if any of the Founders would have expected the First Amendment to be applied to protect sexually explicit books or pictures, blasphemy, false statements of purported fact about those who were not public officials or candidates for public office, commercial advertising, and much more. More recently, revisionist historians have told a different story. According to them, the Founding generation widely viewed the Free Speech Clause as being broad in scope but weak in its protective effect, readily tolerating governmentally imposed restrictions that served the public interest.[27] Largely without taking notice of historical scholarship, the Court has relied on the First Amendment's unrestricted reference to "the freedom of speech" to hold that all categories of speech enjoy robust protection against targeted regulation unless they

---

[24] *See, e.g., Planned Parenthood of Se. Pa.* v. *Casey*, 505 U.S. 833, 980 (1992) (Scalia, J., concurring in the judgment in part and dissenting in part) ("[T]he Constitution says absolutely nothing about [abortion], and ... the longstanding traditions of American society have permitted it to be legally proscribed."); *Roe* v. *Wade*, 410 U.S. 113, 221 (1973) (White, J., dissenting) ("I find nothing in the language or history of the Constitution to support the Court's judgment.").

[25] *See, e.g., Obergefell* v. *Hodges*, 135 S. Ct. 2584, 2612 (2015) (Roberts, C.J., dissenting) ("The majority's decision is an act of will, not legal judgment. The right it announces has no basis in the Constitution or this Court's precedent.").

[26] *See* Leonard W. Levy, EMERGENCE OF A FREE PRESS xii–xv (1985); *see also* David A. Strauss, THE LIVING CONSTITUTION 61 (2010).

[27] *See, e.g.,* Jud Campbell, *Natural Rights and the First Amendment*, 127 YALE L.J. 246 (2017); Genevieve Lakier, *The Invention of Low-Value Speech*, 128 HARV. L. REV. 2167 (2015).

fall within exceptions to First Amendment protection that are themselves firmly rooted in constitutional history.[28] The interests that the Court views the Free Speech Clause as promoting, not original history, thus propel the reasoning of the Court's cases that find a triggering right to strict judicial scrutiny whenever Congress or a state legislature engages in "content discrimination."[29]

Original history has had little if anything to do with the Court's race discrimination cases. Most historians agree that *Brown v. Board of Education* is difficult if not impossible to justify on originalist grounds.[30] The Supreme Court has not tried to explain its affirmative action rulings in originalist terms either.[31] The now celebrated decisions establishing the one-person, one-vote principle are also impossible to root in the original meaning of any constitutional provision.[32]

The better explanation is that constitutional doctrine has followed, and continues to follow, a line of adaptation and sometimes growth, with recently recognized rights often reflecting interests that prior judicial precedents make visible and to which subsequent precedents attribute importance. In order to decide how prior cases relate to those that come after, judges must identify the interests that earlier decisions ascribe to the Constitution and the principles that explain the scope of protection to which those interests are entitled. Free speech law again affords a good illustration. The Court once viewed libel and defamation as wholly beyond the First Amendment's protective coverage.[33] Over time, however, the imputation to the Free Speech Clause of a purpose of protecting interests in robust, uninhibited

[28]   See Brown v. Entm't Merchs. Ass'n, 564 U.S. 786, 790–91 (2011); *United States v. Stevens*, 559 U.S. 460, 468–72 (2010); *but cf.* Janus v. *American Federation of State, County, and Municipal Employees*, 138 S. Ct. 2448, 2470 (2018) (relying on the absence of "persuasive founding-era evidence that public employees were understood to lack free speech protections" to justify a ruling that forcing public-sector employees to pay "agency fees" to support collective bargaining by unions violates the First Amendment).

[29]   See, e.g., *National Inst. of Family and Life Advocates v. Becerra*, 138 S. Ct. 2361, 2371 (2018); *Reed v. Town of Gilbert*, 135 S. Ct. 2218 (2015).

[30]   See, e.g., Michael J. Klarman, FROM JIM CROW TO CIVIL RIGHTS (2004); Michael W. McConnell, *Originalism and the Desegregation Decisions*, 81 VA. L. REV. 947, 950–52 nn.6–16 (1995) (explaining the consensus among legal academics and historians and collecting citations); Alexander M. Bickel, *The Original Understanding and the Segregation Decision*, 69 HARV. L. REV. 1 (1955). For an originalist argument that the Fourteenth Amendment was understood from the beginning as barring school segregation (largely based on unsuccessful Republican efforts in a subsequent Congress to forbid school desegregation under the 1875 Civil Rights Act, see McConnell, *supra*. For a critical response, see Michael J. Klarman, *Brown, Originalism, and Constitutional Theory: A Response to Professor McConnell*, 81 VA. L. REV. 1881 (1995).

[31]   See, e.g., Robert Post & Reva Siegel, *Originalism as a Political Practice: The Right's Living Constitution*, 75 FORDHAM L. REV. 545, 564 (2006) ("[T]here is historical evidence strongly suggesting 'that the framers ... could not have intended it generally to prohibit affirmative action ...'"); Stephen A. Siegel, *The Federal Government's Power to Enact Color-Conscious Laws: An Originalist Inquiry*, 92 NW. U. L. REV. 477, 590 (1998) ("[T]here is no plausible originalist argument that the Constitution proscribes the federal government's power to enact benign color-conscious laws, such as affirmative action.").

[32]   See, e.g., Strauss, *supra* note 26, at 15–16.

[33]   See, e.g., *Beauharnais v. Illinois*, 343 U.S. 250, 258 (1952).

debate about issues of public concern has led to recognition of triggering, scrutiny, and ultimate rights that the Founding generation apparently would not have contemplated.[34] The Court's decisions expanding protections for commercial advertising – which it once regarded as wholly unprotected by the First Amendment[35] – have followed a similar track. At a point in the doctrine's development, the principle emerged that restrictions on commercial advertising deserve elevated (even if not technically "strict") scrutiny in light of listeners' interests in having broad access to information and ideas, unmediated by governmental censorship.[36]

In upholding attacks on racial segregation, the Supreme Court initially emphasized that challenged programs sought to promote a regime of white supremacy and racial caste.[37] In doing so, the Court read the Equal Protection Clause as protecting interests in not being subordinated on account of race. Only later did the Court's opinions begin to read the equal protection guarantee as protecting further, partly distinct interests in freedom from race-based classification of any kind, including classification for the purpose of promoting racial integration in education and employment.[38]

The explanation for the Supreme Court's interest-based and historically revisionist approach – sometimes to afford linguistically surprising protections, sometimes to justify denials of protection – lies partly in the nature of constitutional interpretation, which has both backward- and forward-looking aspects.[39] The Supreme Court derives its interpretive and dispute-resolving capacities (however broad or cabined they may be) from the written Constitution. The Court's claim to legitimate authority – to possession of a power to alter both legal and ultimately moral obligations[40] – therefore depends on its looking backward to ascertain and respect the norms that the Constitution has established. But the Court also looks backward at precedent, at the interests it has protected, and at the principles based on which it has done so. Moreover, insofar as it is otherwise uncertain how the Constitution and other past authorities bear on a current dispute, judges and Justices must also look

---

[34] See, e.g., N.Y. Times Co. v. Sullivan, 376 U.S. 254, 268–69 (1964).

[35] See, e.g., Valentine v. Chrestensen, 316 U.S. 52, 54 (1942).

[36] See, e.g., Va. State Bd. of Pharmacy v. Va. Citizens Consumer Council, Inc., 425 U.S. 748, 764–65 (1976).

[37] See Stephen A. Siegel, The Origin of the Compelling State Interest Test and Strict Scrutiny, 48 AM. J. LEGAL HIST. 355, 404–07 (2006); see also John Hart Ely, The Constitutionality of Reverse Racial Discrimination, 41 U. CHI. L. REV. 723 (1974); Reva Siegel, Equality Talk: Antisubordination and Anticlassification Values in Constitutional Struggles over Brown, 117 HARV. L. REV. 1470 (2004).

[38] See Regents of the Univ. of Cal. v. Bakke, 438 U.S. 265, 269 (1978) (opinion of Powell, J.).

[39] See Richard H. Fallon, Jr., LAW AND LEGITIMACY IN THE SUPREME COURT 10, 44 (2018); Joseph Raz, On the Authority and Interpretation of Constitutions: Some Preliminaries, in CONSTITUTIONALISM: PHILOSOPHICAL FOUNDATIONS 152, 173 (Larry Alexander ed., 1998).

[40] See, e.g., H. L. A. Hart, Commands and Authoritative Legal Reasons, in ESSAYS ON BENTHAM: STUDIES IN JURISPRUDENCE AND POLITICAL THEORY 243 (1982); Frederick Schauer, Authority and Authorities, 94 VA. L. REV. 1931, 1939 (2008).

forward in seeking to establish their own decisions as legitimate authorities, deserving of obedience by political officials and the public.

In order to justify claims to obedience in their resolution of reasonably disputable cases, judges and Justices must implicitly represent that acquiescence in their decisions will produce better outcomes than would result otherwise, either generally or in a particular case.[41] The pressure to produce morally attractive results for the future encourages the imputation of supporting interests and purposes to constitutional provisions that explain and justify morally attractive results for the future. This rationale not only explains why the Free Speech Clause creates rights to freedom from censorship by the executive branch, but also why it affords no protection to speech used by business executives to fix prices. A similar process has occurred as the Justices have embraced the conclusion that the Due Process Clause of the Fifth Amendment bars race discrimination by the federal government, while division about moral desirability explains continuing controversy about substantive due process rights to abortion and gay marriage. Although often cast in methodological terms, the deep disagreements among the Justices have an irreducibly substantive component, involving the forward- as well as the backward-looking aspect of legitimate judicial authority.

JUDICIALLY MANAGEABLE STANDARDS

Interests affect the Supreme Court's identification of different varieties of rights in different ways. With regard to abstract rights, the Court is mostly and appropriately concerned with the kind of interests that would support recognition of a right in the first instance. We can say, for example, that the First Amendment creates a right to communicate ideas that reflects our interests in being able to speak our minds and to have access to the thoughts and information that others wish to express. At this level of abstraction, competing interests and practical concerns that bear on the proper limitation of triggering and ultimate rights have relatively little role.

Although we can formulate many abstract rights without reference to details of application or to competing interests, concerns of the latter variety begin to emerge in the definition of triggering and scrutiny rights. It is largely for this reason that we can often agree about the existence of abstract rights but quickly lapse into disagreement – based on varied weightings of relevant interests – about how to identify triggering and scrutiny rights. (For example, think once again about whether a prohibition against flag-burning infringes on a First Amendment triggering right at all, or whether an admissions preference for members of racial minority groups should be subjected to strict judicial scrutiny.)

---

[41] Cf. Joseph Raz, *The Problem of Authority: Revisiting the Service Conception*, 90 MINN. L. REV. 1003, 1035 (2006) ("It seems implausible to think that one can be a legitimate authority however bad one is at acting as an authority.").

Among the many markers of a sometimes substantial gap between abstract rights, on the one hand, and triggering and scrutiny rights, on the other, is the concept of "judicially manageable standards."[42] That crucial concept is often overlooked in writing about constitutional theory and is little understood. It plays its most explicit role in cases involving the political question doctrine. In that context, the Supreme Court often says that the courts cannot rule on disputes for which no judicially manageable standards exist. Although a discussion of the political question doctrine initially may seem to bend away from issues involving judicially cognizable interests and the sources of triggering rights, the seeming detour will yield a swift payoff. Reflection on the Court's demand for judicially manageable standards in political question cases and the Justices' sometime efforts to construct such standards will help to illuminate the nature of the judicial role in identifying triggering rights and the scrutiny rights that fully specified triggering rights encompass.

The political question doctrine is a partial curiosity. Commentators disagree about its nature.[43] Some question whether the doctrine should exist at all.[44] There can be no disagreement, however, that the Supreme Court applies the political question label from time to time and that it sometimes cites an absence of judicially manageable standards as a reason not to enforce abstract constitutional rights. A now-canonical statement of relevant criteria came in *Baker* v. *Carr*:[45]

> Prominent on the surface of any case held to involve a political question is found a textually demonstrable constitutional commitment of the issue to a coordinate political department; or a lack of judicially discoverable and manageable standards for resolving it; or the impossibility of deciding without an initial policy determination of a kind clearly for nonjudicial discretion; or the impossibility of a court's undertaking independent resolution without expressing lack of the respect due coordinate branches of government; or an unusual need for unquestioning adherence to a political decision already made; or the potentiality of embarrassment from multifarious pronouncements by various departments on one question.[46]

---

[42] The phrase has emerged as a term of art since the Supreme Court's decision in Baker v. Carr, 369 U.S. 186, 217 (1962). For an extended exploration of the concept, see Richard H. Fallon, Jr., *Judicially Manageable Standards and Constitutional Meaning*, 119 HARV. L. REV. 1274 (2006).

[43] The disagreement is unsurprising in light of "the odd amalgam of constitutional, functional, and prudential factors that have been used by the courts in determining whether a case presents a nonjusticiable political question." Rachel E. Barkow, *More Supreme than Court? The Fall of the Political Question Doctrine and the Rise of Judicial Supremacy*, 102 COLUM. L. REV. 237, 244 (2002). For a survey of issues arising under the political question doctrine and of related scholarship, see Richard H. Fallon, Jr., John F. Manning, Daniel J. Meltzer & David L. Shapiro, HART AND WECHSLER'S THE FEDERAL COURTS AND THE FEDERAL SYSTEM 237–266 (7th ed. 2015) [hereinafter HART & WECHSLER].

[44] *See, e.g.*, Louis Henkin, *Is There a "Political Question" Doctrine?*, 85 YALE L.J. 597, 622–23 (1976) (arguing that the doctrine is "an unnecessary, deceptive packaging of several established doctrines"); Martin H. Redish, *Judicial Review and the "Political Question,"* 79 Nw. U. L. REV. 1031, 1045–55 (1985) (arguing that the doctrine is not normatively defensible).

[45] 369 U.S. 186 (1962).

[46] *Id.* at 217.

Questions involving the availability of judicially manageable standards have sharply divided the Supreme Court in cases under the Equal Protection Clause challenging partisan gerrymanders. In *Vieth* v. *Jubelirer*,[47] four Justices deemed challenges to partisan gerrymanders categorically non-justiciable. A fifth Justice agreed that no judicially manageable standard for identifying constitutionally forbidden gerrymanders had "emerged in this case."[48] In reaching their conclusions, the Justices who made up the majority accepted that "an excessive injection of politics" into the design of electoral districts is "unlawful" and violates individual rights under the Equal Protection Clause.[49] The problem, according to Justice Scalia's plurality opinion, was that there were no judicially manageable standards for determining when a gerrymander goes "too far."[50]

In finding the case before it to be non-justiciable, the *Vieth* plurality cast the concept of judicially manageable standards in a double role. Indeed, I think it fair to say that all of the other opinions in the case did, too – as did the opinions in a subsequent partisan gerrymandering case in which the Court once again failed to identify and apply a judicially manageable standard.[51] In one usage, references to judicially manageable standards describe an *input* to constitutional decision-making. Writing for the plurality in *Vieth*, Justice Scalia thought that the language the Equal Protection Clause provided insufficient guidance to courts in identifying when gerrymanders go "too far" and therefore ought either to be invalidated categorically or to trigger some form of exacting judicial scrutiny. In another usage, however, judicially manageable standards are not so much inputs as *outputs* of constitutional adjudication. A judicially manageable standard is an output, rather than an input, in any case in which the Supreme Court successfully devises a test that can thereafter be used to implement a constitutional provision that is not itself a judicially manageable standard.

Accepting the premise that judicially manageable standards can be outputs of judicial decision-making, all of the four dissenting Justices in *Vieth* endeavored to craft tests that would satisfy the requirement of judicial manageability.[52] Strikingly,

---

[47]   541 U.S. 267 (2004).

[48]   *Id.* at 311 (Kennedy, J., concurring in the judgment).

[49]   *Id.* at 293 (opinion of Scalia, J.) (emphases omitted) ("[A]ll [Justice Stevens] brings forward ... is the argument that an *excessive* injection of politics is *un*lawful. So it is, and so does our opinion assume.").

[50]   *Id.* at 296.

[51]   In *League of United Latin American Citizens* v. *Perry*, 548 U.S. 399 (2006), Justices Scalia and Thomas adhered to the view that partisan gerrymandering cases were categorically non-justiciable, while three Justices – including Chief Justice Roberts and Justice Alito – concurred that the challengers had failed to adduce a judicially manageable standard for resolving the dispute at hand. In *Gill* v. *Whitford*, 138 S.Ct. 1916 (2018), the Court avoided the issue of judicially manageable standards for determining the permissibility of partisan gerrymanders by finding that the plaintiffs had failed to establish standing.

[52]   Justice Stevens sought to extract a manageable standard from prior case involving racial gerrymandering, *id.* at 335–36 (Stevens, J., dissenting), but he did not suggest that his preferred formula came directly from the Constitution, from the original understanding of the Equal Protection Clause, or from any other likely candidate to supply the Constitution's normative meaning. Justice Souter –

moreover, Justice Scalia's plurality opinion mounted no criticism of the dissenting Justices' assumption that judges should, when possible, devise workable standards to implement vague constitutional norms. Indeed, Justice Scalia himself had maintained in other contexts that judges should craft clear rules to implement otherwise vague constitutional norms and thus to limit judicial discretion in future cases.[53] Without criticizing the project that the dissenting Justices set for themselves, Justice Scalia argued in *Vieth* that the dissenters had failed to meet their own goal: They had not succeeded in fashioning manageable standards for identifying those gerrymanders that should incur elevated scrutiny, for testing challenged district lines for ultimate validity, or for designing remedies for identified violations.[54]

Despite the Supreme Court's failure to articulate the criteria that it uses to develop judicially manageable standards, some of the considerations that the Justices take into account are either obvious or intuitive. To be judicially manageable, a formulation must be intelligible to lower courts and other officials. Clearly, however, it need not be absolutely determinate. The Court sometimes prefers vague "standards" such as "reasonableness" tests (as Chapter 4 will discuss more fully), which cannot be applied without an exercise of normative judgment, to crisp "rules" that require little judgment in application.[55] Nonetheless, for a standard to count as judicially manageable, it must be expected to generate reasonably consistent and predictable results in the lower courts. As Justice Scalia once wrote, "[p]redictability ... is a needful characteristic of any law worthy of the name."[56] It also seems clear that a judicially manageable standard for implementing an abstract constitutional right must not stray too far from what the Court takes to be the Constitution's meaning. As Justice Scalia wrote in *Vieth*, "[t]his Court may not willy-nilly apply standards – even manageable standards – having no relation to constitutional harms."[57] Even so, the *Vieth* plurality engaged in no pretense that the fit between the meaning of a constitutional provision and a judicially manageable standard for implementing it must be precise. If a constitutional norm is vague, then

joined by Justice Ginsburg – wrote explicitly about the judicial role in fashioning a constitutional test. The challenge, he said, was to "translate" constitutional norms of fairness into "workable criteria." *Id.* at 344 (Souter, J., dissenting). Believing that the courts had not so far met that challenge with regard to partisan gerrymanders, he proposed to "start anew" by developing a complex, five-part test analogous to one that the Supreme Court had "crafted" for employment discrimination cases. *Id.* at 346. He described his goal as "devising" a workable test, *id.*, not finding one in the Constitution. In a separate opinion, Justice Breyer made similarly creative efforts to formulate a manageable standard. *See id.* at 365–67 (Breyer, J., dissenting) (outlining "indicia of abuse" of redistricting norms).

53　　*Cf. Morrison v. Olson*, 487 U.S. 654, 711–12 (1988) (Scalia, J., dissenting) (criticizing the majority for adopting a standard that "might be called the unfettered wisdom of a majority of this Court"); Antonin Scalia, *The Rule of Law as a Law of Rules*, 56 U. CHI. L. REV. 1175, 1179–80 (1989).

54　　*See Vieth*, 541 U.S. at 292–301 (plurality opinion).

55　　See generally Kathleen M. Sullivan, *The Supreme Court, 1991 Term – Foreword: The Justices of Rules and Standards*, 106 HARV. L. REV. 22 (1992).

56　　Scalia, *supra* note 53, at 1179.

57　　*Vieth*, 541 U.S. at 295 (plurality opinion).

any more determinate specification is likely to introduce at least "mild substantive distortion."[58]

At the end of the day, it thus seems clear that determining whether a proposed test for implementing an abstract constitutional right constitutes a judicially manageable standard requires an all-things-considered appraisal of the effects on constitutionally relevant interests. In a remarkable passage near the end of his opinion in *Vieth*, after noting that the frequency of litigation would likely increase with the vagueness of any standard that the Court might prescribe for identifying forbidden partisan gerrymanders, Justice Scalia pronounced the plurality's all-things-considered judgment:

> Is the regular insertion of the judiciary into districting, with the delay and uncertainty that [it] brings to the political process and the partisan enmity it brings upon the courts, worth the benefit to be achieved – an accelerated (by some unknown degree) effectuation of the majority will? We think not.[59]

The Court appears to have been equally concerned with harms and benefits to constitutionally relevant interests in determining whether judicially manageable standards exist, or have been devised, in other cases. In *Nixon v. United States*,[60] in which an impeached and convicted federal judge complained that the Senate had not properly discharged its duty to "try" him, Chief Justice Rehnquist buttressed his curt holding that there were no judicially manageable standards for giving content to the word "try" in the Impeachment Trial Clause with appeal to a web of surrounding considerations. Especially in the case of a presidential impeachment, he reasoned, "opening the door of judicial review … would 'expose the political life of the country to months, or perhaps years, of chaos.'"[61]

INSTRUMENTALISM IN THE DESIGN OF TRIGGERING RIGHTS

Insofar as judicially manageable standards are concerned, cases to which the Supreme Court applies the political question doctrine represent judicial failures. For one reason or another, the Court finds itself unable to identify or construct judicially manageable standards, despite acknowledging that it is the responsibility of courts to attempt to do so when the bare language of a constitutional provision fails to provide sufficiently determinate guidance. Much more typically, the Court succeeds. To repeat, it succeeded (at least by its own lights) when it formulated the strict scrutiny test that defines scrutiny rights in a wide variety of contexts. The Court similarly, though less visibly, succeeds whenever it identifies triggering rights that lead to strict scrutiny's application.

---

[58] Scalia, *supra* note 53, at 1178.
[59] *Vieth*, 541 U.S. at 301 (plurality opinion).
[60] 506 U.S. 224 (1993).
[61] *Id.* at 236 (quoting *Nixon v. United States*, 938 F.2d 239, 246 (D.C. Cir. 1991)).

The political question cases thus draw attention to something that the Supreme Court more typically fails to highlight – namely, the judicial role in crafting judicially manageable standards. As in political question cases, moreover, the Court's decisions to adopt or reject proposed triggering rights and tests of ultimate validity as judicially manageable standards reflect all-things-considered, substantially interest-based judgments. Recognizing that the design of judicially manageable standards implicates multiple interests also casts light on a nearly pervasive feature of constitutional law that is easy to overlook. In defining or constructing triggering and scrutiny rights, the Supreme Court almost necessarily engages in empirical, instrumental calculations.[62] Judicial decisions about whether to adopt tests and to acknowledge triggering rights are shaped by apprehensions concerning acceptable and unacceptable consequences, as measured by reference to constitutionally cognizable interests.

An especially well-known and vivid example comes from *Miranda* v. *Arizona*,[63] which initiated the requirement of so-called *Miranda* warnings in order for confessions obtained through custodial interrogations to be admissible in criminal trials. In *Miranda*, the Court appeared to accept that the meaning of the relevant constitutional language would best be specified as forbidding the introduction of compelled confessions in criminal trials. And it would seem obvious that not every confession obtained in the absence of a *Miranda* warning is coerced or involuntary. Instead, the right to a *Miranda* warning as devised by the Supreme Court serves instrumental purposes: It aims to protect against coercion in the procurement of confessions that would otherwise be difficult if not impossible to prove after the fact.

For a number of years, critics both on the Supreme Court and in legal academia derided *Miranda* as having propounded a "prophylactic" rule, not sufficiently grounded in the Constitution to count as constitutional in nature.[64] But if *Miranda* was anomalous, it would be in degree, not kind. As David Strauss showed in an article entitled *The Ubiquity of Prophylactic Rules*,[65] the Court routinely pays as much heed to practical considerations, the supposedly distinctive concern of prophylactic rules, as to constitutional language and historic understandings, the presumptively characteristic foci of true constitutional interpretation. Professor Strauss's thesis concerning "the ubiquity of prophylactic rules" provided the implicit rationale for the Supreme Court's 2000 decision in *Dickerson* v. *United States*,[66] which held by 7–2 that Congress acted unconstitutionally when it passed a statute

---

[62]   See Richard H. Fallon, Jr., IMPLEMENTING THE CONSTITUTION 28–34, 38–42 (2001).

[63]   384 U.S. 436 (1966).

[64]   See, e.g., Michigan v. Tucker, 417 U.S. 433, 439–44 (1974) (Rehnquist, J.) (describing the Miranda rules as "prophylactic," id. at 439, not "rights protected by the Constitution but . . . instead measures to insure that the right against compulsory self-incrimination was protected," id. at 444); see also Joseph D. Grano, Prophylactic Rules in Criminal Procedure: A Question of Article III Legitimacy, 80 Nw. U. L. REV. 100, 106–11, 145 (1985).

[65]   David A. Strauss, The Ubiquity of Prophylactic Rules, 55 U. CHI. L. REV. 190 (1988).

[66]   530 U.S. 428 (2000).

essentially instructing the federal courts to ignore *Miranda* in determining whether to admit confessions into evidence. In previous decisions, Court majorities – which included Justices who joined the opinion in *Dickerson* – had described *Miranda* as "prophylactic."[67] In *Dickerson*, however, the Court held that *Miranda* established a "constitutional" rule and that Congress therefore could not reject it.[68] In reaching this conclusion, the Justices in the *Dickerson* majority surely did not mean that *Miranda* had involved no instrumental, interest-based, partly empirical calculations. They could only have meant that the nature of the calculations involved in *Miranda* were not sufficiently different in kind from those in other constitutional cases for *Miranda* not to count as a "constitutional" decision – unlike those, for example, that the Court occasionally demarcates as propounding federal "common law" rules to govern matters of uniquely federal concern in the absence of a governing federal statute.[69]

No less than in *Miranda*, the Supreme Court relied pervasively on empirical, predictive, and instrumental calculations in the iconic First Amendment case of *New York Times Co. v. Sullivan*.[70] Rejecting centuries of common law practice and precedent, *Sullivan* holds that states may not impose liability on the press for making defamatory statements about public officials and political candidates absent clear and convincing proof that the defendant both uttered a factually false statement and did so either knowingly or with reckless disregard for the truth.[71] As a concurring opinion made explicit, the Court determined that without "breathing space"[72] for the factual errors that sometimes occur even in conscientious reporting, important contributions to political debate would be "chilled."[73] In drawing the line between protected and unprotected speech where it did, the Supreme Court sought to create the optimal balance of incentives for the press: Reporters and editors should not have to hesitate too much before reporting what they believe to be true, on the one hand, nor should they be licensed to speak with reckless disregard for the truth, on the other. The *Sullivan* decision hinged from start to finish on projections of what would happen under regimes of greater or lesser First Amendment protection and on judgments about the desirability of resulting outcomes.

The Supreme Court has acted on similarly instrumental calculations in defining triggering rights to speak and demonstrate in public fora such as streets and parks. States and municipalities can require advance permitting for large gatherings and demonstrations.[74] But if states and municipalities are to enforce permitting

---

[67] E.g., *Connecticut v. Barrett*, 479 U.S. 523, 528 (1987); *Oregon v. Elstad*, 470 U.S. 298, 307–08 (1985); *New York v. Quarles*, 467 U.S. 649, 653 (1984).

[68] *Dickerson*, 530 U.S. at 432.

[69] On federal common law, see HART & WECHSLER, *supra* note 43, at 635–777.

[70] 376 U.S. 254 (1964).

[71] *See id.* at 283–84.

[72] *Id.* at 298 (Goldberg, J., concurring in the result) (quoting *NAACP v. Button*, 371 U.S. 415, 433 (1963)).

[73] *Id.* at 300.

[74] *See, e.g., Thomas v. Chi. Park Dist.*, 534 U.S. 316, 322–24 (2002); *Cox v. New Hampshire*, 312 U.S. 569, 576 (1941).

requirements, the Court has ruled that they must have clear, content-neutral, publicly promulgated criteria. In the absence of clear criteria, the Court has reckoned, the risk of officials abusing their discretion to award permits to some and not to others would be intolerably great.[75] Whether or not the Court's calculation is correct, current doctrine quite plainly rests on empirical, predictive assessments.

To offer just one more example, the Court has relied on fact-based, instrumental calculations in drawing the important doctrinal distinction between direct and merely incidental infringements of constitutional rights, including speech rights, as briefly discussed in Chapter 2. If the government directly bans flag-burning, for example, interests in avoiding governmental interference with political debate almost self-evidently come into play. Strict scrutiny therefore applies. By contrast, if the government prohibits outdoor fires, and thus indirectly makes flag-burning a crime, the Court effectively assumes that its interests involve the prevention of dangerous conflagrations, not the suppression of ideas. Although a triggering right would still be infringed, less demanding scrutiny would apply, and a challenge would almost surely fail.

INDIVIDUAL INTERESTS AND GOVERNMENTAL INTERESTS IN THE CONSTRUCTION OF TRIGGERING AND ABSTRACT RIGHTS

The Supreme Court obviously takes governmental interests into account when applying strict scrutiny to determine whether the infringement of a triggering right is narrowly tailored to a compelling governmental interest. Perhaps less obviously but equally importantly, the Court also takes governmental interests into account when defining triggering and associated scrutiny rights. An important but nevertheless representative example comes from *Washington v. Davis*,[76] which presented the question whether statutes that have racially discriminatory effects should trigger strict judicial scrutiny. The facts of the case illustrate the issue. The City of Washington required candidates to be police officers to achieve a minimum score on a general aptitude exam. The requirement included no overtly racial element. Nevertheless, African-Americans failed the test at more than four times the rate of whites.

In finding that racially disparate impact should not suffice to trigger strict scrutiny, the Court relied heavily on an assessment of the impediments to promoting significant governmental interests that the application of strict scrutiny to all statutes with racially disparate impacts would impose. Indeed, a linchpin of the Court's

---

[75] See, e.g., *City of Lakewood v. Plain Dealer Publ'g Co.*, 486 U.S. 750, 755–56 (1988); *Lovell v. City of Griffin*, 303 U.S. 444, 451 (1938).
[76] 426 U.S. 229 (1976).

analysis in *Washington* v. *Davis* involved its depiction of an array of anticipated consequences that the Justices deemed unacceptable:

> A rule that a statute designed to serve neutral ends is nevertheless invalid, absent compelling justification, if in practice it benefits or burdens one race more than another would be far reaching and would raise serious questions about, and perhaps invalidate, a whole range of tax, welfare, public service, regulatory, and licensing statutes that may be more burdensome to the poor and to the average black than to the more affluent white.[77]

Taking account of governmental interests in being able to enforce many statutes with racially disparate impacts, the Court ruled that strict scrutiny would not apply unless the plaintiffs could demonstrate that the defendants acted with a racially discriminatory intent.

A similar calculation occurred in *City of Cleburne* v. *Cleburne Living Center*,[78] which held that classifications based on what the Court called mental retardation should receive only rational basis review, not strict scrutiny. Based on formulae employed in prior cases, it was strongly arguable that those with intellectual disabilities constituted a "discrete and insular minority," in the language of the famed *Carolene Products* footnote,[79] any discrimination against which should be treated as suspect. But the Court reckoned that the government had good reasons to classify based on mental incapacity in many contexts.[80] Not wanting to interfere unduly with the government's ability to promote legitimate interests, the Court determined that strict scrutiny did not apply.

Sometimes, however, an assessment of the nature of the governmental interests likely to be involved in a category of cases will push the Court to recognize a right to elevated scrutiny. The rule that content-based regulations of speech incur strict scrutiny illustrates this phenomenon.[81] In the Court's estimation, content-based regulations of speech are likely to reflect governmental antagonism toward and efforts to squelch underlying ideas. Accordingly, the Court has prescribed strict scrutiny of such rules.

Another example of governmental interests figuring into the definition of scrutiny rights comes from the string of cases that ultimately resulted in the decision to subject gender-based discrimination to intermediate scrutiny. Prior to the 1976 decision in *Craig* v. *Boren*,[82] the Supreme Court had never recognized a tier of

---

[77]   *Id.* at 248.
[78]   473 U.S. 432 (1985).
[79]   *See United States* v. *Carolene Prods. Co.*, 304 U.S. 144, 152n.4 (1938).
[80]   *See id.* at 444 ("[L]egislation thus singling out the retarded for special treatment reflects the real and undeniable differences between the retarded and others. That a civilized and decent society expects and approves such legislation indicates that governmental consideration of those differences in the vast majority of situations is not only legitimate but also desirable.").
[81]   *See, e.g.*, *National Inst. of Family and Life Advocates* v. *Becerra*, 138 S. Ct. 2361, 2371 (2018); *Reed* v. *Town of Gilbert*, 135 S. Ct. 2218 (2015).
[82]   429 U.S. 190, 197–99 (1976).

equal protection scrutiny between strict scrutiny and rational basis review. Justice Brennan, the author of the Court's opinion in *Craig*, believed that gender-based classifications ought to incur strict scrutiny, but he could not muster five votes for that conclusion.[83] Too many of his colleagues believed that a strict scrutiny standard would frustrate the government's promotion of too many valid interests in too many cases. Intermediate scrutiny offered less protection to the interests that underlie the triggering right to freedom from gender-based discrimination, but it posed less of a threat to competing governmental interests. In *Craig*, Justice Brennan advanced intermediate scrutiny as a compromise that a majority of his colleagues agreed to accept.

RIGHTS, INTERESTS, AND CONSTITUTIONAL THEORIES

Viewing constitutional rights as compounded to protect interests that courts must balance against other interests should force us to think anew about prescriptive constitutional theories, by which I mean theories that purport to establish standards of correctness and legitimacy in constitutional adjudication. There are so many constitutional theories that I could not possibly discuss all of them. Further complicating the challenge, the best-known theoretical approaches, including both originalism and living constitutionalism, come in multiple varieties. I must therefore paint with a broad brush in seeking to make a narrow point: We should dismiss as unrealistic any theory that does not recognize the need for courts to play a partly instrumental and strategic role when articulating rules for decision in cases not controlled by precedent.

Some constitutional theorists portray the judicial function as exclusively involving "interpretation," which they characterize as a non-instrumental search for constitutional "meaning." In this vocabulary, meaning might be thought to emerge from wholly linguistic and historical inquiries – as some originalists have suggested[84] – or from conceptual reasoning aimed at identifying the "morally best" understanding of abstract constitutional concepts such as "freedom of speech" and "the equal protection of the laws."[85] As we have seen, however, the definition and protection of constitutional rights has a consequence-sensitive, empirical, and even a strategic aspect. Courts must weigh the costs and benefits – as cashed out in terms of

---

[83]   See *Frontiero* v. *Richardson*, 411 U.S. 677, 688 (1973) (plurality opinion) (Brennan, J.).

[84]   See, e.g., Lawrence B. Solum, *Originalism and Constitutional Construction*, 82 FORDHAM L. REV. 453, 462–67, (2013) (suggesting that this was an ambition of early originalists and collecting citations); *id.* at 503–11, 534 (arguing that the view is still held by John O. McGinnis & Michael B. Rappaport); *see also* Antonin Scalia, U.S. Supreme Court Justice, Address by Justice Scalia Before the Attorney General's Conference on Economic Liberties in Washington, D.C. (June 14, 1986), *in* OFFICE OF LEGAL POL'Y, U.S. DEP'T OF JUSTICE, ORIGINAL MEANING JURISPRUDENCE: A SOURCEBOOK app. C at 101 (1987) (proposing a shift from original intent to original public meaning).

[85]   See, e.g., Ronald Dworkin, FREEDOM'S LAW: THE MORAL READING OF THE AMERICAN CONSTITUTION 7–10 (1996).

interests – of defining triggering and scrutiny rights in particular ways. In cases such as *Washington v. Davis* and *New York Times Co. v. Sullivan*, the Supreme Court cannot extract rules for decision through linguistic, historical, or moral conceptual analysis without making empirical and strategic judgments. The Justices must decide how best to reconcile or accommodate competing interests – which they must exercise partly independent judgment in identifying – in light of the likely practical implications of alternative rules of decision.

Some originalists acknowledge as much. A growing coterie depicts constitutional adjudication as involving two functions, interpretation and "construction."[86] On this model, judges first should engage in a historical and linguistic search for the original meaning of constitutional language. Sometimes, however, the meaning that they discover will be too vague or indeterminate to resolve current constitutional disputes, including, one might imagine, those in cases such as *Washington v. Davis*, *New York Times Co. v. Sullivan*, and possibly *Miranda*. In cases of underdeterminacy, but only in such cases, originalists of this stripe portray the judiciary as needing to engage in "construction" to bridge the gap between the Constitution's original meaning and the outcome in particular cases.[87] Within this terminology, the rules of decision in *Washington v. Davis*, *New York Times Co. v. Sullivan*, and *Miranda* would all constitute judicial constructions.

The claims that construction is a function distinct from interpretation and that construction – unlike interpretation – is characterized by a weighing of competing practical considerations sounds reasonable on the surface. It is certainly familiar for prescriptive language to be vague or underdeterminate, as I have emphasized in distinguishing abstract rights from triggering and ultimate rights. But a terminological distinction is crucially important here. As I have used the term, an abstract right is not necessarily a precise reflection of a constitutional provision's original meaning as originalists characteristically use the latter term. An abstract right, in my sense, is a right that can be identified largely without reference to the limits that competing interests would impose on its scope or reach. In talking about original meanings, originalists wish to capture limits on the scope of a right as well as the interests that would explain why the Constitution recognizes a right in the first place.

With this distinction in mind, we should look skeptically on the claim that there is an "original meaning" of the Equal Protection Clause or the Free Speech Clause that could be identified without interest-balancing or strategic judgment. Consider *Washington v. Davis* and *New York Times Co. v. Sullivan* once more. If there is

---

[86] *See, e.g.,* Solum, *supra* note 84, at 467–73; *see also* Jack M. Balkin, *Abortion and Original Meaning,* 24 CONST. COMMENT. 291 (2007); Jack M. Balkin, *Framework Originalism and the Living* Constitution, 103 NW. U. L. REV. 549 (2009); Randy E. Barnett, *An Originalism for Nonoriginalists,* 45 LOY. L. REV. 611 (1999).

[87] *See, e.g.,* Solum, *supra* note 84, at 469–72 (arguing that construction is needed when "the meaning of the constitutional text is unclear, or the implications of that meaning are contested," *id.* at 469); *see also* Balkin, *Framework Originalism and the Living Constitution, supra* note 86, at 560.

a linguistically and historically identifiable meaning of "the equal protection of the laws" that can be specified prior to the questions about triggering and scrutiny rights that the Supreme Court confronted in *Washington* v. *Davis*, for example, it would need to be so vague as to leave nearly the entirety of modern equal protection jurisprudence in "the construction zone."[88] And if interest balancing and practical judgment could not bear on the question of the First Amendment's meaning in *New York Times Co.* v. *Sullivan*, we would be left with the questions of how and why the historically and linguistically defined "meaning" of the First Amendment leaves any room for the application of strict judicial scrutiny or other judicially constructed tests of ultimate constitutional validity.

A similar analysis would apply to any version of nonoriginalism that sought to draw a sharp conceptual line between interpretation and meaning, on the one hand, and judicially defined triggering rights and implementing tests (such as strict scrutiny), on the other hand. For some purposes, it is helpful to distinguish between the Constitution's meaning and doctrines developed to implement or enforce the Constitution's meaning.[89] Among other things, it is sometimes both intelligible and useful to imagine courts as choosing whether to employ implementing rules that either over-enforce or under-enforce the Constitution as they roughly understand it. *Miranda* may exemplify a case in which the Supreme Court thought that it confronted such a choice: It must either allow the introduction into evidence of many confessions that were coerced, when actual coercion could not be proved, or adopt a prophylactic rule. Correspondingly, we might conceptualize doctrines that limit judicial inquiries into alleged constitutional violations by prison officials and military officers as reflecting a judgment to under-enforce the Constitution's meaning.[90]

Even if so, however, if the point of a distinction between "meaning" and "implementation" or "construction" is to mark a divide between where consequence-based, instrumental analysis is forbidden and where such analysis is permitted, the distinction cannot be drawn in a way that serves the intended purpose. As we have seen, both the identification of governmental interests and judgments about the interests that diverse constitutional provisions protect depend on judgments about desirable, acceptable, and unacceptable consequences. As much for originalist as for living constitutionalist theories, value-based ascriptions of supporting interests to constitutional provisions and consequence-sensitive judgments about how to accommodate competing interests are too nearly pervasive in constitutional analysis to sustain the

---

[88]   *See, e.g.*, Balkin, *Framework Originalism and the Living Constitution, supra* note 86, 555–56, 559–66 (arguing that the meaning of Fourteenth Amendment is limited to general principles and interpreting living constitutionalism as a theory of construction); *see also* Jack M. Balkin, LIVING ORIGINALISM 220–55 (2011).

[89]   *See, e.g.*, Fallon, *supra* note 62, at 37–39.

[90]   *See, e.g.*, *Overton* v. *Bazzetta*, 539 U.S. 126 (2003); *Shaw* v. *Murphy*, 532 U.S. 223 (2001); *O'Lone* v. *Estate of Shabazz*, 482 U.S. 342 (1987); *Goldman* v. *Weinberger*, 475 U.S. 503 (1986).

claim that the identification of constitutional "meaning" could be non-instrumental even if the final crafting of judicial rules of decision cannot.

An example comes once again from the strict judicial scrutiny formula. Do we think that courts deviate from and under-enforce the Constitution's meaning in every instance in which they find no ultimate constitutional rights violation due to the presence of a compelling government interest? If not, it is because we determine the Constitution's meaning partly on the basis of an interest-based calculation that renders abstract rights subject to qualification or override when the practical consequences would be unacceptable otherwise.

RIGHTS AND REFLECTIVE EQUILIBRIUM

When we understand constitutional rights as constraints that are designed to reflect and accommodate competing interests, the Rawlsian notion of reflective equilibrium offers an illuminating organizing metaphor for constitutional deliberation in the Supreme Court. Within the simplified version of reflective equilibrium theory that I introduced earlier, we can imagine the Justices reasoning to decision in hard cases by tacking back and forth between provisional formulations of applicable constitutional principles and equally provisional judgments about acceptable outcomes in particular cases. As much as moral reasoning, constitutional decision-making should be principled. But proposed principles of constitutional law, like moral principles, should be tested partly by the outcomes that they would yield.

Although a simple reflective equilibrium model helps to illuminate constitutional decision-making, it leaves out a good deal. As emerges when constitutional rights are examined through the lens that judicial tests such as strict scrutiny furnish, rights are themselves multidimensional. We need to account for abstract, triggering, scrutiny, and ultimate rights, all of which may be open to reformulation in the process of case-by-case constitutional analysis. In cases involving strict scrutiny, compelling governmental interests are another potential variable, as are the demands of narrow tailoring. Those who take constitutional constraints seriously must also weigh the relevance of constitutional text and history, of judicial precedent, and of a variety of judicial-role-based concerns.

It is daunting if not dizzying to imagine how all of the relevant considerations interact with one another. But if anything seems plain, it may be that many if not all are flexible, adjustable, or open to reconsideration. Serious engagement with constitutional issues requires simultaneous analysis on multiple levels and along diverse dimensions. Even and perhaps especially when we recognize as much, the Rawlsian idea of a search for reflective equilibrium provides a model for conceptualizing the task that the Justices of the Supreme Court face – which is the same task that all concerned citizens confront when they think or argue about what the Constitution requires in a particular case.

In explicating the model of reflective equilibrium, Rawls distinguished between narrow and wide versions.[91] The narrow version (with which I began) emphasizes the two-way traffic between case-by-case judgments and explanatory principles. The wider version encompasses further considerations that deep, conscientious reasoning would seek to bring into alignment. As applied to constitutional law, a wide-reflective-equilibrium approach would call for judges not to balance interests as they would in making a personal moral judgment, but to strive to harmonize their legal judgments in particular cases with defensible understandings of the judicial role and appropriate interpretive methodology, the proper formulation and application of a constitutional test (such as strict scrutiny), the significance of precedent, ideals of moral legitimacy and the rule of law, and perhaps other considerations as well.[92]

With respect to any or all of these factors, judges and Justices are likely to begin with provisional, sometimes quasi-intuitive judgments about how the relevant variables should be specified. As the wide-reflective-equilibrium model highlights, however, the felt practical challenge, imposed by the criteria of legitimacy that apply to judicial decision-making, is to specify all of the variables simultaneously in ways that produce an acceptable, normatively attractive alignment overall.

As deployed in legal reasoning in judicial opinions and elsewhere, the wide-reflective-equilibrium method for balancing competing individual and governmental interests is one of reasoned judgment and argument, ongoing over time, as participants in our constitutional practice endeavor to persuade one another through rational argument. We should never expect complete convergence of judgment. There are too many possible bases for reasoned, reasonable disagreement. But we should not be too pessimistic either. By all credible accounts, most cases are "easy" ones,[93] with judges of all political and methodological stripes converging in their legal judgments. Even in the Supreme Court, which sits to resolve difficult cases that have divided the lower courts, the Justices reach unanimous judgments in a large number of cases, often exceeding forty percent.[94]

In advancing a wide-reflective-equilibrium model of interest-balancing in constitutional law, I offer a rational reconstruction of thinking about constitutional

---

[91]   *See* Rawls, POLITICAL LIBERALISM, *supra* note 7, at 8 n.8; John Rawls, *The Independence of Moral Theory*, 48 PROC. & ADDRESSES OF THE AM. PHIL. ASS'N 5 (1974–75). At the very minimum, Rawls's conception of wide reflective equilibrium contemplates a need to specify "the original position" from which representative individuals would choose principles of justice from behind a "veil of ignorance" as part of the same process of equilibration from which substantive judgments about individual cases and statements of general principles of political morality also emerge. *See* Rawls, A THEORY OF JUSTICE, *supra* note 7, at 15–19, 118–23.

[92]   *See* Fallon, *supra* note 39, 142–51.

[93]   *See* Frederick Schauer, *Easy Cases*, 58 S. CAL. L. REV. 399 (1985).

[94]   See, e.g., *The Supreme Court, 2014 Term – The Statistics*, 129 HARV. L. REV. 381, 386 (2015).

rights, not an assertion about routine empirical practice or characteristic judicial psychology. Our question is not, how do judges think about rights as a matter of empirical psychology? It is, how can we conceptualize constitutional rights, in a way reasonably consistent with known influences on judicial decision-making, such that they can emerge from a framework that includes multiple diverse variables and constraints, centrally including competing governmental interests? In formulating this question, we know, too, that a perspicuous conceptualization of constitutional rights must explain how judges' values can influence their conclusions about what constitutional rights we have.

My rational reconstruction of rights as constraints on governmental discretion, devised as reflections of interests that are capable of balancing and accommodation within a reflective equilibrium methodology, will not dispel all anxieties about judges making disputable, morally inflected judgments in identifying constitutionally cognizable interest and then in balancing them against one another. To the contrary, having grasped the nature of constitutional rights within our practice of constitutional adjudication, we may also have sharpened, not escaped, serious questions about when and how far courts ought to second-guess the judgments of legislatures – which also must balance competing private and governmental interests – within a political democracy. Those questions, which now may seem more daunting than ever, will set much of the agenda for subsequent chapters.

4

Tests besides Strict Judicial Scrutiny and the Nature of the Rights That They Protect

Although strict judicial scrutiny plays an outsized role in modern constitutional law, it by no means stands alone. As lawyers know and as students quickly learn, constitutional law comprises a lengthy catalogue of judge-made tests, some of greater and some of lesser importance. Like strict scrutiny, these other tests embody assumptions about, and thus provide lenses through which to identify, the nature of constitutional rights in the United States. A few examples of tests besides strict scrutiny include these:

- Although the Supreme Court often employs strict judicial scrutiny to define and enforce free speech rights, the Court has developed separate, special tests for the permissibility of regulations of commercial advertising;[1] for restrictions of speech in a public forum;[2] for acceptable limitations on speech by children in school[3] and by public employees speaking in their private capacities;[4] for "zoning" regulations of "adult speech" that do not involve total prohibitions;[5] and more.

- In holding that the Second Amendment creates a personal right to bear arms for self-defense,[6] the Supreme Court announced a variety of qualifications that frequently require further inquiries before a court determines whether someone who wishes to carry a gun would have an ultimate right to do so. To implement those qualifications, some lower courts have employed intermediate judicial scrutiny.[7]

---

[1] *See, e.g., Lorillard Tobacco Co. v. Reilly,* 533 U.S. 525 (2001); *Cent. Hudson Gas & Elec. Corp. v. Pub. Serv. Comm'n of New York,* 447 U.S. 557 (1980).
[2] *See Minnesota Voters Alliance v. Mansky,* 138 S. Ct. 1876 (2018); *Int'l Soc. for Krishna Consciousness, Inc. (ISKCON) v. Lee,* 505 U.S. 672 (1992).
[3] *See, e.g., Tinker v. Des Moines Ind. Sch. Dist.,* 393 U.S. 503 (1969).
[4] *See, e.g., Connick v. Myers,* 461 U.S. 138, 150 (1983).
[5] *See City of Renton v. Playtime Theatres, Inc.,* 475 U.S. 41 (1986).
[6] *See District of Columbia v. Heller,* 554 U.S. 570 (2008).
[7] *See, e.g., New York State Rifle & Pistol Ass'n, Inc. v. City of New York,* 883 F.3d 45, 55–56 (2d Cir. 2018); *Woollard v. Gallagher,* 712 F.3d 865, 868, 876 (4th Cir. 2013).

- To determine whether the government has violated rights to due process of law under the Fifth and Fourteenth Amendments, the Court most often applies a three-part balancing test first articulated in *Mathews* v. *Eldridge* (1976).[8]
- Prior to conducting *Mathews* balancing, the Court applies other tests to make a threshold or triggering determination whether a complaining party has suffered a deprivation of "liberty" or "property" adequate to bring the due process guarantee into play.[9]
- In addition to creating a right to procedural due process, the Fifth Amendment includes a guarantee against compelled self-incrimination. To enforce that right in a meaningful way, the Supreme Court, in *Miranda* v. *Arizona*,[10] propounded one of the most famous tests in constitutional law. If a person gives a confession in response to custodial interrogation, the confession will be deemed to have been coerced unless the criminal suspect received a *Miranda* warning and waived the rights that the warning announces.
- To operationalize the Eighth Amendment prohibition against cruel and unusual punishments, the Supreme Court relies on a "proportionality" test, asking whether punishment is proportional to the crime.[11] In one category of cases, the Court considers all of the circumstances of a case. In another, it applies "categorical rules" – such as a rule barring capital punishment for crimes other than homicide – based on a consideration of two factors: "The Court first considers 'objective indicia of society's standards, as expressed in legislative enactments and state practice' to determine whether there is a national consensus against the sentencing practice at issue."[12] Having done so, the Court next conducts an independent judicial appraisal of proportionality. Only at the end of this battery of test-like inquiries does the Court determine whether an ultimate constitutional right has been violated.

Because it would be impossible to examine the entire universe of constitutional tests and the issues that arise in their application, this chapter's survey is more illustrative than complete. Its themes mostly exhibit continuity with the analysis that emerged in Chapter 3.

---

[8]   424 U.S. 319 (1976). *See Medina* v. *California*, 505 U.S. 437, 444 (1992) ("[W]e have … applied [*Mathews*] in a variety of contexts, *e.g., Santosky* v. *Kramer*, 455 U.S. 745, (1982) (standard of proof for termination of parental rights over objection); *Addington* v. *Texas*, 441 U.S. 418 (1979) (standard of proof for involuntary civil commitment to mental hospital for indefinite period.").

[9]   *See* Thomas W. Merrill, *The Landscape of Constitutional Property*, 86 VA. L. REV. 885, 893 (2000) (endorsing a "patterning definition" method under which the Court identifies "general criteria that distinguish constitutional property from other interests or expectancies" and then canvasses "sources of non-constitutional law to determine whether the claimant has a legally recognized interest that satisfies these criteria and hence constitutes constitutional property").

[10]   384 U.S. 436 (1966).

[11]   *See e.g., Graham* v. *Florida*, 560 U.S. 48, 60 (2010); *Harmelin* v. *Michigan*, 501 U.S. 957, 997 (1991) (Kennedy, J., concurring) (recognizing that the Eighth Amendment encompasses a "narrow proportionality principle" that prohibits "greatly disproportioned" sentences).

[12]   *Graham*, 560 U.S. at 61 (quoting *Roper* v. *Simmons* 543 U.S. 551, 563 (2005)).

First, constitutional rights – as refracted through the tests that courts use to enforce them – almost invariably function as specifically defined constraints on the government and its officials. Rarely, if ever, do they constitute categorical entitlements to say particular things or engage in particular acts, regardless of the nature of a regulatory prohibition and the interests adduced to justify it. Suppose I want to say "Throw all the incumbents out of office." In many and possibly most contexts, strict scrutiny would apply, and a prohibition against political speech would not plausibly be narrowly tailored to any compelling governmental interest. If I were a public school teacher, however, the First Amendment would not constrain school officials from firing me for railing against governmental policy during a math or science class. Nor would the First Amendment protect me against eviction from a library or a hospital emergency ward if I insisted on shouting "Throw all the incumbents out of office!" in a loud voice.[13] If the government enforced an ideologically even-handed prohibition against disruptive noisemaking, strict scrutiny would not apply. Under a different test, the government's asserted justification would pass muster.

Second, as much under other tests as under strict scrutiny, rights reflect interests. The sometimes distinguishable decisions that judges need to make in recognizing abstract, triggering, scrutiny, and ultimate rights under any particular constitutional provision embody judgments that unacceptable consequences would ensue absent the assignment of a right. The relevant judicial decisions are thus value-based and consequence-sensitive. Only rarely does the Supreme Court purport to derive the specific tests that it uses to enforce the Constitution from original historical understandings.

Despite these strong elements of continuity, using judicial tests other than strict scrutiny as a lens through which to examine the nature of constitutional rights brings new complexities into view. The first, and most important, involves a distinction among the kinds of official discretion that constitutional rights constrain. The strict scrutiny test was designed to limit governmental discretion in enacting and enforcing statutes and similar broadly applicable regulations. As most commonly and naturally applied, it asks whether a law or regulation is narrowly tailored to a compelling governmental interest – not, for example, whether the conduct of a particular police interrogation of a criminal suspect, or a judicial decision that allowed a particular confession into evidence – is constitutionally permissible. By contrast, many other tests and the rights that they define and implement impose constraints on the discretion of individual governmental officials who are not lawmakers.

[13]   For a pioneering discussion of the different kinds of threats that different governmental regulations of speech can pose, and of the resulting importance of distinguishing between statutes that target speech based on the message that it communicates and those that seek to prohibit harms unrelated to the message being asserted, see John Hart Ely, DEMOCRACY AND DISTRUST: A THEORY OF JUDICIAL REVIEW 105–16 (1980).

Some constitutional tests define rights against executive officials, others against judges. Consider the Fourth Amendment right against unreasonable searches and seizures.[14] Most searches and seizures are effected by executive officials, such as police officers, exercising largely discretionary authority. Claims that searches and seizures violate the Fourth Amendment rarely implicate statutes.[15] To determine whether a particular search or seizure violated the Constitution, courts apply a variety of tests, mostly designed with police activities, not the permissibility of statutes, in mind.

Other constitutional tests define rights against, and limit the discretion of, judges. Contrary to widespread impressions, the *Miranda* rule falls into this category. The Supreme Court's requirement of *Miranda* warnings clearly creates, and was intended to create, a deterrent to police questioning of criminal suspects without apprising them of their rights. But *Miranda* achieves that deterrent effect by functioning directly as a constraint on the discretion of judges. Under *Miranda*, judges must exclude all (or virtually all) custodial confessions that were elicited without *Miranda* warnings. The Fifth Amendment right against compelled self-incrimination is a trial right, applicable only in courtrooms.[16]

In the examination of constitutional tests other than strict judicial scrutiny, a second important point about the diversity of constitutional rights, and of variation in their structures, also emerges. Although it remains analytically useful to differentiate among abstract, triggering, scrutiny, and ultimate rights, some constitutional tests effectively collapse the distinction between scrutiny and ultimate rights. The merger occurs when the infringement of a triggering right invokes a categorical rule of constitutional invalidity. The *Miranda* test for the admissibility of confessions is again illustrative. A prosecutor's attempt to introduce a custodial confession that was procured without a *Miranda* warning triggers a rule that bars the introduction of confessions by defendants who did not receive *Miranda* warnings (unless some exception applies). The *Miranda* "test," if we were to call it that, makes no provision for further judicial calculations after a court determines that police failed to apprise a suspect of her *Miranda* rights before the suspect confessed in the course of a custodial interrogation. The resulting contrast between the *Miranda* "test" and strict judicial scrutiny illustrates an important lesson about the nature of constitutional rights. As refined and operationalized by the Supreme Court, not all of the rights that are created by the Constitution have precisely identical structures.

---

[14] U.S. CONST. amend. IV. ("The right of the people to be secure in their persons, houses, papers, and effects, against unreasonable searches and seizures, shall not be violated...").

[15] But there are a few that do. *See, e.g., City of Los Angeles v. Patel*, 135 S. Ct. 2443 (2015) (invalidating a municipal ordinance that required hotel operators to retain records concerning guests for ninety days and to make them available for police inspection upon request); *see also Camara v. Mun. Court of City & Cty. of San Francisco*, 387 U.S. 523 (1967) (invalidating an ordinance authorizing municipal inspectors to search homes without a warrant).

[16] *See United States v. Patane*, 542 U.S. 630, 641 (2004) ("Potential violations [of the Fifth Amendment] occur, if at all, only upon the admission of unwarned statements into evidence at trial.").

Rights that are enforced by categorical rules have a different structure from those enforced by strict scrutiny, which calls for further judicial analysis after the controlling test is identified.

In all cases, however, it remains important to maintain a conceptual distinction between triggering rights and ultimate rights. And it is especially important to preserve a distinction between abstract rights, on the one hand, and triggering, scrutiny, and ultimate rights, on the other. Without such a distinction, our sense that particular constitutional provisions create reasonably unitary rights – such as rights to free speech, due process of law, and freedom from cruel and unusual punishments – would dissolve into a morass of more particular rights as defined by an ever-expanding panoply of judge-made tests. It would be a reductionist mistake to think that we cannot talk meaningfully about the right to free speech, for example, even if it takes a greatly diverse set of triggering and scrutiny rights to protect that abstract right. At the abstract level, it makes perfect sense to say that we have *a* right to freedom of speech. Beneath the abstract level, we have multiple triggering, scrutiny, and sometimes distinguishable ultimate rights.

RIGHTS AGAINST STATUTES AND SIMILARLY BROAD REGULATIONS

In cataloguing constitutional tests besides strict scrutiny, I begin with other tests that define rights against laws or generally applicable regulations. A partial typology will help to illuminate the diverse ways in which constitutional rights can protect individual interests and restrict legislative discretion while, at the same time, accommodating competing governmental interests.

Tests That Are the Functional Equivalents of Strict Scrutiny

Some judicially created, rights-protective tests are close analogues to strict judicial scrutiny. An example comes from *Brandenburg v. Ohio*.[17] Clarence Brandenburg, a Ku Klux Klan leader, was arrested under a statute that made it a crime to "advocate the duty, necessity, or propriety" of crime or violence as a means of promoting political ends. In invalidating that prohibition under the First Amendment, the Supreme Court announced a newly minted test of constitutional validity, triggered by statutes that restrict political advocacy for the purpose of forestalling violence: "[T]he constitutional guarantees of free speech and free press do not permit a State to forbid or proscribe advocacy of the use of force or law violation except where such advocacy is directed to inciting or producing imminent lawless action and is likely to incite or produce such action."[18] That test closely parallels the elements and concerns of strict judicial scrutiny. The linkage of permissible regulation to imminent

---

[17]   395 U.S. 444 (1969) (per curiam).
[18]   *Id.* at 447.

lawless action implicitly demands that the government seek to justify any prohibition by reference to compelling interest. Further, a statute should also count as narrowly tailored to achieve that end if it bars only such speech as is "directed to" producing imminent lawless action and is likely to achieve its aim.

The Supreme Court also relies on an analogue of strict judicial scrutiny to restrict state interference with interstate commerce under the dormant Commerce Clause. Although the Commerce Clause is framed as a grant of power to Congress, the Court, from early in constitutional history, has interpreted it as impliedly forbidding the states from creating barriers to interstate trade.[19] Accordingly, so-called dormant Commerce Clause doctrine effectively protects a right of access to interstate markets. In defining an important aspect of that general right, the Court has insisted that when a state regulatory or tax statute either discriminates facially against interstate commerce or reflects a discriminatory purpose of disadvantaging out-of-staters, "it will be struck down unless the discrimination is demonstrably justified by a valid factor unrelated to economic protectionism."[20] That demand for a "valid" justification bears similarities to, though it is admittedly weaker than, strict scrutiny's reference to a compelling interest. But to gauge protectionist purposes, the Court will often ask whether the state could have achieved its asserted valid purpose through a "less restrictive alternative."[21] The latter phrase, in particular, closely approximates the strict scrutiny inquiry into whether a statute is narrowly tailored to achieve legitimate goals. If a statute that imposed fewer obstacles to interstate trade would serve a state's legitimate purposes equally well, then a regulation is not narrowly tailored to those purposes. The Court has further suggested the parallelism of the dormant Commerce Clause and strict scrutiny tests by emphasizing the stringency of the prohibition against discriminatory legislation: "[W]hen the state statute amounts to simple economic protectionism, 'a virtually per se rule of invalidity' has applied."[22]

When rights-protective judicial tests closely approximate strict judicial scrutiny, it is not always obvious why the Supreme Court has not eliminated any possible gap by simply extending the quasi-generic strict scrutiny formula. The best explanation may involve historical accident. For a long season in US judicial history, the Court had tested attempted governmental regulations of speech that advocated lawlessness or violence to further political aims under a "clear and present danger" test.[23]

[19] Barry Friedman & Daniel T. Deacon, *A Course Unbroken: The Constitutional Legitimacy of the Dormant Commerce Clause*, 97 VA. L. REV. 1877, 1882 (2011) (finding "plain textualist and originalist support for the dormant Commerce Clause").

[20] *Wyoming v. Oklahoma*, 502 U.S. 437, 454–55 (1992); *Oregon Waste Sys., Inc. v. Dep't of Envtl. Quality of State of Or.*, 511 U.S. 93, 99 (1994) ("If a restriction on commerce is discriminatory, it is virtually per se invalid.").

[21] *See Wyoming*, 502 U.S. at 456 (requiring the "unavailability of nondiscriminatory alternatives adequate to preserve the local interests at stake" (quoting *Hughes v. Oklahoma*, 441 U.S. 322, 336 (1979)).

[22] *Id.* at 454 (quoting *Philadelphia v. New Jersey*, 437 U.S. 617, 624 (1978)).

[23] *Schenck v. United States*, 249 U.S. 47, 52 (1919) (Holmes, J.) ("The question in every case is whether the words used are used in such circumstances and are of such a nature as to create a clear and present danger that they will bring about the substantive evils that Congress has a right to prevent."); *see*

Somewhat disingenuously, *Brandenburg* sought to emphasize continuity with prior cases in the "clear and present danger" line, even as it dramatically expanded the scope of constitutional protection for political speech that encourages or advocates lawbreaking.[24] Invocation of the relatively newly formulated strict scrutiny test that had applications far beyond the First Amendment might have signaled a sharper break with the past than the Court wished to acknowledge.

Despite structural similarities, the Supreme Court may regard its heightened scrutiny of facially discriminatory legislation under the dormant Commerce Clause as designed exclusively to "smoke out" impermissibly "protectionist" state motivations for imposing restraints on interstate trade.[25] By contrast, the strict scrutiny formula requires the judicial weighing of legitimate, competing interests in some cases. In the end, however, I can ultimately only speculate about the Court's reliance on tests that closely approximate, but are not precisely identical to, strict scrutiny.

Weakly Protective Tests, Such as Rational Basis Review

The paradigm of a judicially crafted test that provides only weak protection for abstract constitutional rights is rational basis review, the standard applied under the Due Process and Equal Protection Clauses to legislation that neither classifies on a "suspect" basis nor implicates a "fundamental" right. A typical formulation appeared in *FCC* v. *Beach Communications, Inc.*[26]

> In areas of social and economic policy, a statutory classification that neither proceeds along suspect lines [e.g., race, national origin, religion, or alienage] nor infringes fundamental constitutional rights must be upheld against equal protection challenge if there is any reasonably conceivable state of facts that could provide a rational basis for the classification ... [A] legislative choice is not subject to courtroom factfinding and may be based on rational speculation unsupported by evidence or empirical data.

As in the case of strict scrutiny, a court will not apply even rational basis review without first determining that a triggering right has been infringed. Insofar as

generally David M. Rabban, *The Emergence of Modern First Amendment Doctrine*, 50 U. CHI. L. REV. 1205 (1983) (outlining alternative historical accounts of the emergence of modern First Amendment doctrine); *see also* Hans A. Linde, *"Clear and Present Danger" Reexamined*: Dissonance in the Brandenburg *Concerto*, 22 STAN. L. REV. 1163 (1969).

[24] *See Brandenburg* v. *Ohio*, 395 U.S. 444, 447–48 (1969) (per curiam) (claiming that prior cases established a bar to statutory prohibitions of advocacy "except where such advocacy is directed to inciting or producing imminent lawless action and is likely to incite or produce such action").

[25] Donald Regan, *The Supreme Court and State Protectionism*, 84 MICH. L. REV. 1091 (1986) (claiming that modern dormant Commerce Clause jurisprudence related to the movement of goods aims exclusively to ferret out purposeful protectionism); *see also CTS Corp.* v. *Dynamics Corp. of Am.*, 481 U.S. 69, 95 (1987) (Scalia, J., concurring) (citing Regan and claiming that his thesis may describe the Court's actual practice).

[26] 508 U.S. 307, 314–15 (1993).

rational basis review is concerned, that threshold inquiry is normally not searching, but neither is it boundlessly lax. If Congress chose to put an image of Donald Trump on the one-dollar bill, replacing George Washington, I would be unhappy, but I would not have suffered the deprivation of any cognizable liberty or property right that is protected (even weakly) by the Due Process Clause. Nor could I credibly claim to have been treated unequally, even in comparison with those who thought Trump a better choice than Washington to adorn the one-dollar bill in the twenty-first century. In sum, rational basis review, like strict judicial scrutiny, needs to be triggered.

Nevertheless, along all relevant dimensions, the contrast between strict scrutiny and rational basis review looks – and most often is – dramatic. In comparison with strict scrutiny, rational basis review is both more readily provoked and more easily satisfied. Indeed, judicial application of rational basis review most often amounts to little more than a rubber stamp, as those who presided over the demise of the *Lochner* era surely intended that it would be.

Recent decades, however, have witnessed an important complication in the contrast between strict scrutiny and rational basis review. Although rational-basis challenges to legislation almost always fail, they occasionally succeed. As one measure, a comprehensive study of all rational basis cases in the Supreme Court during the years 1971 through 1996 found a success rate of roughly nine percent.[27] At the risk of slight oversimplification, I would assign successful rational basis challenges to two categories.[28] The first is a hodge-podge. For whatever reason, a majority of the Justices thrust restraint aside, seemingly on an ad hoc basis, to correct what must strike them as a plain injustice. In cases within the hodge-podge category, it is often not easy to see why the Justices find one rule or statute more troublingly "irrational" than others that they uphold.

The second category involves what commentators have sometimes characterized as rational basis review "with bite."[29] Within this grouping, the Court more explicably and consistently appears to apply less-than-ordinarily deferential review to statutes that disadvantage identifiable groups on grounds that a majority of the Justices find troubling but nevertheless hesitate to classify as "suspect." In one case from the 1970s, the Court defended its refusal to apply formally elevated scrutiny to statutes that treated children born out of wedlock less generously than children born to married parents by noting that "where a law is arbitrary" in its treatment of extra-marital children, "we have had no difficulty in finding the discrimination

---

[27] See Robert C. Farrell, *Successful Rational Basis Claims in the Supreme Court from the 1971 Term through* Romer v. Evans, 32 IND. L. REV. 357, 417–18 (1999).

[28] *Cf.* Katie R. Eyer, *The Canon of Rational Basis Review*, 93 NOTRE DAME L. REV. 1317, 1370 (2018) (arguing that rational basis review is "complex" and "deeply and persistently unsettled").

[29] *See generally* Gayle Lynn Pettinga, *Rational Basis with Bite: Intermediate Scrutiny by Any Other Name*, 62 IND. L.J. 779 (1986) (mapping the Court's use of heightened scrutiny under the rubric of rational basis review).

impermissible on less demanding standards."[30] In another case, the Court rejected arguments that persons with mental retardation constituted a "suspect class," discriminations against which would trigger strict judicial scrutiny, but nonetheless invalidated a particular challenged statute as exhibiting an "irrational prejudice."[31] These rulings invited a generalization that the Court stopped short of articulating itself: Statutes that classify to the disadvantage of children born out of wedlock and persons with mental retardation provoke a more-then-usually-searching form of rational basis review.[32] In the case of out-of-wedlock children, the Court formally ratified its commitment to a form of elevated scrutiny by holding in the 1988 case of *Clark* v. *Jeter*[33] that "discriminatory classification based on . . . illegitimacy" should receive intermediate scrutiny and be invalidated unless "substantially related to an important governmental objective."

In recent decades, the Supreme Court has relied repeatedly on the premise that a statute fails rational basis review if animated by prejudice, "animus," or a bare desire to harm a particular group as a ground for invaliding statutes that discriminate against gays and lesbians. *Romer* v. *Evans*[34] invalidated an amendment to the Colorado State Constitution that excluded gays from protection under any state statute or local ordinance barring discrimination. In *Lawrence* v. *Texas*,[35] the Court struck down a prohibition against sodomy. In doing so, it overruled a prior decision that had upheld bars against sodomy, reasoning that "[i]ts continuance as precedent demeans the lives of homosexual persons."[36] *United States* v. *Windsor*[37] relied on a similar premise. In invalidating a statute that forbade federal recognition of same-sex marriages, the Court reasoned that the challenged provision sought "to injure" a class of people that New York's state marriage law sought to protect. Without formally invoking strict scrutiny or any other established test of statutory validity, Justice Kennedy's Court opinion continued: "The Constitution's guarantee of equality 'must at the very least mean that a bare congressional desire to harm a politically unpopular group cannot' justify disparate treatment of that group."[38]

In striking down statutes that disadvantage gays and lesbians based on the legislature's constitutionally forbidden motivations, these cases break from a frequent theme in other decisions applying and explicating rational basis review. In numerous cases not involving claims by gays or persons with retardation, the Supreme Court has recited that rational basis scrutiny does not turn on the actual

---

[30] *Mathews* v. *Lucas*, 427 U.S. 495, 505 (1976).
[31] *City of Cleburne* v. *Cleburne Living Ctr.*, 473 U.S. 432, 442–46, 450 (1985).
[32] But cf. *Heller* v. *Doe*, 509 U.S. 312, 320–21 (1993) (applying highly deferential review to a statute disadvantaging persons with mental retardation).
[33] 486 U.S. 456, 461 (1988).
[34] 517 U.S. 620 (1996).
[35] 539 U.S. 558 (2003).
[36] *Id.* at 575 (overruling *Bowers* v. *Hardwick*, 478 U.S. 186 (2003)).
[37] 570 U.S. 744 (2013).
[38] *Id.* at 770 (quoting *Department of Agriculture* v. *Moreno*, 413 U.S. 528, 534–35 (1973)) (failing to invoke a formal test).

intentions or motivations of the legislature. As the Court put it on one leading case, "[w]here ... there are plausible reasons for Congress' action, our inquiry is at an end," because "it is ... 'constitutionally irrelevant whether this reasoning in fact underlay the legislative decision.'"[39]

The Court's willingness to probe the legislature's actual motivations in enacting laws that disadvantage some groups but not others, and to invalidate statutes based on imputed motivations, further evidences an important distinction in the administration of rational basis review. The probing of actual legislation motivations as a possible basis for invalidating statutes is a manifestation of rational basis review with bite. In Chapter 2, I argued that there is more than one form of strict scrutiny. In recent decades, the same has proved true of rational basis review.

Intermediate Scrutiny and Similar Tests

Chapter 1 offered some examples of rights protected by intermediate scrutiny, defined as requiring that any infringement of a triggering right be "substantially related" to an important governmental interest. The Court first articulated that test in an equal protection challenge to gender discrimination, in *Craig v. Boren*,[40] and has subsequently applied it to classifications based on out-of-wedlock birth.[41] In the First Amendment case of *FCC v. League of Women Voters*,[42] the Court used a formula that closely approximates the *Craig* test to gauge the permissibility of limiting editorializing by public broadcasting stations. In addition, commentators sometimes use the term "intermediate scrutiny" more loosely to characterize a variety of tests of constitutional validity that are more stringent than rational basis review, less exacting than strict judicial scrutiny, and more structured than open-ending balancing.Several courts of appeals have embraced "intermediate scrutiny" to give content to and apply limitations on Second Amendment rights.[43] Justice Scalia's Court opinion in *District of Columbia v. Heller*[44] relied staunchly on originalist historical reasoning to conclude that the Second Amendment creates an individual triggering right to own and carry weapons for purposes of self-defense. But, having established the existence of that right, Justice Scalia acknowledged that it could not be absolute: "Like most rights, the right secured by the Second Amendment is not unlimited."[45] Nor did he claim that Founding-era history gave

---

[39] *United States R.R. Retirement Bd. v. Fritz*, 449 U.S. 166, 179 (1980) (quoting *Flemming v. Nestor*, 363 U.S. 603, 612 (1960)).

[40] 429 U.S. 190, 197 (1976).

[41] *Clark v. Jeter*, 486 U.S. 456, 461 (1988).

[42] 468 U.S. 364, 402 (1984) (holding "that the specific interests sought to be advanced by [a challenged provision's] ban on editorializing are either not sufficiently substantial or are not served in a sufficiently limited manner to justify the substantial abridgment of important journalistic freedoms which the First Amendment jealously protects").

[43] *See supra* note 7.

[44] 554 U.S. 570 (2008).

[45] *Id.* at 626.

sharp definition to the requisite exceptions: "Nothing in our opinion should be taken to cast doubt on longstanding prohibitions on the possession of firearms by felons and the mentally ill, or laws forbidding the carrying of firearms in sensitive places such as schools and government buildings, or laws imposing conditions and qualifications on the commercial sale of arms."[46] The Court then added in a footnote: "We identify these presumptively lawful regulatory measures only as examples; our list does not purport to be exhaustive."[47]

It remains to be seen whether the Supreme Court will endorse the lower courts' embrace of intermediate scrutiny to decide whether infringements of Second Amendment triggering rights also violate ultimate rights. Whether the Court does so or not, intermediate scrutiny stands along with strict scrutiny and rational-basis review as a possible, quasi-generic response to the quasi-generic problem of determining what form judicial review ought to take after it is triggered.

The "undue burden" test of *Planned Parenthood* v. *Casey*,[48] adopted to replace the strict scrutiny formula of *Roe* v. *Wade*,[49] does not use the terminology of intermediate scrutiny, but it bears notable similarities: It is less stringent than the formula that it replaced, but more searching than rational basis review. In *Casey*, the Court postulated that "[a]n undue burden exists, and therefore a provision of law is invalid, if its purpose or effect is to place a substantial obstacle in the path of a woman seeking an abortion before the fetus attains viability."[50] Applying that standard in *Whole Woman's Health* v. *Hellerstedt*,[51] the Court confronted a Texas law that required any doctor performing abortions to have admitting privileges at a nearby hospital and that subjected abortion facilities to the same regulatory standards as "ambulatory surgical centers." In upholding a challenge to the requirements, the Court, in an opinion by Justice Breyer, interpreted the undue burden test as requiring more than a rational relationship between ends and means in order to protect women's interest in effective access to abortion: "The rule announced in *Casey* ... requires that courts consider the burdens that a law imposes on abortion access together with the benefits those laws confer" in order to determine whether the former outweigh the latter.[52] Taking both into account, the Court held that "the surgical-center requirement, like the admitting privileges requirement, provides few, if any, health benefits for women, poses a substantial obstacle to women seeking abortions, and constitutes an 'undue burden' on their constitutional right to do so."[53]

---

[46] *Id.* at 626.
[47] *Id.* at 627 n.26.
[48] 505 U.S. 833 (1992).
[49] 410 U.S. 113 (1973).
[50] *Casey*, 505 U.S. at 878.
[51] 136 S. Ct. 2292 (2016).
[52] *Id.* at 2309.
[53] *Id.* at 2318.

Balancing Tests

Although the origins of strict scrutiny lay in dissatisfaction with balancing as a mechanism for protecting important constitutional rights, balancing tests persist in some doctrinal areas. The undue burden standard, as construed in *Whole Woman's Health*, has a balancing aspect. Overall, however, it is designed to ensure that access to abortion cannot be wholly eliminated. Among transparently identifiable and thorough-going balancing tests, perhaps the best known is the formula promulgated in *Mathews* v. *Eldridge*,[54] which the Supreme Court employs to determine rights to procedural due process. *Mathews* calls for a weighing of three variables: (1) "the private interest" affected by official action; (2) "the risk of an erroneous deprivation of such interest through the procedures used, and the probable value, if any, of additional or substitute procedural safeguards"; and (3) "the Government's interest, including the function involved and the fiscal and administrative burdens that the additional or substitute procedural requirement would entail."

The Supreme Court has prescribed reliance on another balancing test to determine the permissibility of incidental restrictions on voting rights. *Crawford* v. *Marion County Elections Board*[55] presented a challenge to an Indiana law that required voters to present government-issued photo identification in order to prove their eligibility to vote. According to a plurality of the Justices, "evenhanded restrictions that protect the integrity and reliability of the electoral process itself" may be upheld if "justified by relevant and legitimate interests 'sufficiently weighty to justify the limitation.'"[56] Balancing state interests against voter interests, Justice Stevens rejected a "facial" challenge to the photo identification requirement but left open the possibility that some voters might be able to establish that they faced such severe obstacles to obtaining state-issued photo identification that the statutes would be unconstitutional as applied to them.[57]

The Supreme Court similarly applied a balancing test to determine whether a state had violated a political party's right to have its candidates listed on the ballot in *Timmons* v. *Twin Cities Area New Party*.[58] The case involved Minnesota "antifusion" statutes that prohibit candidates from being nominated for the same elective office by more than one party. Rejecting a constitutional challenge under the First and Fourteenth Amendments, Chief Justice William Rehnquist concluded that the state's interest in maintaining the "integrity, fairness, and efficiency" of its ballots by preventing their use as "billboard[s] for political advertising" was "sufficiently

---

[54]   424 U.S. 319, 334 (1976).
[55]   553 U.S. 181 (2008).
[56]   *Id.* at 189–91 (quoting *Norman* v. *Reed*, 502 U.S. 279, 288–89 (1992)); *see also Anderson* v. *Celebrezze*, 460 U.S. 780, 789–90 (1983) (outlining the balancing framework to be deployed for constitutional challenges to state election laws).
[57]   For a discussion of "facial" versus "as-applied" challenges, see Chapter 6.
[58]   520 U.S. 351 (1997).

weighty" to justify the prohibition against fusion candidacies.[59] The majority also found that states have a legitimate interest in "the stability of their political systems," which Minnesota, like other states, was entitled to protect.[60]

With balancing as with most other tests, judicial inquiry begins with the question of whether the government or one of its officials has infringed a triggering right. Unsurprisingly, moreover, the definition and identification of triggering rights requires consequence-sensitive analysis in its own right.

In the due process context, the Supreme Court has developed an especially complex jurisprudence specifying when someone has been deprived of "liberty" or "property" in the constitutional sense.[61] For the most part, the Supreme Court has said, property interests, and some liberty interests too, "are not created by the Constitution. Rather, they are created and their dimensions are defined by existing rules or understandings that stem from an independent source such as state law."[62]

But there are exceptions. On the one hand, the Supreme Court has held that some protected property and liberty interests – including the right to interest on money that has been deposited pursuant to a court order and to freedom from corporal punishment in the public schools[63] – enjoy a constitutional status that is independent of state law. On the other hand, the Court has deemed some asserted liberty interests too trivial to merit constitutional protection, regardless of the recognition that state law may afford them.[64] In all of these cases, the Court makes consequence-sensitive calculations about the acceptability of relying on state law to define the liberty and property interests that merit procedural due process protections. When the Court deems state law insufficiently protective of interests of constitutional magnitude, it furnishes federal specifications of protected liberty and property. It did so, for example, when it held that school children have a constitutionally protected liberty interest in not being subjected to corporal punishment by school personnel, even in a state that authorizes corporal punishment. By contrast, when state law threatens to burden the federal courts with litigation concerning interests that the Court regards as trivial, it enforces a ceiling on the states' capacity to define cognizable liberty and property interests within the meaning of the Due Process Clause. In the case most clearly establishing this point,

---

[59] *Id.* at 364–65.

[60] *Id.* at 366; *see also Anderson*, 460 U.S. at 789 (holding that, in resolving constitutional challenges to state election laws, courts must "consider the character and magnitude of the asserted injury to the rights protected by the First and Fourteenth Amendments," "identify and evaluate the precise interests put forward by the State as justifications for the burden imposed by its rule," and "consider the extent to which those interests make it necessary to burden the plaintiff's rights").

[61] *See generally* Merrill, *supra* note 9.

[62] *Board of Regents* v. *Roth*, 408 U.S. 564, 577 (1972).

[63] *See Webb's Fabulous Pharmacies* v. *Beckwith*, 449 U.S. 155, 162–64 (1980) (finding constitutional right to interest on principal); *see also Ingraham* v. *Wright*, 430 U.S. 651, 674 & n.43 (1977) (finding constitutional right to be free from arbitrary corporal punishment).

[64] *See, e.g., Sandin* v. *Connor*, 515 U.S. 472 (1995) (holding that a prisoner has no due process liberty interest to be free from disciplinary segregation imposed pursuant to state's prison procedures).

Sandin v. *Conner*,[65] the Court ruled that inmates in state prisons possess no constitutionally protected liberty interest in freedom from disciplinary segregation, regardless of any guarantees that state law may give them. "Discipline by prison officials in response to a wide range of misconduct falls within the expected perimeters of the sentence imposed by a court of law," the Court reasoned.[66]

Categorical Tests

Categorical tests mark some exercises of official discretion as per se unconstitutional. The Supreme Court has held that the First Amendment's Establishment Clause categorically prohibits statutes, rules, and policies that either coerce religious practice[67] or constitute endorsements of religion in the public schools.[68] *Griswold* v. *Connecticut*[69] laid down the rule that the government may not prohibit married couples from using contraceptives in the privacy of their bedrooms. The Court has spoken in similarly unconditional terms in holding that executions of children and the insane offend the constitutional prohibition against cruel and unusual punishment.[70] In all of these cases as in many more, the Supreme Court identifies ultimate constitutional violations without reliance on any kind of test that requires appraisal of competing interests.

Among the catalogue of judicial tests of constitutional validity, categorical rules might appear to challenge my repeated assertions, when discussing strict judicial scrutiny, that analysis of the nature of constitutional rights requires distinctions among abstract, triggering, scrutiny, and ultimate rights. In cases governed by categorical rules, triggering, scrutiny, and ultimate rights seem to collapse into one another. The test that the infringement of a triggering right calls into operation marks the violation of an ultimate right, without need for further judicial analysis.

It should occasion no surprise that judicial doctrines sometimes rely on categorical rules to define ultimate constitutional rights. Indeed, there is one sense in which every judicial determination of an ultimate right pronounces a categorical

---

[65] 515 U.S. 472 (1995).

[66] *Id.* at 485.

[67] *See Lee* v. *Weisman*, 505 U.S. 577 (1992). In *Lee*, all Justices agreed that governmental coercion would violate the Establishment Clause, though the majority and dissenting opinions disagreed about what constitutes coercion. *Id.* at 642 (1992) (Scalia, J. dissenting) ("I have no quarrel with the Court's general proposition that the Establishment Clause 'guarantees that government may not coerce anyone to support or participate in religion or its exercise'" (quoting *id.* at 587)).

[68] *See, e.g., Engel* v. *Vitale*, 370 U.S. 421 (1962) (holding that a public school's recitation of a morning prayer violated the Establishment Clause); *Wallace* v. *Jaffree*, 472 U.S. 38 (1985) (holding that a public school's mandatory moment of silence for meditation or prayer violated the Establishment Clause).

[69] 381 U.S. 479 (1965).

[70] *See Roper* v. *Simmons*, 543 U.S. 551 (2005) (holding that the Eighth and Fourteenth Amendments prohibit the execution of persons who were minors when they committed their crimes); *see also Ford* v. *Wainwright*, 477 U.S. 399 (1986) (holding that the Fourth Amendment prohibits the execution of persons who are, in the Court's terminology, insane).

rule. Consider the Supreme Court's iconic decision in *Brown* v. *Board of Education*,[71] holding that a scheme of racially segregated public schools violates the Equal Protection Clause. The Court decided *Brown* in 1954, before it had developed the strict judicial scrutiny test. Today, in expounding equal protection doctrine, we might describe *Brown* as standing for the proposition that no sufficiently compelling governmental interest justified segregating students in public schools based solely on their races. Even today, however, we might also view *Brown* as having pronounced a rule that applies categorically to all cases with similar facts: Race-based segregation in the public schools is constitutionally forbidden. We could make similar claims regarding more modern applications of tests, including strict scrutiny, to identify ultimate rights. For example, after the Supreme Court has applied strict scrutiny to determine that targeted prohibitions against flag burning violate the First Amendment, we could say that a categorical rule of constitutional law bars targeted prohibitions against burning the flag. Following the Court's ruling that discriminatory state tax schemes that are designed to prop up in-state industries fail the applicable test of validity under the Commerce Clause, we could also say, going forward, that such schemes are per se impermissible.

However we choose to analyze cases such as these, it would be procrustean to insist that every judicially enforceable constitutional right can be disaggregated into an abstract right, a triggering right, a scrutiny right, and an analytically discrete ultimate right. Nor has my claim that we cannot understand the nature of constitutional rights without distinguishing among abstract, triggering, scrutiny, and ultimate rights meant to imply otherwise. I have insisted that we cannot understand some claims about constitutional rights, or the judicial analysis that such claims require, without having four possible types of right in mind. In that sense, we need distinctions among abstract, triggering, scrutiny, and ultimate rights to understand the nature of constitutional rights, taken generally. But we need not deploy all of these categories to understand absolutely every claim of right that a court will uphold.

We should also take care not to let recognition of categorical tests lead us into a tempting but deep misunderstanding about the sense in which constitutional rights might be categorical. That mistake finds its epitome in Justice Black's insistence that the First Amendment is an absolute – apparently in contrast with the rights that some other constitutional provisions protect. Justice Black's fallacy lay in his focus on a particular constitutional provision as distinguished from a particular rule or test to enforce a constitutional provision. The First Amendment, taken as a whole, is not an absolute, even if the Supreme Court may sometimes apply categorical rules to enforce it. As we have seen previously, there may be an absolute right to burn a flag in defiance of a statute banning political protest, but not an

---

[71]   347 U.S. 483 (1954).

ultimate right to burn a flag, even for expressive purposes, in violation of an ordinance prohibits setting fires on public property.

The same holds true for many other rights that are listed or enumerated in the Bill of Rights and elsewhere in the Constitution, including the Second, Fourth, Sixth, and Eighth Amendments, the Fourteenth Amendment Due Process and Equal Protection Clauses, and more. Like the First Amendment, all of these rights are multifaceted constraints, enforced through multiple tests, that can give even "ultimate" rights a relative aspect. None creates a blanket privilege to do whatever one wants, regardless of the regulation that the government seeks to enforce or the governmental interests that might support that particular kind of regulation. For example, gays and lesbians cannot be denied the opportunity to marry based on their sex or gender, but officials can refuse to issue a marriage license to a gay couple – just as they could in the case of a couple consisting of one man and one woman – if one of them is already lawfully married to someone else. To repeat one of this book's most important themes, constitutional rights are constraints on governmental power, and the constraints that the Constitution imposes are multifarious, not unitary, in character. An action that is protected against punishment under one statute may sometimes, nonetheless, be validly prohibited under another.

RIGHTS AGAINST OFFICIAL ACTION NOT MANDATED BY A RULE OF POLICY

So far I have discussed judicial tests for the constitutional validity of laws, regulations, written and unwritten policies, and the like. To a reasonable approximation, those tests define and enforce rights against rules.[72] But the government acts, and the actions of its officials can infringe constitutional rights, in ways that do not involve either the writing or the enforcement of statutes. Government officials exercise discretionary authority, not strictly controlled by law, to hire and fire lower-level employees, administer public schools, conduct investigations, and arrest criminal suspects. The Constitution also constrains the judicial branch in the performance of judicial functions, including those of presiding over trials, imposing punishments, and issuing search warrants.

In many instances, the standards that the Supreme Court applies to define and enforce constitutional rights against executive and judicial action are less crisply delineated than the tests that apply to statutes. Indeed, it is often harder to say precisely what the applicable tests are. Even so, analysis largely confirms the lessons about the nature of constitutional rights that have emerged from examining test-focused challenges to the validity of statutes. First, nearly without exception, rights function as limited constraints on official authority, not privileges to engage in

---

[72] For the provocative claim that all constitutional rights are rights against rules, see Matthew D. Adler, *Rights against Rules: The Moral Structure of American Constitutional Law*, 97 MICH. L. REV. 1, 3 (1998).

categorically protected speech or conduct, no matter what. Second, rights continue to reflect interests. Third, in many cases even if not in all, we need to distinguish among abstract, triggering, scrutiny, and ultimate rights. Fourth, and finally, a single abstract right – as given constitutional status by a single, identifiable constitutional provision such as the Free Speech Clause – may be protected by a diverse multitude of tests, each reflecting a distinctive threat to the abstract right and the costs of affording underlying individual interests a particular kind of protection.

One substantial element of practical discontinuity also emerges. The Supreme Court often appears more reluctant to recognize rights that restrict the discretion of executive officials than the parallel discretion of lawmakers under the same constitutional provisions. The best explanation resides in a complex form of interest-balancing. Without always being candid, the Court recurrently takes account of the social costs and benefits of recognizing different types of triggering rights and associated scrutiny rights. When doing so, moreover, the Justices frequently conclude that tests that would involve the courts in close, case-by-case oversight of executive conduct would be detrimental, not beneficial, in an overall balance of individual against governmental interests. To put the point a little bit differently, the Court is sometimes more willing to substitute its judgment for that of legislators than to second-guess the day-to-day, often split-second, discretionary decisions of the cop on the beat.

Strict Scrutiny and Tests That Are the Functional Equivalents of Strict Scrutiny

Although strict judicial scrutiny emerged as a measure of the validity of statutes, regulations, and other general policies, it can be adapted for application to cases in which individual officials take adverse action against someone on a basis that, if written into a rule or policy, would trigger strict scrutiny. Race-based decision-making affords a prime example. Antidiscrimination norms apply as much against executive and judicial action as against legislative decision-making. In appraising the permissibility of otherwise discretionary decisions by government officials, the Supreme Court, accordingly, has sometimes suggested that any race-based motivation in decisions about whom to hire for government jobs or to include in government programs would elicit strict scrutiny, regardless of whether the validity of any law or general policy was at stake. Although decisions to hire and fire on the basis of race are suspect, there may be situations – analogous to those in which the Court has upheld affirmative action programs – in which taking race into account would be necessary to promote compelling governmental interests. For example, in *United States* v. *Paradise*,[73] the Supreme Court upheld a lower court order requiring a state that had previously discriminated against African-American applicants for positions as police officers to meet race-based promotion targets as

[73]   480 U.S. 149 (1987).

a remedy. In doing so, the Court held that the judicial order survived strict judicial scrutiny.[74]

Lower courts have also applied either strict scrutiny or a close analogue to cases in which governmental officials have defended race-based hiring preferences as essential to achieve of vital policy goals.[75] One leading case upheld reliance on race as a hiring criterion for a prison boot camp at which nearly 70 percent of the inmates were racial minorities. In explaining its ruling, the court articulated a test under which the racial hiring criterion could pass constitutional muster "only if the defendants show that they are motivated by a truly powerful and worthy concern and that the racial measure that they have adopted is a plainly apt response to that concern."[76] Pursuant to that standard, the court credited "expert evidence" that "the boot camp [would] not succeed in its mission of pacification and reformation with as white a staff as it would have had if a black male had not been appointed to one of the lieutenant slots."[77]

Surprisingly or unsurprisingly, however, the Supreme Court has not always prescribed strict judicial scrutiny or its like to determine whether race-based decision-making by executive officials and by judges violates constitutional rights. In a number of instances, the Court has held that race-based discrimination by executive officials and judges violates the Constitution without further inquiry into the possibility that it might be necessary to promote a compelling governmental interest. The Court has done so, for example, in cases involving jury selection, including those in which prosecutors use their peremptory challenges to exclude prospective jurors based on race or religion.[78] In those cases, the Court has found race-based decision-making to be categorically impermissible. To remedy the violation, the Court has demanded that affected defendants must be either released or retried.

Categorical Tests

As the case of racially motivated jury selection illustrates, a number of the most important tests that the Supreme Court employs to define and enforce rights against discretionary action by individual governmental officials are categorical. Further examples include these:

---

[74] *Id.* at 167. However, the Court refused to state the appropriate level of heightened scrutiny required in the case, because the lower court's order "survives even strict scrutiny analysis." *Id.* at 166.

[75] *See, e.g., Wittmer* v. *Peters,* 87 F.3d 916, 920 (7th Cir. 1996); *see also Cotter* v. *City of Boston,* 323 F.3d 160, 172 (1st Cir. 2003) (City's race-conscious promotion decisions "were a narrowly-tailored means of addressing demonstrated past discrimination."); *Majeske* v. *City of Chicago,* 218 F.3d 816, 819 (7th Cir. 2000) ("[W]e must apply strict scrutiny when reviewing the City's affirmative action plan.").

[76] *Wittmer,* 87 F.3d at 918.

[77] *Id.* at 920.

[78] *See Batson* v. *Kentucky,* 476 U.S. 79 (1986).

- The Fourth Amendment creates a right to freedom from unreasonable searches and seizures. To enforce this guarantee, the Supreme Court has adopted a categorical test under which warrantless searches of the home are flatly forbidden unless a delineated exception applies.[79]
- The Fifth Amendment guarantees criminal suspects a right to refuse to give incriminating evidence against themselves. Under the categorical rule of *Miranda v. Arizona*, any confession rendered in police custody without the administration of a *Miranda* warning is presumed to have been compelled and must be excluded from evidence (again, unless an exception to the rule applies).
- The Supreme Court has also held categorically that the Fifth Amendment entitles criminal defendants to a presumption of innocence.[80]
- In *Gideon v. Wainright*,[81] the Supreme Court held that the Sixth Amendment guarantee of the right to counsel encompasses a right of indigent defendants to have court-appointed lawyers represent them in felony cases. A subsequent decision extended the protection, again categorically, to all prosecutions that result in imprisonment for any period.[82] The categorical approach eliminates discretion that judges would otherwise have in determining when the appointment of trial counsel should be deemed necessary.[83]
- The Court, on this point echoing the language of the Constitution, has held that the Sixth Amendment flatly guarantees criminal defendants a right to trial by jury in any case in which the maximum penalty exceeds six months in prison.[84]

[79] *See, e.g., Collins* v. *Virginia*, 138 S. Ct. 1663 (2018). The Court has recognized a number of "exigent circumstances" justifying the warrantless search of a home. *See, e.g., Brigham City, Utah* v. *Stuart*, 547 U.S. 398, 403 (2006) ("One exigency obviating the requirement of a warrant is the need to assist persons who are seriously injured or threatened with such injury."); *Welsh* v. *Wisconsin*, 466 U.S. 740, 754 (1984) (confirming the exception to the warrant requirement for imminent destruction of evidence, but refusing to apply it where the underlying offense at issue was noncriminal); *Stanton* v. *Sims*, 571 U.S. 3, 6 (2013) (noting an exception to the warrant requirement where officers have probable cause and are in hot pursuit of a suspect, but cataloguing lower court disagreement over how severe the underlying offense must be in order to trigger the exception).
[80] *In re Winship*, 397 U.S. 358, 364 (1970) ("[W]e explicitly hold that the Due Process Clause protects the accused against conviction except upon proof beyond a reasonable doubt of every fact necessary to constitute the crime with which he is charged.").
[81] 372 U.S. 335 (1963). While Gideon announced a categorical right to counsel, it did not state the precise time at which the right attaches, or the type of proceedings that the right covers.
[82] *See Argersinger* v. *Hamlin*, 407 U.S. 25, 37 (1972) (holding that "absent a knowing and intelligent waiver, no person may be imprisoned for any offense, whether classified as petty, misdemeanor, or felony, unless he was represented by counsel at his trial").
[83] The Court has recognized a Sixth Amendment right to counsel during preliminary hearings as well as post-indictment lineups. See *Kirby* v. *Illinois*, 406 U.S. 682, 689 (1972) (confirming that the right to counsel attaches at the time of arraignment or preliminary hearing).
[84] *See* U.S. CONST. amend. VI ("In all criminal prosecutions, the accused shall enjoy the right to a speedy and public trial, by an impartial jury of the State and district wherein the crime shall have been committed..."); *see also Baldwin* v. *New York*, 399 U.S. 66, 73–74, (1970) (establishing

- Again under the Sixth Amendment, *Crawford* v. *Washington*[85] ruled that the Confrontation Clause bars the admission of testimonial statements into evidence against a criminal defendant unless the party who gave a statement is unavailable and a prior opportunity for cross-examination existed.

As with respect to tests for the validity of statutes, the Court-crafted categorical tests that apply in these cases have a trigger that almost certainly reflects a balancing of individual and governmental interests. Under the Fourth Amendment, the prohibition against warrantless searches does not attach unless the target has a "reasonable expectation of privacy."[86] Determinations about "reasonable expectations" require an appraisal of competing interests, and the Court's decision to put the home in an especially protected category reflects a judgment about the central importance of privacy interests in that context. In *Carpenter* v. *United States*,[87] which held that cell phone users have a reasonable expectation of privacy in their wireless carriers' records of their physical locations, the Justices disagreed expressly about the severity of the resulting impediments to legitimate law-enforcement practices. The *Miranda* right does not apply to confessions offered outside of police custody. The Court undoubtedly took public as well as private interests into account not only in drawing that line, but also in specifying the contents of the warning that police must administer if subsequently obtained confessions are to be admissible into evidence. Similarly, the right to appointed counsel springs into existence in criminal cases only when a defendant faces a possibility of imprisonment, even though defendants can retain private lawyers – and expect to benefit from the assistance of counsel – even when only fines or other penalties are at stake. Here again we must assume that the Court weighed competing interests in defining the category of cases in which the unconditional right to appointed counsel applies.

Although I would not know how to count, I would speculate that rights-based limitations on the discretion of executive officials and judges are more likely to be enforced by categorical tests than parallel limitations on lawmaking authority, which so frequently involve either strict scrutiny or rational basis review. Certainly strict judicial scrutiny is rarer in cases involving rights-based challenges to executive

a categorical constitutional right to trial by jury in criminal cases "where the possible penalty exceeds six months' imprisonment").

[85] 541 U.S. 36, 67–68 (2004).

[86] The reasonable expectation of privacy test was initially formulated in *Katz* v. *United States*, 389 U.S. 347 (1967) (Harlan, J., concurring), but has remained in flux, sparking a multitude of different doctrinal formulations. *See, e.g., Byrd* v. *United States*, 138 S. Ct. 1518 (2018) ("'[P]roperty concepts' are instructive in 'determining the presence or absence of the privacy interests protected by that Amendment.'" (quoting *Rakas* v. *Illinois*, 439 U.S. 128, 144 (1978))); *Florida* v. *Riley*, 488 U.S. 445, 454 (1989) (O'Connor, J., concurring) (arguing that societal expectations of privacy should be rooted, in part, in whether particular types of invasion occur with "sufficient regularity"); *Smith* v. *Maryland*, 442 U.S. 735, 750 (1979) (Marshall, J., dissenting) (prescribing that "[w]hether privacy expectations are legitimate" depends on "the risks [one] should be forced to assume in a free and open society").

[87] 138 S. Ct. 2206 (2018).

and judicial action than in challenges to statutes. Part of the explanation may involve anticipated social costs. More specifically, the social costs of enforcing a categorical prohibition – without exception for cases involving compelling governmental interests – may often be lower when individual decisions are at issue than when the enforceability of a statute is at stake. Invalidating a statute can have broadly adverse implications.

The Court may also be concerned about the social costs of judicial review in the absence of clear, categorical rules. Criminal prosecutions already generate an enormous volume of constitutional litigation.[88] Given the stunning diversity of fact situations in which constitutional challenges to actions by individual governmental officials can arise, the Justices may think reliance on categorical rules a practical necessity if courts are not to be bogged down in a morass of cases calling for fact-specific judgments about the proper application of other kinds of tests.

As we shall see, the Supreme Court's concern to avoid fact-intensive oversight of the day-to-day actions of government officials in administering the law can also lead to the framing of highly deferential tests. For reasons that involve a weighing of public against private interests, the Court insists that police officers, for example, must be accorded a broad scope of discretionary authority to do what seems to them to be reasonable under the circumstances.

At first blush, the juxtaposition of a large number of categorical rules with highly deferential standards may seem contradictory: Why would a Court that thinks it important to impose categorical restrictions on official discretion in one set of cases opt to leave discretion so little constrained in others? The common element in the two strategies is a recognition of the social costs of case-by-case judicial review. Categorical rules create certainty about acceptable as well as unacceptable exercises of official discretion. Highly deferential tests signal strongly that courts will not second-guess discretionary judgments. Both approaches thus minimize incentives for case-by-case litigation unless officials act in plain disregard for constitutional norms.

Balancing Tests

The tests that the Supreme Court employs to define public employees' free speech rights form a complex grid. Nearly without exception, employees have the same right to be free from criminal prosecution for speech, under the same tests, as the rest of us. But rights not to be fired or disciplined for speech that has disruptive consequences in the workplace occupy a different footing. When an employee's comments in her personal capacity on a matter of public interest lead supervising officials to seek her dismissal, *Connick* v. *Myers* calls for courts to engage in "particularized balancing" that takes account of both "the nature of the employee's

---

[88] *See, e.g.*, Jeffrey L. Fisher, *Categorical Requirements in Constitutional Criminal Procedure*, 94 Geo. L.J. 1493, 1519 (2006) (asserting that "criminal prosecutions are [already] the leading progenitor of constitutional litigation, at least in terms of sheer volume").

expression" and "the government's interest in the effective and efficient fulfillment of its responsibilities to the public."[89] Among other points of interest, *Connick* illustrates that balancing tests – which stood at the center of debates between balancers and free speech absolutists during the 1950s – continue to play at least a minor role in protecting free speech interests.

Balancing tests, such as that which the Supreme Court articulated in *Mathews* v. *Eldridge*, have also been used in some cases to determine whether government officials afforded adequate procedural safeguards before firing an employee or subjecting a public school student to significant punishment, even in cases in which no statutory procedural scheme exists.[90] Beginning in the 1970s, however, the Court began to exhibit anxiety that the Due Process Clause might become "a font of tort law,"[91] authorizing a broad range of suits against state officials in federal court. From the Court's perspective, the nightmare scenario was that every time a public official infringed on a liberty or property interest, the aggrieved party would allege that the infringement occurred without due process of law and therefore violated the Constitution. In response, the Court has developed a complex and arguably confused doctrine – associated with a 1981 decision in *Parratt* v. *Taylor*[92] – under which parties who complain of isolated acts of procedural malfeasance by state officials ordinarily cannot sue those officials in federal court but must bring their suits in state court instead.

Parratt was a suit brought by a prison inmate complaining about the loss of a hobby kit, valued at $23.50, from a prison mailroom. In a suit for damages against the warden and other prison officials, the inmate alleged that the loss occurred without due process of law. In an opinion exhibiting impatience with the perceived triviality of the matter at issue, the Supreme Court ruled that the inmate could not maintain an action for deprivation of property without due process if he had the opportunity to sue for a remedy in state (rather than federal) court. The Court's reasoning, expanded upon in subsequent cases,[93] was legally intricate: The Due Process Clause requires states to provide fair hearings before effecting deprivations of liberty and property (such as the inmate's hobby materials) only when pre-deprivation process is feasible; but it is typically not feasible for states to put procedures in place to stop "random and unauthorized" deprivations of liberty and property, such as apparently happened in *Parratt*, before they occur; and,

---

[89] *Id.* at 159.

[90] *See Ingraham* v. *Wright*, 430 U.S. 651, 675 (1977) (applying *Mathews* balancing to reject a challenge to a public school's imposition of corporal punishment); *cf. Goss* v. *Lopez*, 419 U.S. 565, 581 (1975) (engaging in a balancing analysis to determine the process due to public school students before suspension).

[91] *E.g., Castle Rock* v. *Gonzales*, 545 U.S. 748, 768 (2005); *Daniels* v. *Williams*, 474 U.S. 327, 332 (1986); *Parratt* v. *Taylor*, 451 U.S. 527, 544 (1981); *Paul* v. *Davis*, 424 U.S. 693, 701 (1976).

[92] 451 U.S. 527 (1981).

[93] For discussion of the *Parratt* doctrine, see Richard H. Fallon, Jr., John F. Manning, Daniel J. Meltzer, & David L. Shapiro, Hart & Wechsler's The Federal Courts and the Federal System, 1024–30 (7th ed. 2015).

therefore, the only procedural due process that a state can reasonably be asked to provide in cases of "random and unauthorized" deprivations is an after-the-fact suit in state court to remedy the alleged wrong.

That reasoning is clever but not persuasive. The inmate's complaint in *Parratt* was not about the actions of the state itself, but about the actions of officials clothed with the authority of the state. And officials who act with the authority of the state can ordinarily be sued in both their individual and official capacities for violating the Constitution, regardless of available remedies in state court.[94] Confronted with that objection, the Court responded that suits alleging deprivations of procedural due process constitute a class by themselves. In a subsequent case also coming from a prison setting, the Court further held that merely "negligent" deprivations of liberty and property by state officials trigger no right to any type of judicial scrutiny or judicial remedy under the Due Process Clause.[95]

Significantly, however, the Supreme Court continues to permit parties to challenge the adequacy of state laws and procedural schemes – as contrasted with "random and unauthorized" actions by executive officials – through suits in federal court alleging Due Process Clause violations.[96] The juxtaposition exhibits the Court's constitutional priorities. Almost certainly not by happenstance, the Court prescribes a larger role for the federal courts in testing the validity of statutes and regulations that are likely to have broad application than in cases involving isolated exercises of executive discretion not mandated by any law or policy. Constructing rights to protect interests, the Court views protection as more important in the former category than in the latter, in which it apparently also regards the social costs of routine judicial involvement as unacceptable. To echo the Court's recurrent formulation, it refuses to let the Due Process Clause become "a font of tort law" that would clog the federal courts with cases that it regards as likely to involve only lower-order constitutional stakes.

Tests That Implicitly Require the Appraisal and Accommodation of Competing Interests

Some measures of the permissibility of governmental action are not explicitly framed as balancing tests, but nevertheless require a close analogue to balancing in their application. One example comes from First Amendment doctrine governing citizens' rights to use public property for expressive purposes. The relevant doctrine is hugely complex. But one aspect involves rights of access to so-called non-public fora, consisting of public property that has not historically been available for public

---

94 See Richard H. Fallon, Jr., *Some Confusions about Due Process, Judicial Review, and Constitutional Remedies*, 93 COLUM. L. REV. 309, 332, 352 (1993); Henry Paul Monaghan, *State Law Wrongs, State Law Remedies, and the Fourteenth Amendment*, 86 COLUM. L. REV. 979, 990–91 (1986).

95 *See Daniels v. Williams*, 474 U.S. 327 (1986).

96 *See, e.g., Logan v. Zimmerman Brush Co.*, 455 U.S. 422 (1982).

speech and protests (as parks and sidewalks have) nor been specifically dedicated to that purpose (as a municipal auditorium might be).[97] Examples include military bases and airports.[98] Under the applicable test, public officials may exclude would-be speakers from non-public fora as long as their doing so is "reasonable" and "not an effort to suppress the speaker's activity due to disagreement with the speaker's view."[99] Correspondingly, would-be speakers have triggering and ultimate rights to speak where their exclusion would not be "reasonable." Assessments of reasonableness closely approximate, if they do not require, balancing judgments.

Other constitutional tests that require appraisals of reasonableness – including whether police had reasonable suspicion adequate to justify a search or seizure – require similarly balancing-like calculations.[100] More broadly, the triggering right to any application of the Fourth Amendment is defined by reference to reasonable expectations of privacy. As commentators have recognized, "the phrase 'reasonable expectation of privacy' remains remarkably opaque."[101] In practice, however, the Court appears to apply it with sensitivity to which kinds of investigative discretion by government officials it thinks ought to be constrained in light of their potential for abuse.[102] As could probably go without saying, the Justices do not always converge in their judgments. To take just one example, the Justices divided five to four in holding that cell phone users have a reasonable expectation of privacy in their providers' records of the locations of their phone use.[103]

I should emphasize, however, that the courts, in applying reasonableness standards, do not always exercise independent judgment. Rather, the Supreme Court

---

[97] *See Southeastern Promotions, Ltd.* v. *Conrad*, 420 U.S. 546, 555 (1975); *see generally Minnesota Voters Alliance* v. *Mansky*, 138 S. Ct. 1876 (2018) (classifying a polling place as a non-public forum); *ISKCON* v. *Lee*, 505 U.S. 672, 679 (1992) (holding that airports are non-public fora); *Perry Educ. Ass'n* v. *Perry Local Educators' Ass'n*, 460 U.S. 37, 48 (1983) (finding that a school's mail system was a nonpublic forum); *but see Walker* v. *Texas Div., Sons of Confederate Veterans, Inc.*, 135 S. Ct. 2239, 2252 (2015) (finding that a state's specialty license plate, the designs of which could be submitted by vehicle owners, did not constitute a nonpublic forum, but rather involved government speech).

[98] *See Greer* v. *Spock*, 424 U.S. 828, 837–38 (1976) (finding that military bases are non-public fora); *see also ISKCON*, 505 U.S. at 679.

[99] *ISKCON*, 505 U.S. at 679; *see Minnesota Voters Alliance* v. *Mansky*, 138 U.S. 1876, 1885 (2018) (quoting *Perry*, 460 U.S. at 46 ("[T]he state may reserve the forum for its intended purposes, communicative or otherwise, as long as the regulation on speech is reasonable and not an effort to suppress expression merely because public officials oppose the speaker's view.")).

[100] *See, e.g., Katz* v. *United States*, 389 U.S. 347, 360 (1967) (Harlan, J., concurring) ("[T]here is a twofold requirement, first that a person have exhibited an actual (subjective) expectation of privacy and, second, that the expectation be one that society is prepared to recognize as 'reasonable.'"); *see also Terry* v. *Ohio*, 392 U.S. 1, 27 (1968) ("Our evaluation of the proper balance . . . [is] that there must be a narrowly drawn authority to permit a reasonable search for weapons for the protection of the police officer, where he has reason to believe that he is dealing with an armed and dangerous individual, regardless of whether he has probable cause to arrest the individual for a crime.").

[101] Orin Kerr, *Four Models of the Fourth Amendment*, 60 STAN. L. REV. 503, 505 (2007).

[102] *See id.* at 548.

[103] *See Carpenter* v. *United States*, 138 S. Ct. 2206 (2018).

seems committed to the proposition that courts should often appraise what was reasonable under the circumstances from the perspective of a police officer or other governmental official at the time of an alleged constitutional violation. A recently controversial example involves the use of force, sometimes including deadly force, to subdue a suspect who resists arrest or attempts to flee. Emphasizing that police officers must make snap decisions under fraught and sometimes threatening conditions, the Court has insisted that "[t]he 'reasonableness' of a particular use of force must be judged from the perspective of a reasonable officer on the scene, rather than with the 20/20 vision of hindsight."[104] When this shift of focus occurs, reasonableness tests become decidedly less constraining of government officials' discretion and less protective of citizens' abstract and triggering rights than they would be otherwise.

Weakly Protective Tests

Village of Willowbrook v. *Olech*[105] held that a homeowner who believed she had been singled out for adverse treatment could claim an equal protection violation as a member of a "class of one." This class-of-one theory appeared to contemplate judicial review pursuant to the rational basis test to enforce prohibitions against a broad range of discretionary governmental actions that are arbitrary, irrational, or motivated by animus. But a subsequent decision sharply limited the class-of-one theory by holding that it "does not apply in the public employment context" and possibly in other contexts that "by their very nature involve discretionary decisionmaking based on a vast array of subjective, individual assessments."[106] The Court's ground for limiting the theory was blunt: Allowing suits alleging unequal treatment in all situations in which officials must make decisions based on a multitude of factors "would undermine the very discretion" without which many governmental operations could not proceed successfully.[107]

When the Court recognizes triggering rights at all in cases challenging exercises of official discretion under the Equal Protection Clause and as a matter of substantive due process, the applicable tests are typically very weak, especially in contexts in which the Supreme Court doubts the judicial capacity for case-by-case interest balancing or fears that judicial involvement would undermine governmental authority in sensitive areas. To take two noteworthy examples, the Supreme Court has insisted that courts should be especially hesitant to second-guess discretionary decisions by military and prison officials.[108] As the Court explained in *Chappell*

---

[104] See *Graham* v. *Connor*, 490 U.S. 386, 396 (U.S. 1989).
[105] 528 U.S. 562 (2000).
[106] *Engquist* v. *Oregon Dep't of Agr.*, 553 U.S. 591, 598, 603 (2008).
[107] *Id.* at 603.
[108] For critical analysis of relevant doctrine, generally arguing that the Court's decisions are undertheorized, see Eric Berger, *Deference Determinations and Stealth Constitutional Decision Making*, 98 Iowa L. Rev. 465, 485–92 (2013).

v. *Wallace*,[109] "courts are ill-equipped to determine the impact upon [military] discipline that any particular intrusion upon military authority might have." Similar considerations underlie the Court's approach to complaints about the exercise of official discretion in prison cases. The leading case of *Turner* v. *Safley*[110] holds squarely that most infringements even of prisoners' fundamental rights must be upheld as long as they are "reasonably related to legitimate penological interests." What is more, the Supreme Court has mandated a relaxed application even of this loose standard. In explaining its "broad hands-off attitude toward problems of prison administration,"[111] it has emphasized that courts are poorly situated to make the calculations that full and reasonable enforcement of the Constitution would require.[112]

A dramatically paradigmatic example of judicial deference to executive discretion comes from the "some evidence" test that the Court has prescribed for reviewing decisions by prison disciplinary officials in cases – such as those brought in state court – to which *Parratt* v. *Taylor*[113] does not apply.[114] Under this test, a court will not examine an administrative decision to determine whether it was correct, or even reflected a sensible appraisal of evidence or competing considerations, but only to determine whether "some evidence" supported it. The Court's justification for so relaxed a standard must almost certainly involve a weighing of social costs against individual interests in quasi-adjudicative fairness. It is easy for a court to gauge whether an administrative record contains some supporting evidence, much more difficult to determine whether an official acted correctly. In addition, the Court may believe that prisoners' suits are likely to be vexatious and trivial and that the costs of

[109] 462 U.S. 296, 305 (1983) (quoting Earl Warren, *The Bill of Rights and the Military*, 37 N.Y.U. L. REV. 181, 187 (1962)) (internal quotation mark omitted).

[110] 482 U.S. 78, 89 (1987); *see also Florence* v. *Bd. of Chosen Freeholders of Cty. of Burlington*, 566 U.S. 318, 326 (2012) ("The Court has confirmed the importance of deference to correctional officials and explained that a regulation impinging on an inmate's constitutional rights must be upheld 'if it is reasonably related to legitimate penological interests.'" (quoting *Turner*, 482 U.S. at 89)).

[111] *Procunier* v. *Martinez*, 416 U.S. 396, 404 (1974).

[112] *See Shaw* v. *Murphy*, 532 U.S. 223, 229–30 (2001) (rejecting a claim that inmates have a First Amendment right to give legal advice to other inmates and noting that "courts are particularly 'ill equipped' to deal" with the problems of prisons (quoting *Procunier*, 416 U.S. at 405)); *O'Lone* v. *Estate of Shabazz*, 482 U.S. 342, 349–50, 353 (1987) (noting the courts' lack of institutional competence and applying *Turner* to reject a free exercise challenge to prison regulations); *Turner*, 482 U.S. at 84–85, 89 (establishing a relaxed standard of review in light of courts' relative lack of expertise in prison administration and separation-of-powers concerns).

[113] 451 U.S. 527 (1981).

[114] *See Superintendent, Mass. Corr. Inst.* v. *Hill*, 472 U.S. 445, 455–56 (1985) ("[T]he requirements of due process are satisfied if some evidence supports the decision by the prison disciplinary board to revoke good time credits."). The Court also applies the "some evidence" test in habeas corpus cases involving challenges to the factual predicates for executive branch decisions to remove aliens from the United States, *see, e.g., INS* v. *St. Cyr*, 533 U.S. 289, 306 (2001), and occasionally in other contexts too, *see, e.g., Eagles* v. *United States ex rel. Samuels*, 329 U.S. 304, 312 (1946) ("If it cannot be said that there were procedural irregularities of such a nature or magnitude as to render the hearing unfair, or that there was no evidence to support the order, the inquiry [into military custody of a selective service registrant] is at an end." (citations omitted)).

even moderately robust judicial enforcement of abstract rights would therefore outweigh the benefits.

The same approach carries over into the domain of substantive due process. A few Supreme Court decisions have applied substantive due process principles to administrative action not specifically authorized by statute, but with an emphasis that the applicable judicial test of constitutional permissibility should be highly forgiving. In *Rochin v. California*,[115] for example, the Court held that police pumping of the stomach of a criminal suspect to obtain evidence violated the Due Process Clause because, but only because, it "shock[ed] the conscience." The Court repeated that formula in a 1998 case, *County of Sacramento v. Lewis*.[116] Other cases have employed different standards, some of which appear easier for plaintiffs to meet.[117] Overall, no agreed framework has emerged for identifying when relatively isolated official acts offend substantive due process. It is clear, however, that most deprivations of interests that substantive due process protects will attract only a weakly protective test, such as the "shock-the-conscience" formula – a more forgiving standard even than the rational basis test that is used to determine the permissibility of statutes that do not trigger elevated scrutiny.[118]

CONCLUSION: OTHER TESTS, OTHER RIGHTS

At the conclusion of this brisk trek through the terrain of rights-protective constitutional tests, three conclusions have emerged with sufficiently recurring clarity to bear emphasis. First, nearly across the board, the Constitution's text and original history provide a starting point for judicial identification, analysis, and protection of constitutional rights, but little more. The formulation of particular constitutional tests pervasively reflects judicial interest-balancing, even in cases governed by seemingly categorical rules.

Second, with nearly invariant frequency, linguistically unitary constitutional guarantees – including those of the Free Speech Clause, the Religion Clauses, the Fourth and Fifth Amendments, and Fourteenth Amendment Due Process and Equal Protection Clauses – are protected by a multitude of tests, not just by one. As a result, the constitutional rights that single constitutional provisions create are multifarious, both in kind and in substance, as brought out by the diverse senses in which the terminology of rights can be used.

---

[115]   342 U.S. 165 (1952).

[116]   523 U.S. 833 (1998).

[117]   See Rosalie Berger Levinson, *Reining in Abuses of Executive Power through Substantive Due Process*, 60 FLA. L. REV. 519, 529–35 (2008).

[118]   *See* Jane R. Bambauer & Toni M. Massaro, *Outrageous and Irrational*, 100 MINN. L. REV. 281, 284–85 (2015) ("The rational basis test is enjoying a bit of a comeback ... The outrageousness [or shocks-the-conscience] test, by contrast, still lives in disrepute. Its occasional use sends critics clamoring for more judicial restraint.").

Third, in talking about rights under various constitutional provisions, it is important for many purposes to distinguish between rights not to be harmed by the enforcement of statutes, rules, or regulations, on the one hand, and rights against otherwise discretionary conduct by officials performing executive or administrative functions, on the other hand. Even more in the latter context than in the former, the Supreme Court – whether appropriately or misguidedly – is often acutely sensitive to what it would view as the unacceptable social costs of imposing robust, judicially enforced constraints on the discretion of government officials. The tests that the Court uses to enforce constitutional rights reflect this interests-based calculus. And so, ultimately, do the constitutional rights that the Court's tests define.

5

Legislative Intent and Deliberative Rights

In adjudicating claims of constitutional rights, courts sometimes ask whether Congress or a state legislature had constitutionally forbidden intentions when it enacted a challenged statute. Consider this case: A wealthy, overwhelmingly white, suburban community enacts a statute requiring that town police and firefighters must reside in the town. This statute is almost surely valid if the town's governing board adopted it for the permissible purpose of ensuring employees' prompt availability in case of an emergency,[1] but it is almost equally certainly invalid if it was adopted for the purpose of keeping racial minorities out of the police and fire departments.[2] Under these circumstances, the ultimate rights of minorities seeking employment as police officers or firefighters will depend on the town council's motivations. In order to understand the nature of constitutional rights, we therefore need to look beyond interests – although they will remain relevant – and examine the significance of constitutionally forbidden intentions and purposes. In doing so in this chapter, I shall focus principally on the significance of forbidden legislative intentions. Although courts occasionally inquire into the intentions of executive officials – as we saw in Chapter 4 – intent-based analysis tends to be far more significant, as well as more conceptually controversial, in cases challenging the constitutionality of statutes. Accordingly, although I shall not ignore issues involving forbidden intentions by non-legislative officials, I shall postpone them until the end.

Inquiries into forbidden legislative intentions are nearly as ubiquitous in modern constitutional law as the strict judicial scrutiny test. To identify constitutional violations under the Equal Protection Clause, courts sometimes ask whether the legislature acted with a racially discriminatory intent,[3] whether it manifested animus toward an identifiable group,[4] or whether it had the "predominant purpose" of

---

[1] See *McCarthy v. Philadelphia Civil Serv. Comm'n*, 424 U.S. 645 (1976) (per curiam).

[2] See, e.g., *Washington v. Davis*, 426 U.S. 229, 240–41 (1976).

[3] See, e.g., *id.*

[4] See, e.g., *Romer v. Evans*, 517 U.S. 620, 632 (1996); *City of Cleburne v. Cleburne Living Ctr., Inc.*, 473 U.S. 432, 440 (1985); *U.S. Dep't of Agric. v. Moreno*, 413 U.S. 528, 534 (1973); see also *United States v. Windsor*, 530 U.S. 744, 774 (2013).

creating a voting district in which members of a racial minority group constitute a majority.[5] The Supreme Court has held that statutes violate the Establishment Clause if they have the forbidden purpose of promoting religion.[6] The Free Exercise Clause mandates strict scrutiny of laws "the object" of which "is to infringe upon or restrict practices because of their religious motivation."[7] Under the "undue burden" test of *Planned Parenthood of Southeastern Pennsylvania* v. *Casey*,[8] regulations of abortion violate the Due Process Clause if their "purpose . . . is to place a substantial obstacle in the path of a woman seeking an abortion before the fetus attains viability."[9] The Court has pointed to forbidden purposes as a ground for invalidating interferences with the right to travel.[10] In an article written while she was a law professor, Justice Elena Kagan argued that modern Free Speech Clause doctrine systematically seeks to ferret out and invalidate legislation that was enacted with the intent to suppress messages that the government disapproves.[11] There are further examples as well.[12]

---

[5] See, e.g., *Bush* v. *Vera*, 517 U.S. 952, 959 (1996) (plurality opinion); *Miller* v. *Johnson*, 515 U.S. 900, 916 (1995); see also *Harris* v. *Ariz. Indep. Redistricting Comm'n*, 136 S. Ct. 1301, 1309 (2016) (finding that population deviations among state legislative districts of less than ten percent do not violate the Equal Protection Clause absent a showing that "it is more probable than not that illegitimate considerations were the predominant motivation behind the plan's deviations from mathematically equal district populations").

[6] See, e.g., *Wallace* v. *Jaffree*, 472 U.S. 38, 43, 56 (1985); *Lemon* v. *Kurtzman*, 403 U.S. 602, 612 (1971).

[7] *Church of the Lukumi Babalu Aye, Inc.* v. *City of Hialeah*, 508 U.S. 520, 533 (1993).

[8] 505 U.S. 833, 877 (1992) (joint opinion of O'Connor, Kennedy, and Souter, JJ.).

[9] *Id.* at 878.

[10] See *Mem'l Hosp.* v. *Maricopa County*, 415 U.S. 250, 263–64 (1974); *Shapiro* v. *Thompson*, 394 U.S. 618, 631 (1969).

[11] See Elena Kagan, *Private Speech, Public Purpose: The Role of Governmental Motive in First Amendment Doctrine*, 63 U. CHI. L. REV. 413 (1996). Although the Supreme Court said in *United States* v. *O'Brien*, 391 U.S. 367 (1968), that "this Court will not strike down an otherwise constitutional statute on the basis of an alleged illicit legislative motive," *id.* at 383, subsequent First Amendment cases arguably look in different directions. See *Heffernan* v. *City of Paterson*, 136 S. Ct. 1412, 1418 (2016) (holding that "[w]hen an employer demotes an employee out of a desire to prevent the employee from engaging in political activity that the First Amendment protects, the employee is entitled to challenge that unlawful action under the First Amendment"); *Sorrell* v. *IMS Health Inc.*, 131 S. Ct. 2653, 2663 (2011) (asserting that "a statute's stated purposes may also be considered" in appraising its constitutional validity); see also *Texas* v. *Johnson*, 491 U.S. 397, 407, 410 (1989) (invalidating a state statute where the state's asserted justificatory interests were related to the suppression of ideas). In addition, Justice Kagan argued that many objective-looking inquiries – such as the examination of whether restrictions on speech are content-based – function as "proxies" for direct examination of legislative intent. *See* Kagan, *supra*, at 414, 441.

[12] Under the dormant Commerce Clause, tax or regulatory statutes that reflect a discriminatory or protectionist legislative purpose incur strict judicial scrutiny. See, e.g., *Wyoming* v. *Oklahoma*, 502 U.S. 437, 454–55 (1992) ("This 'negative' aspect of the Commerce Clause prohibits economic protectionism – that is, regulatory measures designed to benefit in-state economic interests by burdening out-of-state competitors." (quoting *New Energy Co. of Ind.* v. *Limbach*, 486 U.S. 269, 273–74 (1988))); *City of Philadelphia* v. *New Jersey*, 437 U.S. 617, 628 (1978) (condemning measures enacted to "slow or freeze the flow of commerce for protectionist reasons"). In addition, judicial inquiries frequently begin with the question whether the legislature enacted a challenged provision

With legislative intentions playing so prominent a role in constitutional analysis, some commentators have gone so far as to maintain that judicial review of the constitutionality of statutes either is or ought to be limited to identifying forbidden motives.[13] Indeed, as Chapter 2 recognized, the Supreme Court has occasionally suggested that the purpose of strict judicial scrutiny is to "smoke out" forbidden intentions and to invalidate legislation that reflects them.[14]

These suggestions present an important challenge to my account of constitutional adjudication as inherently and appropriately involving interest-balancing. My response is straightforward: Intent-based inquiries are indeed common, but they are best understood as reflecting *triggering rights*, which must take their place alongside abstract, scrutiny, and ultimate rights. In other words, a finding of forbidden legislative intent normally triggers the application of a further, searching test of constitutional validity, but rarely if ever does a finding of impermissible legislative intentions categorically establish that a statute is unconstitutional. To see why, we need a distinction between two categories of constitutional norms. Some constitutional norms are substantive: They bar, or create triggering and scrutiny rights against, substantively defined categories of governmental action – for example, against statutes that are written in forbidden or suspect terms, or have forbidden or suspect effects. A statute would fall into this category if it forbade political editorializing on election day or required Muslims to go through more airport screening than non-Muslims. We would know that it was invalid, or at least that it required strict scrutiny, without needing to inquire into the intentions or purpose of the legislature that enacted it. But another category of norms – as reflected in doctrinal tests that focus on forbidden legislative intentions – is "deliberative." Deliberative norms create obligations of legislators not to pursue constitutionally forbidden aims or to take official actions based on constitutionally forbidden motives. Those obligations in turn create *deliberative rights*, which are almost invariably triggering rather than ultimate rights, not to be harmed by statutes that were enacted for forbidden purposes.

---

with a punitive intent in challenges to legislative enactments under constitutional provisions that prohibit ex post facto laws, bills of attainder, and double jeopardy. *See, e.g., Kansas v. Hendricks*, 521 U.S. 346, 368–69 (1997); Alice Ristroph, *State Intentions and the Law of Punishment*, 98 J. CRIM. L. & CRIMINOLOGY 1353, 1370 (2008).

[13] *See e.g.*, Charles Fried, *Types*, 14 CONST. COMMENT. 55, 62–63 (1997); Kagan, *supra* note 11, at 414; Jed Rubenfeld, Essay, *Affirmative Action*, 107 YALE L.J. 427, 428–29 (1997); *see also* John Hart Ely, DEMOCRACY AND DISTRUST: A THEORY OF JUDICIAL REVIEW 145–48 (1980).

[14] *See, e.g., Johnson v. California*, 543 U.S. 499, 505 (2005) ("The reasons for strict scrutiny are familiar. Racial classifications raise special fears that they are motivated by an invidious purpose."); *Grutter v. Bollinger*, 539 U.S. 306, 326 (2003) (quoting *City of Richmond v. J.A. Croson Co.*, 488 U.S. 469, 493 (1989) (plurality opinion)) (asserting that the purpose of strict scrutiny was "to 'smoke out' illegitimate uses of race"); *R.A.V. v. City of St. Paul*, 505 U.S. 377, 386 (1992) (explaining need to apply strict scrutiny to ensure that the government could not "regulate … based on hostility – or favoritism – towards the underlying message [that a speaker] expressed").

Accepting the genuine importance of deliberative norms and rights, and thus the importance of legislative intent in understanding the nature of constitutional rights, my interest-based approach insists that bad legislative motives are not the only consideration determining the constitutional rights that we have. To the contrary, courts must weigh interests to define substantive norms, to identify which legislative motives or purposes should trigger strict scrutiny, and to determine whether badly motivated legislation is nevertheless narrowly tailored to a compelling governmental interest.

Another challenge, which cannot be met without recourse to interest-based calculations, must also be confronted. While some commentators believe that courts should focus their inquiries into the constitutionality of legislation exclusively on legislative purposes, others adopt nearly a polar opposite view. According to them, inquiries into legislative intent are a snipe hunt. These skeptics of inquiries into legislative motivations rely on a conjunction of three objections. (1) It is frequently difficult or impossible to discern the intentions of even a single legislator, who may have voted for a bill for a myriad of reasons, some having nothing to do with its substantive effects. As Justice Scalia once explained:

> He may have ... wanted to make amends with a faction of his party he had alienated on another vote, or he may have been a close friend of the bill's sponsor, or he may have been repaying a favor he owed the majority leader, or he may have hoped the Governor would appreciate his vote and make a fundraising appearance for him, or he may have been pressured to vote for a bill he disliked by a wealthy contributor or by a flood of constituent mail, or he may have been seeking favorable publicity.[15]

(2) In a multimember legislature, different members are likely to have had different intentions. (3) There is no good answer to the question of how many legislators would need to have forbidden intentions for their intentions to matter:

> If a state senate approves a bill by vote of 26 to 25, and only one of the 26 intended solely to advance religion, is the law unconstitutional? What if 13 of the 26 had that intent? ... [I]s it possible that the intent of the bill's sponsor is alone enough to invalidate it – on a theory, perhaps, that even though everyone else's intent was pure, what they produced was the fruit of a forbidden tree?[16]

To grasp the role of forbidden intentions in constitutional adjudication, and thus the nature and significance of deliberative rights, therefore requires unraveling two logically sequenced puzzles. The first is analytical: We need to discern what legislative intentions or purposes are and consider how individual intentions could be cumulated into a collective "intent of the legislature." Only after answering that question can we resolve a second set of issues, involving the part that forbidden intentions, as properly conceptualized, play and ought to play in the definition of

---

[15] *Edwards* v. *Aguillard*, 482 U.S. 578, 637 (1987) (Scalia, J., dissenting).
[16] *Id.* at 638.

ultimate constitutional rights. Among the central questions is whether forbidden legislative intentions should trigger strict judicial scrutiny or, instead, render a challenged statute categorically invalid.

I should say one more preliminary word about the scope of this chapter's analysis. In discussing the generic role of forbidden intentions in the definition of individual rights, I shall not seek to identify which specific intentions and motivations various constitutional provisions should be interpreted to prohibit. To keep the discussion within manageable bounds, I assume, unless I indicate otherwise, that the intentions and motivations that the Supreme Court has classed as impermissible deserve that designation. Correspondingly, I shall leave questions concerning possible additional forbidden intentions and motivations – including the possibility that the category of discriminatory intent should subsume subconscious mental states – for another day.

CAN A LEGISLATURE HAVE CONSTITUTIONALLY FORBIDDEN INTENTIONS?

In cases in which courts must decide whether a statute applies to particular facts – whether, for example, a prohibition against "vehicles" in a park includes baby carriages or bicycles – a panoply of judges and commentators has disparaged and indeed ridiculed inquiries into subjective legislative intentions as a gauge of statutory meaning.[17] When matters of statutory interpretation occupy center stage, the lesson has taken hold that the legislature is "a 'they,' not an 'it.'"[18] Individual legislators may have intentions and purposes, but the legislature as a whole, the emerging wisdom maintains, has no collective intent or purpose.[19] With this challenge in mind, we need to ask what the Supreme Court means when it speaks of discriminatory or otherwise forbidden legislative intentions, purposes, or motivations in cases challenging statutes' validity under the Constitution.

In pursuing that question, we should keep some distinctions in mind. The Supreme Court almost invariably treats the terms "intentions" and "purposes" as synonymous.[20] In addition, it most frequently includes "motivations" in the same

---

[17]   The skeptics range from the conservative Justice Antonin Scalia, *see, e.g.*, Antonin Scalia, *Common-Law Courts in a Civil-Law System: The Role of United States Federal Courts in Interpreting the Constitution and Laws, in* A MATTER OF INTERPRETATION 3, 16–23 (Amy Gutmann ed., 1997), to the liberal political jurisprudential thinker and moral philosopher Ronald Dworkin, *see, e.g.*, Ronald Dworkin, LAW'S EMPIRE 321–33 (1986).

[18]   Kenneth A. Shepsle, *Congress Is a "They," Not an "It": Legislative Intent as Oxymoron*, 12 INT'L REV. L. & ECON. 239, 244 (1992).

[19]   *See, e.g.*, John F. Manning, *Textualism and Legislative Intent*, 91 VA. L. REV. 419, 428–32 (2005).

[20]   *See* David A. Strauss, *Discriminatory Intent and the Taming of Brown*, 56 U. CHI. L. REV. 935, 951 (1989); Julia Kobick, *Note, Discriminatory Intent Reconsidered: Folk Concepts of Intentionality and Equal Protection Jurisprudence*, 45 HARV. C.R.-C.L. L. REV. 517, 521 n.22 (2010) ("As used in *Davis*, a government's 'discriminatory purpose' is a synonym for a government's 'intentionally discriminatory action.' Throughout the majority opinion, the Court uses 'purpose' and 'intent' to denote the same idea."); *see also Edwards* v. *Aguillard*, 482 U.S. 578, 613 (1987) (Scalia, J., dissenting) ("[R]egardless of

conceptual hopper.[21] We should be slightly more conceptually fastidious. In pursuit of analytical clarity, we can define a person's intentions in terms of the proximate aims that she seeks to achieve in taking an action.[22] For example, if a legislator votes to authorize a Ten Commandments display in the state capitol, we might say that she acts with the intention (or aim) of promoting religion. So speaking, we might distinguish her "motivations" for doing so as involving the values, beliefs, or dispositions that made the aim of promoting religion attractive to her.[23] For example, we might say that her motivation was to please God – or, alternatively, that it was to win the support of religiously devout voters. If we distinguish between "intention" and "motivation" in this way, with each denominating a distinct mental state, then the term "purpose" is ambiguous: It can refer either to what a person proximately aims at[24] or to the deeper grounds that would explain why someone adopted the aim that she did.[25] I shall not seek to purge "purpose" – a term that the Supreme Court most characteristically treats as synonymous with intention[26] – of its ambiguity.

When the terms intention, motivation, and purpose are used in these ways, it seems obvious that the legislature – a collective body, made up of many individuals – could not have shared, collective, psychological states of the relevant kind, possibly beyond the intent to enact whatever legislation it enacts. Accordingly, a risk of confusion exists whenever a court speaks of forbidden legislative intentions. Often, moreover, the Supreme Court writes opinions that seem oblivious to this difficulty. For example, in the canonical equal protection case of *Village of Arlington Heights v. Metropolitan Housing Development Corp.*,[27] the Court first deemed legislative intentions to be crucial, then described the relevant question as whether "a discriminatory purpose has been *a* motivating factor in the decision."[28] It is impossible to

---

what 'legislative purpose' may mean in other contexts, for the purpose of the *Lemon* test it means the 'actual' motives of those responsible for the challenged action.").

[21] *Cf.* Kagan, *supra* note 11, at 426 n.40 (rejecting distinctions among these and similar terms as unhelpful for purposes of constitutional analysis); Ristroph, *supra* note 12, at 1354 and n.2 (noting that "[i]nquiries into purpose, intention, and motivation are . . . prevalent in constitutional doctrine," *id.* at 1354, and using the terms "interchangeably," *id.* at 1354 n.2).

[22] *See, e.g.*, Deborah Hellman, WHEN IS DISCRIMINATION WRONG? 143 (2008); T. M. Scanlon, *Intention and Permissibility*, 74 ARISTOTELIAN SOC. SUPP. VOL. 301, 306 (2000).

[23] *See, e.g.*, Hellman, *supra* note 22, at 140; Gordon G. Young, *Justifying Motive Analysis in Judicial Review*, 17 WM. & MARY BILL RTS. J. 191, 207–08 (2008).

[24] *See, e.g.*, *Edwards* v. *Aguillard*, 482 U.S. 578, 636–37 (1987) (Scalia, J., dissenting) ("[W]hile it is possible to discern the objective 'purpose' of a statute (*i.e.*, the public good at which its provisions appear to be directed) . . . discerning the subjection motivation of those enacting the statute is . . . almost always an impossible task."); *see also* Bd. *of Educ.* v. *Mergens ex rel. Mergens*, 496 U.S. 226, 249 (1990) (plurality opinion) ("[W]hat is relevant is the legislative *purpose* of the statute, not the possibly religious *motives* of the legislators who enacted the law.").

[25] *See, e.g.*, Hellman, *supra* note 22, at 140.

[26] *See* Kobick, *supra* note 20, at 521 n.22; Strauss, *supra* note 20, at 951.

[27] 429 U.S. 252 (1977).

[28] *Id.* at 265–66 (emphasis added). Notable, too, is the formula that the Supreme Court uses in assessing the permissibility of race-based considerations in the drawing of voting districts. In that context, the

know exactly what the Court meant by this formulation or if it meant anything coherent at all.

In seeking an intelligible account of the nature of constitutionally forbidden legislative intent, we should reject any notion that a multimember legislature might have a collective mental state. Once we have done so, however, investigation will reveal three ways to give coherent content to the idea of constitutionally forbidden legislative intent, each of which seems to explain the Supreme Court's inquiry in some cases.

Counting-Based Ascriptions of Subjective Intent. Even though the collective legislature does not have a unitary psychological intent, individual legislators undoubtedly have intentions and motivations, just as the rest of us do. So recognizing, the courts could sometimes ascribe a collective intent to the legislature based on an actual identification and counting of individual legislators' separate mental states. Such an approach would begin with inquiries into the intentions of individual legislators and then rely on legal rules to determine when, as a matter of law, the intentions of some should be ascribed to the legislature as a whole.

In considering that courts might inquire into legislators' individual motivations, and then determine whether to ascribe those of some members to the legislature as a whole, we should keep in mind that available evidence sometimes permits courts to ascertain individual intentions.[29] In imputing intentions to people whom we know, we often rely on a mix of contextual factors, biographical information, and explicit statements. We can do the same with legislators. The remarks of a single legislator in legislative debates may provide only weak evidence of the intentions or purposes of other members, but strong evidence regarding the speaker. Sometimes the legislative history may further suggest that a majority of legislators voted as they did for constitutionally forbidden purposes, such as seeking to harm a racial minority or promote a favored religion.[30]

Court frames the question as whether race was the "predominant" factor in the legislature's decision to draw district lines as it did. *E.g., Ala. Legislative Black Caucus v. Alabama*, 135 S. Ct. 1257, 1262 (2015); *Shaw v. Hunt*, 517 U.S. 899, 906–07 (1996). John Hart Ely mocked the "predominant purpose" standard as incoherent. John Hart Ely, *Gerrymanders: The Good, the Bad, and the Ugly*, 50 STAN. L. REV. 607, 611–12 (1998). Among the reasons to think that the "predominant purpose" test depends on legislators' actual psychological motivations is that the Court has held that there is no constitutional impropriety in legislatures drawing irregular or otherwise seemingly suspicious district lines for the purpose of protecting incumbent legislators. *See, e.g., Easley v. Cromartie*, 532 U.S. 234, 257–58 (2001). Determining whether incumbent protection was the legislature's actual purpose seems to require psychological inquiries.

[29] *See, e.g.,* Ristroph, *supra* note 12, at 1365 (noting that "courts and juries regularly make determinations of individuals' intentions" in criminal cases).

[30] *See, e.g., Wallace v. Jaffree*, 472 U.S. 38, 56–57 (1985) (relying on legislative history to support a finding that the legislature acted with a constitutionally forbidden purpose of promoting prayer in public schools).

We should not be misled here by a false analogy to statutory interpretation cases in which courts have sometimes pursued inquiries into legislative intent for purposes of determining what a statute means. In that context, different legislators may have had radically diverse beliefs, assumptions, expectations, and so forth, any or all of which may, on some accounts, bear on a statute's meaning. By contrast, if we want to know whether individual legislators acted with forbidden purposes – such as that of disadvantaging a racial or religious minority – the question solicits a yes or no response regarding each member. Answering it may prove difficult for either evidentiary or, in some cases, conceptual reasons.[31] But the question whether one or more individual legislators acted for impermissible reasons is by no means inherently unanswerable. Nor is the follow-on question of how many had intentions that occupied the forbidden category.

Sometimes, moreover, there may be no psychologically plausible explanation for individual legislators' decisions to vote for a particular law that does not involve forbidden purposes. A classic example comes from *Gomillion* v. *Lightfoot*,[32] in which the Alabama legislature changed Tuskegee's city boundaries from a square to a 28-sided figure.[33] In doing so, it removed all but "four or five of its 400 Negro voters while not removing a single white voter."[34] On the pleaded facts, the Supreme Court sensibly reasoned, "the conclusion would be irresistible … that the legislation [was] solely concerned with … fencing Negro citizens out of town so as to deprive them of their pre-existing municipal vote."[35]

In cases in which it appears that different legislators may have had different purposes or motivations, a question arises about how many must have had forbidden aims to justify an ascription of forbidden intent in the subjective, psychological sense to the legislature as a whole. Unfortunately, the Supreme Court has never addressed

---

[31] *See, e.g.*, Laurence H. Tribe, *The Mystery of Motive, Private and Public: Some Notes Inspired by the Problems of Hate Crime and Animal Sacrifice*, 1993 SUP. CT. REV. 1, 15 (discussing the kinds of intentions in which constitutional law takes an interest and those in which it does not and distinguishing between "motive in the fairly innocuous *mens rea* sense" and "the murkier sense" that "entails more probing into … inner beliefs"). Among the further conceptual difficulties is that which arises when relevant actors have mixed or multiple motivations – a situation that can occur in cases of individual as well as group action. *See* Andrew Verstein, *The Jurisprudence of Mixed Motives*, 127 YALE L.J. 1106 (2018) (developing a typology of legal approaches to mixed-motive cases). In my view, if an intention or motivation likely played some role in a legislator's decision, she should be regarded as having had a constitutionally forbidden intent. *See* Richard H. Fallon, Jr., *Constitutionally Forbidden Legislative Intent*, 130 HARV. L. REV. 530, 579–80 (2016).

[32] 364 U.S. 339 (1960).

[33] *Id.* at 340.

[34] *Id.* at 341.

[35] *Id.* As I shall explain below, cases in which courts base findings of forbidden purpose nearly entirely on a statute's language and effects, without in-depth analysis of context or legislative history, could also be conceptualized as involving reliance on an "objective" conception of legislative intent. Without denying that possibility, I mean to emphasize here that the "objective" evidence can be seen as proof of the existence of psychological intentions that, because they are subjective and not publicly visible, can only be identified based on objective indicators.

this question directly.[36] My own judgment, which I think consistent with the Court's cases but which I could not claim to have determinate legal foundations, is that courts should ascribe forbidden motivations to the collective legislature only when an actual majority of the legislators who voted for a law did so with improper intentions.[37] No inexorable logic dictates assigning this significance to the intentions of a majority of supporting legislators, rather than a greater or a smaller number. Nonetheless, drawing the line at this point reasonably accommodates several pertinent considerations. If a majority of the legislators who vote for a bill take their deliberative obligations seriously, then a substantial safeguard of the interests that underlie whatever constitutional right is at stake will have operated, even if a minority of a bill's supporters voted as they did for constitutionally repugnant reasons. Setting the bar at this level also gives political democracy reasonable latitude to operate by precluding constitutional claims based on forbidden legislative intentions whenever the legislature divides narrowly and there is plausible evidence that a few members may have voted as they did for corrupt or invidious purposes. A point comes, however, at which too many legislators' defaults on their deliberative obligations demand a judicial response if constitutional guarantees are to be enforced sufficiently robustly.

Objective Legislative Intent Imputed to Make Sense of Specific Statutory Language. Even those who insist most stridently that a multimember legislature cannot have unitary, collective, psychological intent acknowledge the need for courts to develop and rely on an ostensibly "objective" conception of legislative intent in enacting a statute.[38] They do so in response to two uncontroversial insights. First, our interest in interpreting statutory language presupposes that it reflects the intentions of legislators who enacted it with the aim of prescribing the consequences of future conduct.[39] Second, it is frequently impossible to grasp the meaning of statutory language without imputing aims or purposes to the legislature.[40] As the avowedly

---

[36] See *Edwards v. Aguillard*, 482 U.S. 578, 637 (1987) (Scalia, J., dissenting).

[37] Another possibility would be for the Supreme Court to adopt a rule deeming that the legislature acted with forbidden intentions whenever the votes of legislators with prohibited purposes were necessary to enact – and thus were the but-for cause of the passage of – a challenged piece of legislation. Under this approach, the attitudes of even a single legislator could lead to an ascription of forbidden legislative intent if that single legislator cast the determining vote in an otherwise evenly divided legislature. To deem that a legislature had acted with discriminatory intentions under these circumstances would seem too draconian a restraint on the operations of political democracy.

[38] See, e.g., John F. Manning, *What Divides Textualists from Purposivists?*, 106 COLUM. L. REV. 70, 79 (2006) (discussing textualists' need for a conception of objective intent); Caleb Nelson, *What Is Textualism?*, 91 VA. L. REV. 347, 353–57 (2005) (discussing textualists' search for statutes "objectified intent"); Scalia, *supra* note 17, at 17 (explicating the need for inquiries into "'objectified' intent").

[39] See Larry Alexander & Saikrishna Prakash, *"Is That English You're Speaking?" Why Intention Free Interpretation Is an Impossibility*, 41 SAN DIEGO L. REV. 967, 990 (2004).

[40] Among philosophers of language, there is widespread agreement that the meaning of utterances depends on speakers' intentions, but controversy about exactly how it does so. According to the influential theories of H. P. Grice, the meaning of an utterance simply is the speaker's intended meaning. *See* Andrei Marmor, INTERPRETATION AND LEGAL THEORY 19 ((2014) ("According to a Gricean view . . . [w]hatever the speaker intended to say is the content asserted."); *see generally* Paul Grice,

textualist Justice Antonin Scalia once wrote, the word "nails" means one thing when it appears in a building code, but something different in a statute regulating beauty salons.[41] To know what the word "nails" means in a particular context, we need to reach judgments concerning the legislature's intentions or the purposes that the legislature sought to achieve.

In defending a methodology that ascribes "objective" intentions to the collective legislature, textualists often say that courts should not rely on ascribed intentions or purposes to contradict a statute's clear meaning.[42] In some instances, this asserted stricture poses puzzles. With all agreeing that the meaning of statutory language depends on its context,[43] and must be determined in light of the purposes that legislation seeks to promote, it is not obvious how statutory language could have a clear meaning apart from a determination of its purposes, in context. If that puzzle can be untangled, one possibility would be this: Textualists might believe that interpreters should ordinarily impute to the legislature the sparest set of intentions or motivations that are necessary to make it plausible or even intelligible that rational people would have adopted the language that the legislature did in a particular context.[44]

With that conception of objective legislative intent in mind, we might say, as the Supreme Court sometimes does, that some statutes exhibit unconstitutional intentions on their faces. In light of a statute's language, there may be no psychologically plausible explanation of why a legislature might have enacted it that does not involve a forbidden purpose. If more distance from the psychological intentions of the actual legislature were wanted, we might even postulate a conception of legislative intent

STUDIES IN THE WAY OF WORDS 117 (1989) (characterizing utterer's meaning as "basic" and other notions of meaning as "(I hope) derivative"). According to other theorists, the meaning of an utterance in ordinary conversation is a function of multiple factors, of which a speaker's intentions are only one. *See, e.g.*, Andrei Armor & Scott Soames, *Introduction*, in PHILOSOPHICAL FOUNDATIONS OF LANGUAGE IN LAW 1, 8 (A. Marmor & S. Soames eds. 2011) (asserting that the communicative content of utterances "is determined by a variety of factors, including the semantic content of the sentence uttered, the communicative intentions of the speaker, the shared presuppositions of the speakers-hearers, and obvious features of the context of utterance").

[41] Antonin Scalia & Bryan A. Garner, READING LAW: THE INTERPRETATION OF LEGAL TEXTS 20 (2012).

[42] *See id.* at 57 (discussing the "Supremacy-of-Text Principle": "except in the rare case of an obvious scrivener's error, purpose – even purpose as most narrowly defined – cannot be used to contradict text or to supplement it"); *id.* at 343 (discussing "[t]he false notion that the spirit of a statute should prevail over its letter"); *id.* at 375 (rejecting "the use of legislative history" as "assum[ing] that what we are looking for is the intent of the legislature rather than the meaning of the statutory text"); John F. Manning, *The Absurdity Doctrine*, 116 HARV. L. REV. 2387, 2434 n.179 (2003) ("[T]he modern textualists' concerns come into play only when courts use background statutory purpose to contradict or vary the clear meaning of a specific statutory provision." (emphasis omitted)).

[43] *See* Manning, *supra* note 38, at 73, 79–80 (discussing the importance of context for textualism and purposivism); *see also* Scalia & Garner, *supra* note 41, at 16, 32–33.

[44] *See* Manning, *supra* note 19, at 423. In my view, many textualists fail to adhere consistently to the policy of imputing the sparest possible set of background assumptions necessary to render statutory language intelligible. *See* Richard H. Fallon, Jr., *Three Symmetries between Textualist and Purposivist Theories of Statutory Interpretation – and the Irreducible Roles of Values and Judgment within Both*, 99 CORNELL L. REV. 685, 707–19 (2014).

predicated on what an imagined typical legislature, enacting particular statutory language in a specified historical context, would most reasonably be understood as having aimed at or as being motivated by.[45] The modern Supreme Court (with the assent of the textualist Justices Scalia and Thomas) may have adopted this approach in *Shaw* v. *Reno*,[46] which invalidated a peculiarly shaped legislative district as a forbidden racial gerrymander. In the Court's view, the challenged district was "so extremely irregular on its face that it rationally can be viewed only as an effort to segregate the races for purposes of voting."[47]

As this example suggests, an approach that imputes an objective legislative intent or purpose in order to make the legislature's adoption of statutory language psychologically or sociologically intelligible will often overlap in practical effect with a conception of legislative intent based on the imagined subjective intentions of a majority of the actual enacting legislators. For example, *Gomillion* v. *Lightfoot*, which I discussed earlier, could be conceptualized as involving a finding of either "subjective" or "objective" legislative intent. As in *Shaw* v. *Reno*, an objective observer could "only" view the challenged statute as "an effort to segregate the races,"[48] regardless of whether she viewed herself as seeking to discover the psychological intentions of a majority of the actual legislature or the imagined objective intentions of a hypothetical legislature. With the exception of legislative history, which textualists characteristically eschew,[49] those seeking subjective and those seeking this kind of objective legislative intent will typically look at the same evidence in this kind of case and will typically come to the same conclusions.[50]

[45] *See* Seana Valentine Shiffrin, *Speech, Death, and Double Effect*, 78 N.Y.U. L. REV. 1135, 1155 (2003) (employing an "objective notion of intention as it is made manifest through the performance of actions of a certain type, actions that, because of what they involve, are typically motivated by a certain rationale and are reasonably interpreted as being so motivated").

[46] 509 U.S. 630 (1993).

[47] *Id.* at 642; *see also McCreary County* v. *ACLU of Ky.*, 545 U.S. 844, 861–62 (2005) ("The eyes that look to purpose belong to an 'objective observer,' one who takes account of the traditional external signs that show up in the 'text, legislative history, and implementation of the statute,' or comparable official act." (quoting *Santa Fe Indep. Sch. Dist.* v. *Doe*, 530 U.S. 290, 308 (2000))).

[48] *Shaw*, 509 U.S. at 642.

[49] *See* Scalia & Garner, *supra* note 41, at 76; *see also id.* at 369 (listing, as one of thirteen "falsities," "[t]he false notion that committee reports and floor speeches are worthwhile aids in statutory construction"); Manning, *supra* note 38, at 73 ("[T]extualists emphasize that the statutory text alone has survived the constitutionally prescribed process of bicameralism and presentment.").

[50] A similar conclusion has often emerged concerning efforts to distinguish objective and subjective conceptions of intent in private law. *See, e.g.*, Lawrence Ponoroff, *The Limits of Good Faith Analyses: Unraveling and Redefining Bad Faith in Involuntary Bankruptcy Proceedings*, 71 NEB. L. REV. 209, 222 n.44 (1992) (observing that "the dichotomy" is less pronounced in practice than in theory since "ordinarily the only way to prove bad motive is by inferences drawn from objective conduct"); Michael P. Van Alstine, *Of Textualism, Party Autonomy, and Good Faith*, 40 WM. & MARY L. REV. 1223, 1247 (1999) (characterizing the debate about objective and subjective conceptions of intent in contract law as exhibiting "more theoretical smoke than practical fire").

Nevertheless, a conceptual distinction exists, as the Supreme Court occasionally highlights. In *Board of Education* v. *Mergens ex rel. Mergens*,[51] for example, a plurality of the Court insisted that "what is relevant is the legislative *purpose* of the statute, not the possibly religious *motives* of the legislators who enacted the law."[52] In this formulation, "motives" are actual psychological phenomena, but the legislative purpose is not. In *Mergens*, moreover, the plurality insisted that if the legislature did not act with a forbidden purpose in the objective sense, then it should be deemed not to have acted with a forbidden purpose at all, evidence of forbidden subjective motivations to the contrary notwithstanding. But there are few cases of this kind. Even in *Mergens*, moreover, there was no majority opinion. I shall consider below what the Court ought to do in the relatively rare cases in which subjectively forbidden legislative intent is demonstrable under counting-based rules for ascribing psychological intent, but objectively forbidden intent is not.

Categorically Ascribed Objective Intent. Another conception of legislative intent ascribes forbidden purposes to the legislature in categorical, rule-like terms, based on objective characteristics of statutes' language or structure, without any effort to reconstruct the thinking of a specific legislature or its members. Justice Kagan's article, which argues that large elements of free speech jurisprudence deploy "proxies" for inquiries into subjective legislative intent,[53] exemplifies this possibility. It surveys the landscape of First Amendment doctrine, most of which makes no reference to legislative intent, but argues that the rules are best understood as mechanisms to identify instances in which most enacting legislators likely had forbidden motivations. For example, reigning case law marks statutes as suspect under the First Amendment if they regulate speech on the basis of content (rather than imposing content-neutral time, place, and manner regulations).[54] According to Justice Kagan, when the legislature enacts content-based regulations, the Justices suspect that many or most of its members acted with the forbidden purpose of stifling speech with which they disagreed.[55] Crucially, however, the rule structure precludes case-by-case inquiries concerning legislators' actual, subjective intentions.[56] Rather, in Justice Kagan's account, the Court takes objective measures as irrebuttable indicators of legislative intent. As the Supreme Court said in *Reed* v. *Town of Gilbert*,[57] "[a] law that is content based on its face is subject to strict scrutiny regardless of the government's benign motive ... or lack of 'animus toward the ideas contained' in the regulated speech."[58] The text of the statute is all that matters.

---

[51]   496 U.S. 226 (1990).
[52]   *Id.* at 249 (plurality opinion).
[53]   *See* Kagan, *supra* note 11, at 414, 441.
[54]   *See, e.g., Reed* v. *Town of Gilbert*, 135 S. Ct. 2218, 2228 (2015).
[55]   *See* Kagan, *supra* note 11, at 443.
[56]   *See, e.g., Reed*, 135 S. Ct. at 2228 (quoting *City of Cincinnati* v. *Discovery Network, Inc.*, 507 U.S. 410, 429 (1993)).
[57]   135 S. Ct. 2218 (2015).
[58]   *Id.* at 2228 (quoting *Discovery Network*, 507 U.S. at 429).

Because the free speech doctrine that Justice Kagan describes as intent-based does not, with a few exceptions, purport on its face to consider legislative intentions or purposes at all,[59] the First Amendment is, admittedly, a controversial example to use in illustrating an objective conception of constitutionally forbidden intent. But several other doctrines that refer specifically to legislative intentions demonstrate the possibility of an objective conception that relies entirely on non-psychological indicia.

One example comes from equal protection doctrine and, in particular, the rational basis test.[60] Although rational basis review is normally highly deferential, the Supreme Court occasionally invalidates statutes on the ground that the legislature enacted them with discriminatory or otherwise forbidden purposes.[61] The leading decisions in which it has done so plainly involve a reliance on legislators' actual mental states in one way or another. More typically, however, the Court insists that the rational basis test eschews inquiry into the legislature's psychological motivations.[62] Refusing to look at actual intentions, it asks whether, as an objective matter, there is any rational basis on which the legislature's action could be sustained.[63] In so doing, the Court could be interpreted as employing an objective, categorically ascribed conception of legislative intent, defined by any objectively valid interest that the state advances.

It would also be possible to conceptualize the rule that race-based classifications trigger strict judicial scrutiny[64] as a proxy for inquiries into the subjective intent of the legislature[65] that ultimately relies on an objective, categorically ascribed conception of legislative intent. On this interpretation, race-based classifications would irrefutably establish the existence of a forbidden discriminatory intent, which could plausibly be described as objective, regardless of what individual legislators' subjective mental attitudes might have been. Strict scrutiny would then apply to determine whether such classifications might be justified nevertheless.[66]

---

[59] Indeed, in *United States* v. *O'Brien*, 391 U.S. 367 (1968), the Supreme Court famously held that "the purpose of Congress ... is not a basis for declaring ... legislation unconstitutional." *Id.* at 383; *see also* Kagan, *supra* note 11, at 413 ("[M]ost descriptive analyses of First Amendment law, as well as most normative discussions of the doctrine, have considered the permissibility of governmental regulation of speech by focusing on the effects of a given regulation.").

[60] *See, e.g., FCC* v. *Beach Commc'ns, Inc.*, 508 U.S. 307, 315 (1993).

[61] *See, e.g., Romer* v. *Evans*, 517 U.S. 620, 632 (1996); *City of Cleburne* v. *Cleburne Living Ctr., Inc.*, 473 U.S. 432, 450 (1985).

[62] *See, e.g., Beach Commc'ns*, 508 U.S. at 315; *U.S. R.R. Ret. Bd.* v. *Fritz*, 449 U.S. 166, 179 (1980).

[63] *See, e.g., Beach Commc'ns*, 508 U.S. at 315; *Fritz*, 449 U.S. at 179. In *Trump* v. *Hawaii*, 138 S. Ct. 2392, 2420 (2018), involving alleged discriminatory intentions by the President in selectively limiting foreign nationals' ability to enter the United States, the Court "assume[d]" that "we may consider plaintiffs' extrinsic evidence" of impermissible intentions, but emphasized that under the rational basis test it would "uphold the policy so long as it can reasonably be understood to result from a justification independent of unconstitutional grounds." *Id.*

[64] *See, e.g., Johnson* v. *California*, 543 U.S. 499, 505 (2005).

[65] *See* Dworkin, *supra* note 17, at 394–96.

[66] On a similar but distinct interpretation, race-based classifications would be rebuttably (rather than irrebuttably) assumed to flow from forbidden motivations, and the strict scrutiny formula would test

Forbidden Legislative Intent as a Protean Concept. Although there are multiple coherent senses in which the Supreme Court might conceptualize constitutionally forbidden legislative intent, I should repeat a caution with which I began: The Court is inconsistent in its practices. Different conceptions of legislative intent sometimes seem to matter, as the examples that I have used to illustrate the persistence of at least three conceptions would suggest. In some of the Court's references to legislative intent, moreover, it is wholly unclear what the Justices have in mind. I mean only to emphasize that there are coherent conceptions of legislative intent, available to the Court and sometimes utilized by it.

THE SIGNIFICANCE OF FORBIDDEN LEGISLATIVE INTENT

With three coherent but diverse conceptions of constitutionally forbidden legislative intent now on the table, we can move to the question of what consequences a finding of forbidden intent by some or all legislators does and ought to have. Or to put the question differently, we can inquire, what significance do deliberative rights have? In some instances, the Supreme Court suggests that an impermissible purpose conclusively invalidates legislation.[67] In other cases, however, the Court has stated that a statute enacted for a forbidden purpose will occasion the application of strict scrutiny.[68] If so, deliberative rights are triggering rights, which occasion the application of strict scrutiny, but are not necessarily ultimate rights. On a few occasions, the Justices have said, much more weakly, that a finding of invalid purpose merely shifts the burden to the government to establish that it would have enacted the same legislation for other reasons.[69]

Despite the conflicting signals, the Supreme Court should, and normally does, treat deliberative rights as triggering rights: Constitutionally forbidden legislative intentions serve as a trigger for strict judicial scrutiny, but the ultimate test of constitutional validity is objective, involving the weight of the governmental interests that support challenged legislation. The arguments that support this conclusion will emerge best through a consideration of how strict scrutiny fits with and most sensibly applies to each of the three coherent conceptions of forbidden legislative intent canvased above. Analysis will also reveal that strict scrutiny should apply

the bona fides of the government's claim to have a legitimate, and indeed compelling, justification for its employment of racial criteria in a particular context. *See, e.g., Grutter* v. *Bollinger*, 539 U.S. 306, 326 (2003) (quoting *City of Richmond* v. *J.A. Croson Co.*, 488 U.S. 469, 493 (1989) (plurality opinion)); *see also Johnson*, 543 U.S. at 505 ("The reasons for strict scrutiny are familiar. Racial classifications raise special fears that they are motivated by an invidious purpose."). *See generally* Richard H. Fallon, Jr., *Strict Judicial Scrutiny*, 54 UCLA L. REV. 1267, 1309–10 (2007) (discussing one possible conception of strict scrutiny as an illicit motive test); Fried, *supra* note 13, at 62–63; Rubenfeld, *supra* note 13, at 428–29.

[67] *See, e.g., Wallace* v. *Jaffree*, 472 U.S. 38, 56 (1985); *Lemon* v. *Kurtzman*, 403 U.S. 602, 612 (1971).

[68] *See, e.g., Church of the Lukumi Babalu Aye, Inc.* v. *City of Hialeah*, 508 U.S. 520, 533 (1993).

[69] *See, e.g., Mt. Healthy City Sch. Dist. Bd. of Educ.* v. *Doyle*, 429 U.S. 274, 287 (1977); *Village of Arlington Heights* v. *Metro. Hous. Dev. Corp.*, 429 U.S. 252, 270 n.21 (1977).

whenever a challenger can establish forbidden legislative intent in the subjective sense, regardless of whether one of the objective tests of forbidden intent is satisfied.

Counting-Based Ascriptions of Subjective Intent. A powerful reason to apply strict judicial scrutiny whenever the legislature breaches deliberative rights inheres in the relationship between the legislative and judicial roles under the constitutional separation of powers. Our Constitution imposes deliberative obligations on both legislatures and courts as a means of protecting constitutional rights. These obligations are role obligations. Legislators could, in principle, violate them even if they always voted correctly – for example, by always doing as they were told by their spouses or lovers. Given their role obligations, legislators should not enact legislation that they think unconstitutional. On the judicial side of the separation-of-powers balance, courts should invalidate legislation when they conclude that the legislature erred in finding a law to be constitutionally permissible.

This structure of dual responsibility for fair constitutional deliberation creates a double safeguard for constitutional rights. And, of crucial relevance, courts rely on the first safeguard of fair, reasoned legislative deliberation when they defer to legislative judgments of constitutional permissibility by applying minimal standards of judicial review, as under the rational basis test. When a majority of the legislature defaults on its obligation not to act for forbidden purposes, and especially when it violates the deliberative rights of minority communities to freedom from hostile legislative action, strict judicial scrutiny provides a needed corrective. It gives operational force to the deep premise of our constitutional order – reflected in its provision of judicial review of the correctness of legislative judgments – that it is normally far worse for "preferred" constitutional rights of the kind enforced by strict scrutiny and analogous tests to be under-enforced than over-enforced. When a majority of the legislature acts with a forbidden motive in the subjective sense, a constitutional wrong occurs that should not be allowed to stand unless resulting legislation is objectively necessary to the protection of a compelling governmental interest.

But strict scrutiny is a more appropriate corrective for forbidden legislative intentions than automatic invalidation of resulting legislation would be. Despite assertions in some cases that statutes with constitutionally forbidden motivations in the subjective sense are categorically invalid,[70] I know of no case in which the Supreme Court has ever struck down a law that it plausibly could have adjudged necessary to promote a compelling governmental interest. I would construe cases of purportedly rational basis scrutiny in which the Court has invalidated statutes reflecting a bare desire to harm a minority group in the same way:[71] Such especially egregious

---

[70]   As discussed below, those assertions have come in Establishment Clause cases. *See, e.g., McCreary County v. ACLU of Ky.*, 545 U.S. 844, 850 (2005); *Edwards v. Aguillard*, 482 U.S. 578, 585 (1987).

[71]   See, e.g., *United States v. Windsor*, 570 U.W. 744, 770 (2013); *Romer v. Evans*, aa517 U.S. 620, 634 (1996).

breaches of deliberative obligations should trigger a form of elevated scrutiny that the legislation involved in those cases transparently failed to satisfy. Although we should not adhere blindly to currently dominant legal approaches, such approaches deserve consideration as possible sources of accreted wisdom when they draw support from independent arguments.[72] Consider a hypothetical case in which a state legislature, in the past, had overwhelmingly voted for that state's statutory prohibition against murder for the forbidden purpose of promoting adherence to the Bible's Sixth Commandment. Common sense insists that courts should not invalidate a statute prohibiting murder on the ground that a majority of the legislators who voted for it did so with constitutionally impermissible subjective intentions.

Although I draw this conclusion largely based on practical, consequence-based considerations, involving a balance of relevant interests, two analogies strongly support it. The first comes from moral philosophy, in which recent work persuasively debunks the relevance of subjective motivations to determinations of whether actions are morally permissible or impermissible.[73] This work strongly supports the conclusion, though it is initially counterintuitive for many, that what is most fundamentally wrong with badly motivated legislation is that it almost invariably has bad effects – for example, by imposing unjustifiable burdens on minority groups.

For reasons that have also appealed to lawyers and judges,[74] many philosophers have long believed that an actor's subjective intentions or purpose can crucially affect the moral permissibility of her actions.[75] The doctrine of "double effect"[76] has served as an anchor for this belief. That doctrine holds, roughly, that it is always morally impermissible to act with an evil goal or purpose, but that it is sometimes permissible to take actions that aim at achieving good ends but will foreseeably have bad, unintended, and unwanted side effects. Consider a doctor who must decide whether to give a patient a dose of pain medication that the doctor anticipates would bring about the patient's death. If the doctor administered that dosage for no other reason than to kill the patient, adherents of the doctrine of double effect maintain

---

[72] *See, e.g.,* David A. Strauss, THE LIVING CONSTITUTION 40–46 (2010) (developing Burkean arguments for a common law–like approach to constitutional adjudication).

[73] *See generally* T. M. Scanlon, MORAL DIMENSIONS (2008).

[74] *See Vacco v. Quill,* 521 U.S. 793, 808 n.11 (1997) ("Just as a State may prohibit assisting suicide while permitting patients to refuse unwanted lifesaving treatment, it may permit palliative care related to that refusal, which may have the foreseen but unintended 'double effect' of hastening the patient's death.").

[75] *See, e.g.,* G. E. M. Anscombe, *Medalist's Address: Action, Intention, and 'Double Effect,'* in THE DOCTRINE OF DOUBLE EFFECT 50 (P. A. Woodard ed., 2001); Philippa Foot, *Morality, Action, and Outcome,* in THE DOCTRINE OF DOUBLE EFFECT, *supra,* at 67.

[76] According to one formulation of the doctrine of "double effect," "[t]he foreseen evil effect of a man's action is not morally imputable to him, provided that (1) the action in itself is directed immediately to some other result, (2) the evil effect is not willed either in itself or as a means to the other result, [and] (3) the permitting of the evil effect is justified by reasons of proportionate weight." John C. Ford, *The Morality of Obliteration Bombing,* in WAR AND MORALITY 15, 26 (Richard A. Wasserstrom ed., 1970). For debate about the proper formulation of the doctrine and its substantive defensibility, see generally THE DOCTRINE OF DOUBLE EFFECT, *supra* note 75.

that she would commit a clear moral wrong. But if the patient has a terminal illness, and no lesser dosage will relieve her excruciating pain, then, it is often said, the doctor acts permissibly if she administers that dosage with the intent of alleviating pain, even if she knows that the patient's death is nearly certain to result as an undesired consequence.[77] In this case, intentions – either to alleviate pain, on the one hand, or to hasten death, on the other – may appear to hold the key to moral permissibility or impermissibility.

Professor T. M. Scanlon has recently exposed fallacies in the traditional thinking.[78] Even in a case such as that of a doctor who must decide whether to administer pain medication that would likely cause a patient's death, Scanlon maintains that moral permissibility and impermissibility depend on the availability of objective reasons or justifications for a particular action – by which he means, roughly, reasons or justifications that a fair-minded observer would credit as valid – and not on the psychological intentions or motivations of a particular agent.[79] The distinction can prove highly consequential. Imagine a doctor who dislikes her terminally ill patient and must decide whether to give her medication adequate to alleviate her pain, in circumstances in which any dosage with that effect would also cause the patient's death. In considering what she ought to do, the doctor will turn up a blind alley if she inquires into her own psychological attitudes for any purpose other than to determine whether she can be objective in her assessment of morally relevant considerations.[80] If not, and if there is another doctor who can make the decision in her stead, perhaps she should ask that doctor to do so. But suppose that the attending doctor must decide quickly, due to the patient's excruciating pain, and that it would be a long time before another doctor could be consulted. Even if the attending doctor thinks or worries that her intention in prescribing the medication (if she should decide to prescribe it) might be to cause the death of a person whom she dislikes, the right question for that doctor – as for any other doctor – is whether the balance of objective reasons makes it permissible, impermissible, or possibly even mandatory for her to alleviate the patient's pain, even when doing so would likely bring about the patient's death.

Scanlon's analysis should extend to issues concerning the legal justifiability of statutes. Recall my earlier example of a legislature that prohibited murder with the psychological intent of giving effect to God's law. Or suppose that a bare majority of the legislature voted for a statute requiring the vaccination of children based on a dislike of Christian Scientists, who believe that vaccination contravenes God's

---

[77] *See* Alison McIntyre, *Doctrine of Double Effect, in* STANFORD ENCYCLOPEDIA OF PHILOSOPHY (Edward N. Zalta ed., 2014), http://plato.stanford.edu/archives/win2014/entries/double-effect/ (discussing the application of the doctrine of double effect to this example).

[78] *See* Scanlon, *supra* note 73, at 8–36.

[79] *See id.* at 37.

[80] *See id.* at 19–20, 30–31 (making a similar point through use of the example of a general and a prime minister considering whether a military bombing that would cause civilian casualties is morally permissible).

mandates. But further suppose that, in light of an infectious disease epidemic, the statute is necessary to promote a compelling governmental interest. If non-psychological facts adequately justify the statute, a court should uphold it even in this special case.[81]

In taking this position, I do not mean to imply either that legislators who act for impermissible purposes have behaved blamelessly or that they should pay no price for their deliberative malfeasance. A legislator who acts for forbidden purposes breaches her deliberative obligations under the Constitution and almost certainly exhibits a bad character as well. And she should be held to account. Criticism is warranted in the press and elsewhere. Further, voters should take the legislator's deliberative malfeasance and bad character into account in determining whether to return her to office.[82] (A doctor who delights in being able to hasten the death of a patient whom she dislikes deserves a similar response: Those who learn of her attitude and motivations would appropriately view her less favorably than before and might want to cut off professional or social relations with her as a result.) But the question for voters differs from the question of constitutional validity that courts must decide. The latter resembles – though it is of course not the same as – the issue of the moral permissibility of an action, as distinguished from one involving the quality of the actor's deliberation or character.

A second analogy, this one drawn expressly from law, comes from *Whren* v. *United States*.[83] In *Whren*, the Supreme Court held that a search and seizure may be objectively reasonable and thus permissible under the Fourth Amendment regardless of the possibly invidious motivations that led an official to perform it.[84]

Although *Whren* illustrates the conceptual distinction between judging an action or a statute and judging the motivations that led to an action or the enactment of a statute, its holding is controversial. Some believe that *Whren* removed an important deterrent to police misconduct. Taking that objection seriously, we should consider the possible desirability of automatic judicial invalidation of any statute that results from legislators' breaches of deliberative norms as a partly deterrent remedy for legislative misconduct.[85]

---

[81] *But cf.* Paul Brest, Palmer v. Thompson, *An Approach to the Problem of Unconstitutional Legislative Motive*, 1971 SUP. CT. REV. 95, 127–28 (maintaining that the argument for judicial review of legislative intentions is to ensure that the legislature did not act for impermissible purposes, not to determine independently whether the legislature reached a good ultimate decision); Susan H. Williams, *Content Discrimination and the First Amendment*, 139 U. PA. L. REV. 615, 699 (1991) ("When the court finds that the purpose of a regulation is an illegitimate one, the remedy is plain: hold the regulation invalid on its face...") .

[82] *Cf.* Caleb Nelson, *Judicial Review of Legislative Purpose*, 83 N.Y.U. L. REV. 1784, 1812 (2008) ("[A]ntebellum courts emphasized that the people themselves could police the legislature's good faith by voting faithless legislators out of office.").

[83] 517 U.S. 806 (1996).

[84] *Id.* at 813.

[85] *See generally* Daniel J. Meltzer, *Deterring Constitutional Violations by Law Enforcement Officials: Plaintiffs and Defendants as Private Attorneys General*, 88 COLUM. L. REV. 247 (1988) (discussing the judicial role in crafting remedies for constitutional violations).

When carefully considered, however, this prescription seems too draconian insofar as impermissibly motivated statutes are involved. Even if we think *Whren* wrongly decided on its facts, neither logic nor historical understandings of the Constitution dictate that all violations of deliberative norms by individual legislators, or even by a majority of legislators, always require courts to invalidate statutes for which the legislators voted.[86] Within an interest-based, consequence-sensitive framework for thinking about the definition of constitutional rights, the question becomes how to weigh the costs and benefits of alternative possible judicial responses. When analysis proceeds on these terms, the competing considerations are best accommodated by a rule under which forbidden legislative motivations will trigger strict judicial scrutiny and thus lead to a statute's invalidation unless it is narrowly tailored to a compelling governmental interest. This approach respects the significance of breaches of legislators' deliberative obligations without undue damage to objectively important governmental interests that a statute might sometimes serve, regardless of the subjective intentions or motivations of those who voted for it.

Breaches of deliberative norms by executive and judicial officials raise different issues that call for a different response. Judicial invalidations of statutes that serve compelling interests would impose distinctively large social costs that courts properly seek to avoid. By contrast, most impermissibly motivated actions by courts and executive officials should be deemed categorically invalid. The rule that forbids prosecutors to use their peremptory challenges to exclude prospective jurors on the basis of race functions as a case in point.[87]

Adoption of my proposal that impermissible legislative motions should trigger strict judicial scrutiny, rather than automatic statutory invalidation, would require revisions, but relatively modest and desirable ones, in Establishment Clause doctrine. In cases under the Establishment Clause, the Supreme Court has never formally applied strict scrutiny or acknowledged that the presence of a compelling governmental interest could save a statute that would be invalid otherwise.[88]

---

[86] Inquiries into the intent of the legislature for purposes of determining the constitutional validity of legislation have a disputed history. Nineteenth century cases frequently rebuffed calls for judicial scrutiny of legislative motivation. See Nelson, *supra* note 82, at 1812. According to a study by Professor Caleb Nelson, however, the Supreme Court, from the nineteenth century onward, has regularly invalidated statutes when a discriminatory or other constitutionally forbidden purpose manifests itself on a statute's face. See *id.* at 1790–91 & nn.17–22. Nelson maintains that the early Court limited its resistance to inquiries into legislative history. See *id.* at 1820 (asserting that in the late nineteenth century courts "still generally refused to use internal legislative history to impugn the legislature's good faith").

[87] See *Batson v. Kentucky*, 476 U.S. 79, 89 (1986).

[88] See Ira C. Lupu & Robert W. Tuttle, *The Mystery of Unanimity in* Hosanna-Tabor Evangelical Lutheran Church & School v. EEOC, 20 LEWIS & CLARK L. REV. 1265, 1276–77 (2017) ("Once a practice . . . is judicially determined to be an establishment of religion . . . [c]ompeting government interests play no part."); *see also Hosanna-Tabor Evangelical Lutheran Church & Sch. v. EEOC*, 565 U.S. 171, 196 (2012) ("The interest of society in the enforcement of employment discrimination

The Supreme Court has also said frequently in Establishment Clause cases that a constitutionally impermissible legislative intention or purpose renders a challenged statute unconstitutional.[89] In doing so, the Court has often suggested that the relevant gauge of the legislature's intent is more objective than subjective.[90] But sometimes it has held that statutes violate the Establishment Clause based on appraisals of subjective legislative intent as discerned from a statute's legislative history.[91] The first item on an agenda to reform Establishment Clause doctrine should be to recognize – as current doctrine may at least implicitly acknowledge anyway – that challenged statutes should not trigger heightened scrutiny under the Establishment Clause, regardless of legislative intentions, unless they inflict some objectively palpable harm on identified, challenging parties. Absent palpable harm, no one should have standing to sue, and a constitutionally forbidden legislative intent should neither invalidate a statute nor trigger exacting judicial review.[92] For example, if a legislature required the posting of the Declaration of Independence with the purpose of promoting religious belief – based on a hope and expectation that the Declaration's reference to "all men" being "endowed by their Creator with certain unalienable Rights" would have this effect – but its effort to communicate a religious message almost wholly failed, the statute should not be invalidated. If Establishment Clause doctrine were understood as requiring palpable harms before a forbidden legislative intent could achieve operative significance in the judicial review of legislation, it would become entirely plausible, and indeed desirable, to hold that statutes that both cause palpable harms and reflect forbidden legislative intentions should occasion strict judicial scrutiny.[93]

Objective Legislative Intent Imputed to Make Sense of Specific Statutory Language. If a law reflects forbidden legislative intentions in the objective sense that statutory textualists favor – that of being imputed without further subjective inquiries in order to make it intelligible why the legislature could plausibly have enacted particular

statutes is undoubtedly important. But so too is the interest of religious groups in choosing who will preach their beliefs, teach their faith, and carry out their mission. When a minister who has been fired sues her church alleging that her termination was discriminatory, the First Amendment has struck the balance for us. The church must be free to choose those who will guide it on its way.").

[89] *See, e.g., McCreary County* v. *ACLU of Ky.*, 545 U.S. 844, 850 (2005) (affirming that "a determination of the counties' [forbidden] purpose is a sound basis" for finding an Establishment Clause violation); *Edwards* v. *Aguillard*, 482 U.S. 578, 585 (1987) ("[A]ppellants have identified no clear secular purpose for the Louisiana Act.").

[90] *See, e.g., McCreary County*, 545 U.S. at 861–62 ("The eyes that look to purpose belong to an 'objective observer,' one who takes account of the traditional external signs that show up in the 'text, legislative history, and implementation of the statute,' or comparable official act." (quoting *Santa Fe Indep. Sch. Dist.* v. *Doe*, 530 U.S. 290, 308 (2000))); *Bd. of Educ.* v. *Mergens ex rel. Mergens*, 496 U.S. 226, 249 (1990) (plurality opinion) ("[W]hat is relevant is the legislative *purpose* of the statute, not the possibly religious *motives* of the legislators who enacted the law.").

[91] *See, e.g., Wallace* v. *Jaffree*, 472 U.S. 38, 56 (1985) (striking down a statute based on evidence of forbidden intent drawn from legislative history).

[92] *See* Richard H. Fallon, Jr., *Tiers for the Establishment Clause*, 166 U. Pa. L. Rev. 59 (2017).

[93] *See id.* at 112–17.

language – then strict scrutiny again ought to apply. The same reasoning governs as in cases of subjective legislative intent. With the legislature having breached its deliberative obligations, the statute that it enacted is suspect. Searching judicial review should apply to correct for the absence of deliberative fairness by the legislature to ensure that rights are not under-enforced as a result.

Nonetheless, the distinction between subjective and objective gauges of legislative intent introduces a new problem: What should happen if evidence of subjective intent demonstrates that a majority of the legislature had forbidden psychological motivations, but the imputation of such motivations is not necessary to explain why a typical or imaginable legislature might have enacted a challenged statute? Consider once again the hypothetical case that I introduced at the beginning of this chapter, in which the town council of a predominantly white, suburban community adopts a policy requiring its police officers and firefighters to reside within the town. One need not impute bad motivations to explain how or why a rational council member might have voted for the policy. It is rationally related to legitimate interests, including that of having public safety personnel readily available for emergency duty. Under the kind of objective conception of legislative intent that is imputed to make legislative language rationally intelligible, the statute would not trigger strict scrutiny. Nonetheless, imagine that persuasive evidence reveals that a majority of the council voted for it with a constitutionally forbidden subjective intent to minimize the number of qualified minority applicants.

In this case of divergence between subjective and objective gauges of legislative intent, strict judicial scrutiny ought to apply based on the subjective conception, even if another legislative body might imaginably have adopted an identical statute for non-discriminatory reasons. Although the plurality opinion in the *Mergens* case – involving the question whether a statute that forbade school discrimination against religious groups violated the Establishment Clause – ruled that a permissible objective purpose renders forbidden subjective motivations irrelevant, it would be a mistake to make too much of *Mergens*. As explained above, Establishment Clause doctrine is confused and anomalous in many ways and ought to be substantially reformed. Even in the absence of sweeping changes, the Court has not given the reasoning of *Mergens* general applicability, nor should it do so.

As a doctrinal matter, the leading Supreme Court case on the significance of racially discriminatory intent, *Washington v. Davis*,[94] clearly contemplates that proof of discriminatory intent in the subjective sense should lead to strict judicial scrutiny of statutes that are minimally rational on their faces. Inquiries into subjective legislative intentions of the kind that the Court anticipated in *Washington v. Davis* would have little point if a finding of forbidden intentions could not at least trigger strict judicial scrutiny. As a normative matter, the argument that I have pressed repeatedly holds once more: Widespread breaches of legislators' deliberative

[94]　426 U.S. 229, 240 (1976).

obligations – and the deliberative rights that are their correlatives – should provoke skeptical, not deferential, judicial review. In order to give adequate protection to the interests of minority communities under the Equal Protection Clause, courts should apply strict judicial scrutiny in order to compensate for legislators' default on their deliberative obligations.

Categorically Ascribed Objective Intent. The conception of objective legislative intent that relies on categorical rules to mark statutes as suspect based on their content or effects – for example, in regulating speech on the basis of content or establishing race-based classifications – functions for all practical purposes as a substantive test of constitutional validity. Although Justice Kagan has described objective conceptions of this kind as "proxies" for inquiries into forbidden intentions,[95] we would do better simply to say, with no practical redirection of legal analysis, that laws exhibiting designated characteristics are either per se invalid or, more typically, categorically trigger heightened judicial review. As a perceptive commentator observed in critiquing the Court's now-abandoned jurisprudence forbidding some but not all "irrebuttable presumptions,"[96] "[a]ny rule that expressly and conclusively presumes one fact from another may be recast as a direct rule of substantive law."[97] Applying that insight, we should recognize that if a settled doctrinal rule subjects race-based classifications or content-based regulations to strict judicial scrutiny, the content of that triggering right does not depend on the motivations of those who enacted a particular, challenged statute.

Some may resist this suggestion by protesting that tests embodying "objective" conceptions of legislative intent typically apply to, and are designed to identify, situations in which a majority of the legislature likely had forbidden psychological motivations.[98] As a practical matter, however, it takes no reference to motivations to produce the conclusion that those who hold this view want to reach: Statutes that regulate speech on the basis of content trigger strict scrutiny, as do statutes that classify on the basis of race. Characterizing the application of strict scrutiny in these cases as predicated on findings of "objective" intent is, accordingly, unnecessary. As a conceptual matter, moreover, we should not confuse the considerations that underlie a rule, and justify it, with the rule's content. And the content of rules under

---

[95] See Kagan, *supra* note 11, at 414, 441.

[96] A number of Supreme Court decisions from the 1960s and 1970s selectively condemned certain legislative classifications on the ground that they embodied "irrebuttable presumptions" forbidden by the Due Process and Equal Protection Clauses. *See, e.g., Vlandis v. Kline,* 412 U.S. 441, 453 (1973) (invalidating an irrebuttable presumption that students who applied to a state university while residing in another state remained residents of that other state, and thus were ineligible for in-state tuition, for so long as they remained students).

[97] John M. Phillips, Note, *Irrebuttable Presumptions: An Illusory Analysis,* 27 STAN. L. REV. 449, 462 (1975).

[98] *Cf. Johnson v. California,* 543 U.S. 499, 505 (2005) (explaining that race-based classifications are subject to strict judicial scrutiny because "[r]acial classifications raise special fears that they are motivated by an invidious purpose").

which statutes that regulate speech on the basis of content or classify on the basis of race trigger strict judicial scrutiny does not refer to forbidden motivations.

Beneath this conclusion lies a more fundamental consideration. Having recognized that rights protect interests, we should ask what interests constitutional provisions such as the Free Speech and Equal Protection Clauses exist to protect. The interests of most ultimate concern are not ones in avoiding badly motivated legislative action. To take one example, we cherish the Free Speech Clause because it protects interests in speaking and in having access to information and ideas. To offer another, the ultimate concern of the Equal Protection Clause is providing assurance against governmental action that unfairly disadvantages minority groups. Bad motives on the part of the legislature may furnish a proxy for the deep concern: We think that legislation should be deemed suspect, because likely to undervalue interests in free exchange of ideas or minority interests in receiving benefits or avoiding burdens, when legislators enacted it with constitutionally forbidden intentions.[99] But motive-based inquiry and deliberative rights are means to ultimate constitutional ends, best measured in terms of substantive effects on interests. Accordingly, treating measures of irrebuttably inferred "objective intent" as substantive constitutional rules does not overlook the deep reason for us to have relevant triggering rights in the first place – as those who emphasize the likelihood of impermissible legislative motivations sometimes maintain. Instead, a substantive focus more nearly captures the most fundamental underlying concerns, involving protection of interests in free speech and non-subordination based on race or other morally irrelevant characteristics.

Finally, interests in descriptive accuracy require recognition that triggering rights based on categorical factors enforce substantive rather than deliberative rights. The clearest example may come from the Supreme Court's occasional assertions that it applies strict scrutiny in affirmative action cases as a device to root out forbidden legislative motivations. If affirmative action appropriately attracts strict judicial scrutiny, it is surely because substantive constitutional norms so dictate, not because politically accountable bodies that adopt affirmative action policies likely do so based on prejudice against or a desire to harm whites.[100]

As the Court frankly recognized in *Adarand Constructors, Inc.* v. *Pena*, the only sensible purpose that strict scrutiny may serve in affirmative action cases is not to "smoke out" illicit motives, but to determine whether race-based classifications are objectively justified.[101] And the answer to that question can emerge only through a conception of strict judicial scrutiny that requires courts to appraise competing

---

[99]   *Cf.* Kagan, *supra* note 11, at 509–10 (exploring the possibility that First Amendment rules might "serv[e] as 'double proxies' – first, and more proximately, for an inquiry into a certain kind of motive; then, and more remotely, for an inquiry into a certain kind of effect" on constitutionally protected values or interests).

[100] Ely, *supra* note 13, at 170–72.

[101] 515 U.S. 200, 229–30 (1995).

individual and governmental interests and to weigh them against each other. Imputations of forbidden legislative intent, whether on a categorical basis or otherwise, have no useful role in shaping the appropriate judicial inquiry, regardless of whether strict scrutiny or some other test should apply.

INTENT-BASED INQUIRIES AS AN ALTERNATIVE TO THE WEIGHT OF INTERESTS

A discussion of the role of constitutionally forbidden legislative intent would not be complete without a head-on confrontation of suggestions that the Supreme Court should forsake all forms of interest-balancing in defining and enforcing constitutional rights and that it should instead rely more heavily if not exclusively on intent-based doctrines. The most celebrated proponent of this view was John Hart Ely, whose book *Democracy and Distrust: A Theory of Judicial Review* ranks as one of the greatest works of constitutional theory of the last fifty years. According to Ely, the Constitution, read as a whole, creates a predominantly democratic and majoritarian structure of government; the rights with which it is, and must be, most concerned are those relating to failures of the democratic process, typically involving constitutionally forbidden legislative intentions. From this democratic and process-based account, Ely derives the principle that the courts should rely on relatively open-ended provisions of the Constitution to invalidate legislation only where necessary either to provide fair and equal access to the political process or to correct for process failures, paradigmatically involving forbidden legislative attitudes or intentions.[102] In Ely's view, if judicially enforceable equal protection norms bar discrimination against African-Americans, women, or religious minorities, for example, it is only because legislation disadvantaging such groups likely reflects forbidden prejudice.[103] In his formulation, the judicial branch should find violations of constitutional rights under provisions including the Free Speech, Equal Protection and Due Process Clauses only when:

> (1) the ins are choking off the channels of political change to ensure that they will stay in and the outs will stay out, or (2) though no one is actually denied a voice or a vote, representatives beholden to an effective majority are systematically disadvantaging some minority out of simple hostility or a prejudiced refusal to recognize commonalities of interest, and thereby denying that minority the protection afforded other groups by a representative system.[104]

Appraisal of Ely's proposal should begin with a point that he ultimately conceded: His theory cannot explain a good deal of modern constitutional doctrine. As Ely acknowledged, modern doctrine reflects substantive judgments about which groups

---

[102] Ely, *supra* note 13, at 102–03.
[103] *See id.* at 146, 152–59.
[104] *See id.* at 102–03.

and activities deserve protection under a diverse list of constitutional provisions.[105] To cite one plain example, modern doctrine treats all legislation that discriminates on the basis of gender as quasi-suspect,[106] even though neither men nor women are plausibly categorized as a "discrete and insular" minority – and thus presumptively incapable of protecting their interests in the political process – within the framework of the *Caroline Products* footnote[107] that Ely sought to defend. Although counseling judicial deference to legislative judgment in most cases, that famous footnote recognized that a different approach might be appropriate with regard to "statutes directed at particular religious, or national, or racial minorities."[108] Women constitute an actual majority of the population. Men have historically dominated the political process.[109] Accordingly, it is most improbable that statutes disadvantaging men result from violations of deliberative norms that forbid legislators to act with hostile intentions toward men as a group. Similarly, the Establishment Clause forbids more than improper purposes: A tax levied to support a national church would be invalid even if all members of the enacting Congress voted for the tax with the subjective purpose, not of promoting religion, but of fostering a political sense of national community. To cite even a less controversial example, it seems untenable to maintain that the First Amendment's only protections against infringements of the freedom of speech should need to rest on judgments that "the ins are [deliberately] choking off the channels of political change."

If we treat Ely's argument as more exclusively normative, it again falls short. To begin with, it seems clear that courts could not apply Ely's theory without making the kind of normative, substantially interest-balancing judgments that he thought they should avoid. When it comes to identifying discrete and insular minorities, one person's "prejudice" – which the *Caroline Products* footnote invoked to define the problem in the legislative process that courts should correct for – is another's moral judgment.[110] Disputes about the constitutionality of limiting marriage to one man and one woman vividly illustrate the point. Some viewed statutes that barred same-sex marriage as reflecting a hostile intention to demean gay couples.[111] Others saw such laws as non-invidious exercises in rational traditionalism.[112]

---

[105] See John Hart Ely, *Another Such Victory: Constitutional Theory and Practice in a World Where Courts Are No Different from Legislatures*, 77 VA. L. REV. 833 (1991).

[106] See, e.g., *Miss. Univ. for Women v. Hogan*, 458 U.S. 718, 730 (1982).

[107] *United States v. Carolene Prods. Co.*, 304 U.S. 144, 152 n.4 (1938).

[108] *Id.* at 153 n.4 (citations omitted).

[109] See Ely, *supra* note 13, at 164.

[110] See, e.g., Laurence H. Tribe, *The Puzzling Persistence of Process-Based Constitutional Theories*, 89 YALE L.J. 1063, 1072–77 (1980) ("It all sounds pretty good – until we ask how we are supposed to distinguish such 'prejudice' from principled, if 'wrong,' disapproval." *Id.* at 1073.).

[111] See *Obergefell v. Hodges*, 135 S. Ct. 2584, 2602 (2015) (concluding that excluding same-sex couples from state-recognized marriages "demeans or stigmatizes those whose . . . liberty is then denied").

[112] See *id.* at 2641–42 (Alito, J., dissenting).

Even in matters involving the design of the political process, fairness judgments are inescapable.[113] The Supreme Court made such a determination in articulating the now largely uncontroversial one person, one vote requirement. Challenges to race-based and partisan gerrymandering pose more controverted issues about fairness in the distribution of political power. It also seems mistaken at a deeper level to assume that forbidden legislative intentions could generate all of the triggering rights that most of us think ought to exist under the Constitution. These range from First Amendment rights that have nothing to do with politics or political insiders choking off the channels of political change to rights of sexual autonomy.[114]

Finally, and in some ways most curiously, Ely offered only a thin, unconvincing account of how strict scrutiny operates. He appears to have thought that it could function solely as a device to expose forbidden intent: Absent proof of close tailoring to a compelling governmental interest, we should assume that statutes that classify on the basis of race or that restrict political speech have forbidden purposes. As we have seen, however, this suggestion will not stand up. Even after triggering rights are identified, determining whether they are outweighed by competing governmental interests often requires a serious, sometimes difficult comparison of individual interests with potentially countervailing governmental interests.

I would offer a similar response to other commentators who have sought to define constitutional rights principally as shields against governmental action based on forbidden reasons. Some have interpreted Ronald Dworkin, the famous champion of rights as trumps, as holding a view of the latter kind[115] – an interpretation that I accept here for sake of argument.[116] On this interpretation, Dworkin did not view rights in the terms that I have advanced, as protections afforded to individual interests against the claims of competing governmental interests, but rather as "constraints on the kinds of reasons that government may legitimately act upon."[117] Professor Richard Pildes has offered a similar but more modest thesis: that many, though not all, constitutional rights should be understood as involving

---

[113] *See, e.g., id.* at 1067–72 ("Even the Constitution's most procedural prescriptions cannot be adequately understood, much less applied, in the absence of a developed theory of fundamental rights that are secured to persons against the state." *Id.* at 1067.).

[114] *Cf. id.* at 1065–67 (outlining some of the Constitution's "openly substantive commitments," including commitments to private property, religious freedom, and anti-slavery).

[115] *See* Jeremy Waldron, *Pildes on Dworkin's Theory of Rights*, 29 J. LEGAL STUD. 301 (2000); *see also* Paul Yowell, *A Critical Examination of Dworkin's Theory of Rights*, 52 AM. J. JURISPRUDENCE 93, 130 (2007) ("The persistent strategy of Dworkin's work on rights has been to locate the essence of rights not in individuals and their needs but in the exclusion of arguments or political justifications opposed to equality.").

[116] Others read Dworkin differently. *See* Richard H. Pildes, *Dworkin's Two Conceptions of Rights*, 29 J. LEGAL STUD. 309 (2000).

[117] Waldron, *supra* note 115, at 301–02.

"qualitative" rather than balancing judgments that mark some kinds of reasons as constitutionally "excluded" or categorically inadequate in some contexts.[118]

In order to consider whether rights are best viewed as constraints on reasons (independent of any sort of balancing judgment about the strength of competing interests), we need to ask what "reasons" are. There may be a crucial ambiguity here. Reasons might be either intentions or motivations, on the one hand, or objective justifications that could exist regardless of an actor's motives, on the other hand. In an example that I used earlier, a doctor might prescribe a potentially lethal dosage of pain medication with the subjective intention or motive of bringing about the death of a disliked patient, but the act of prescribing that dosage might be supported by good reasons in an objective sense if no lesser quantity would suffice to relieve the excruciating pain of a terminal patient who demanded relief from the agony.

Any theory that exclusively conceptualizes rights as constraints on reasons in the psychological sense will be vulnerable to the same criticisms as John Ely's. On the one hand, although subjectively forbidden legislative motivations ordinarily do and should trigger strict judicial scrutiny, not all triggering rights either are or should be of this stripe. The Constitution should protect us against more than bad intentions. Good intentions cannot justify objectively unwarranted infringements of constitutionally protected interests. On the other hand, bad legislative motivations should not lead to the invalidation of legislation that could survive strict judicial scrutiny. In an example that I have used before, a law against murder should not be invalidated even if it could be proved that majority of legislators voted for it in order to do God's will.

Overall, inquiries into legislative intent have an important role in helping to define triggering rights. But they cannot eradicate the kind of interest-based definition of triggering rights or the interest-based balancing that is needed to identify ultimate rights pursuant to constitutional tests such as strict judicial scrutiny.

If we instead interpret Dworkin or other theorists as equating rights with constraints against reasons in an objective rather than a psychological sense, the resulting view of rights would again be too narrow. Constitutional rights do not just protect us against governmental actions that are not supported by any creditable, non-excluded reason at all. Rights also confer protections against governmental actions for which the supporting reasons, though not categorically forbidden, are nevertheless not strong enough under the circumstances when compared with the individual interests at stake.[119] Moreover, subjective motivations should sometimes

[118] *See* Richard H. Pildes, *Avoiding Balancing: The Role of Exclusionary Reasons in Constitutional Law*, 45 HASTINGS L.J. 711 (1994). Professor Pildes adapts the vocabulary of "excluded" or "exclusionary" reasons from Joseph Raz, PRACTICAL REASON AND NORMS 190 (2d ed. 1990) ("The very point of exclusionary reasons is to bypass issues of weight by excluding consideration of the excluded reasons regardless of weight.").

[119] Again, I do not mean to be engaging in exegesis of Dworkin's actual view. Some of his writing can be read as expressing a position close to my own. *See, e.g.*, Ronald Dworkin, JUSTICE FOR HEDGEHOGS 329

matter: Breaches of deliberative obligations should trigger strict scrutiny or comparably searching tests, even if interest-balancing must then ensue to determine whether an ultimate right has been violated. Many applications of strict judicial scrutiny rest on this premise.

In rejecting theories that conceptualize rights as constraints on reasons, rather than direct protections of interests pursuant to balancing judgments, we should not ignore one of the important attractions of the former approach. If persuasively defended, it would absolve the courts of any need to engage in interest-balancing that either overlaps with legislative functions or otherwise has a quasi-legislative aspect. The attraction of this view inheres largely in its promise to assign the judiciary a wholly distinctive function. But our existing constitutional practice, as viewed through the lenses of strict judicial scrutiny and most other judge-crafted tests of constitutional validity, requires interest-balancing.

CONSTITUTIONALLY FORBIDDEN INTENTIONS OF OFFICIALS OTHER THAN LEGISLATORS

Much of the analysis that I have offered in considering the constitutional pertinence of legislative intentions carries over to cases in which single officials – such as Presidents, cabinet heads, and law enforcement officers – act with constitutionally forbidden purposes when promulgating regulations or other general policies that carry the authority of law. In adjudicating challenges to policy decisions with broad application, courts should balance competing private and public interests in much the same way that they would in litigation testing the constitutionality of a statute. Revealingly, the strict scrutiny formula fits cases in the former category as easily as those in the latter. Accordingly, the Court has almost invariably assumed that intentions and motivations that would be constitutionally forbidden as bases for legislative action would be equally impermissible in the context of executive action in propounding rules and regulations. In cases involving discrimination based on race or religion, for example, strict judicial scrutiny should therefore apply, and the Supreme Court has customarily applied it.

In *Trump v. Hawaii*,[120] a bitterly divided Supreme Court confronted a presidential proclamation restricting entry into the United States by nationals of eight other nations, six of which are predominantly Muslim. Based on a series of statements first by presidential candidate and then by President Donald Trump, challengers alleged that the exclusion policy reflected a discriminatory animus toward Muslims and therefore violated the Establishment Clause. In an opinion by Chief Justice Roberts, the Court, dividing by five to four, began its substantive analysis by "assum[ing]," without actually holding, that it could "look behind the face of the Proclamation" to

(2011) (embracing the view that "political rights are trumps over otherwise adequate justifications for political action").

[120]   138 S. Ct. 2392 (2018).

consider evidence of possibly discriminatory intent "to the extent of applying rational basis review."[121] (The Court had previously quoted a prior decision as having held that "when the Executive exercises" a statutorily delegated power to exclude a foreign national from the United States "on the basis of a facially legitimate and bona fide reason, the courts will neither look behind the exercise of that discretion [for possible impermissible motives], nor test it by balancing its justification against" competing interests.[122]) But the Chief Justice then immediately stated that the Court must uphold the challenged policy "so long as it can reasonably be understood to result from a justification independent of unconstitutional grounds."[123] Applying that relaxed standard, the Court found "legitimate purposes" for the challenged Proclamation – which did not explicitly refer to religion at all – in "preventing entry of nationals who cannot be adequately vetted" in their countries of origin "and inducing other nations to improve their practices."[124] Despite the high-profile character of *Trump* v. *Hawaii* and the passions that it aroused, the decision was narrowly written, emphasizing that "the admission and exclusion of foreign nationals is a 'fundamental sovereign attribute exercised by the Government's political departments largely immune from judicial control,'"[125] especially in "cases that overlap with 'the area of national security.'"[126] It seems unlikely to affect judicial examination of executive motives or the level of scrutiny that forbidden intentions trigger in other contexts.

If we turn our gaze from officials' motivations when issuing regulations and establishing policies to more individualized and targeted actions – for example, those of a police officer in determining whether to conduct a specific search or a prosecutor in using a peremptory challenge to exclude a particular potential juror – the balance of considerations changes. Among other pertinent concerns, strict scrutiny was designed as a test of legislation, not isolated official acts. There is no statute to subject to necessary-to-a-compelling-interest review. Accordingly, as we saw in Chapter 4, a different set of tests has emerged for application to cases involving individually targeted misconduct by executive officials (even though strict scrutiny is occasionally used). Many seek to remove the courts from oversight of the minutia of executive operations, even though constitutional guarantees may be implicated. Some are highly deferential, but others are categorical. In some cases, moreover, judges will condemn impermissibly motivated official action as constitutionally invalid, and provide remedies for it, with no further balancing inquiry. As we have seen, a convicted criminal defendant who can prove that a prosecutor used her peremptory challenges to exclude potential jurors on racially discriminatory

---

[121] *Id.* at 2420.
[122] *Id.* at 2419 (quoting *Kleindeinst* v. *Mandel*, 408 U.S. 753, 770 (1972)).
[123] *Id.* at 2420.
[124] *Id.* at 2421.
[125] *Id.* at 2418 (quoting *Fiallo* v. *Bell*, 430 U.S. 787, 792 (1977).
[126] *Id.* at 2419 (quoting *Kerry* v. *Din*, 135 S. Ct. 2128, 2140 (2015) (Kennedy, J., concurring in the judgment).

grounds is categorically entitled to have her conviction vacated and her case retried.[127] Without need for resort to strict scrutiny or any comparable test, both fairness-based and deterrent considerations support this result.

In cases not involving challenges to regulations and generally applicable policies, it is also plausible that courts should inquire into executive officials' motives in some contexts or for some purposes but not others. Notwithstanding the categorical rule against prosecutors' racially discriminatory use of peremptory challenges, *Whren v. United States* determined that inquiries into the motivations of individual officers in conducting searches and seizures would produce too much litigation focused on matters too difficult for courts to plumb successfully. However one judges *Whren's* conclusion, whether officials' subjective motivations should determine the reasonableness and thus the validity of searches under the Fourth Amendment is a different question from that which the Court confronted in *Batson* – and even more different from the question whether a widely applicable executive-branch policy that was put in place for racially or religiously discriminatory reasons should trigger strict judicial scrutiny.

One more point is necessary to round out the picture. Although proving forbidden intentions by a single executive official presents no conceptual problems, the practical difficulties can often prove formidable. And sometimes – when the social costs of remedies would be high – the Supreme Court responds by making the existence of forbidden intentions almost impossible to prove. An example involves racially discriminatory intent in policing. In the iconic 1886 case of *Yick Wo v. Hopkins*,[128] the Court held that racially discriminatory law enforcement practices violate the Equal Protection Clause. The city of San Francisco made it unlawful to operate a laundry in a wooden building without a permit. City officials routinely granted permits to Caucasian applicants, but denied them to virtually all Chinese applicants, including Yick Wo, who was fined for running a laundry without a license. On appeal, the Supreme Court ruled that the discrimination was unconstitutional and, accordingly, that Yick Wo could not be penalized.

The constitutional principle that the Supreme Court announced in *Yick Wo* seems unquestionably correct. But the Court, understandably, has not wanted to open the way for every criminal defendant who is a member of a racial minority group to assert claims of racially discriminatory prosecution – in part because it knows how very frequent such claims might be in a nation in which the arrest and prosecution rates for African-Americans, in particular, vastly outstrip those for whites. Shying from the consequences of releasing admitted lawbreakers onto the streets because others were not targeted for prosecution as well, the Court has imposed practically insuperable burdens on defendants who seek to prove discriminatory prosecution. To succeed with such a claim, a defendant must demonstrate

[127] See *Batson* v. *Kentucky*, 476 U.S. 79, 89 (1986) (holding that the Equal Protection Clause forbids prosecutors' use of peremptory challenges to exclude potential jurors based on their race).
[128] 118 356 (1886).

not only that members of a particular race are prosecuted with disproportionate frequency, but also that governmental officials deliberately fail to enforce the law against members of a preferred race or races who engage in similar conduct.[129] Under that exacting standard, the Supreme Court has never upheld another claim of racially discriminatory prosecution since deciding *Yick Wo* in 1886.[130]

CONCLUSION

Although the argument of this chapter has been intricate, its two main themes are straightforward and easily summarized. First, forbidden legislative intentions matter to constitutional law. Officials have deliberative obligations. Citizens have deliberative rights that officials violate if, for example, they seek to disadvantage racial or religious minorities or restrict speech by those with whom they disagree. Insofar as challenges to the validity of legislation are concerned, however, deliberative rights are generally triggering rights, which lead to the application of strict judicial scrutiny, rather than ultimate rights. There are probably very few cases in which a statute that was enacted for forbidden reasons would survive strict scrutiny. But even the theoretical possibility reveals the extent to which the existence of ultimate rights depends on interest-based calculations.

Second, although forbidden legislative and executive motivations play a role in determining the constitutional rights that we have, motivations are not all that matters. The notion that courts could restrict their function to assessing whether the legislature (or executive officials) acted with constitutionally impermissible intentions is chimerical. Rights reflect interests. Judicial determinations about constitutional rights recurrently turn on appraisals of competing interests, sometimes in the application of a test such as strict scrutiny, but sometimes earlier. For example, the Supreme Court weighs competing interests at the triggering-rights stage when it determines that forbidden legislative intentions should provoke strict scrutiny, that discriminatory uses of peremptory challenges violate a categorical prohibition, and that the subjective motivations of cops on the beat in conducting objectively reasonable searches should not be subject to further judicial scrutiny at all.

---

[129]   *See United States v. Armstrong*, 517 U.S. 456 (1996).
[130]   *See* David Cole, No Equal Justice 159 (1999).

6

Rights, Remedies, and Justiciability

Just as the Supreme Court considers competing interests when defining substantive rights, it balances individual interests against governmental or social interests when crafting the rules that govern when people can sue in federal court and in determining the remedies to which they are entitled. In ways that are little understood – even by lawyers and judges – rights, jurisdictional doctrines that specify who can sue, and remedies for constitutional violations form a package. Rights would possess much less value than they have now if no court had jurisdiction (or lawful authority) to enforce them. Nor would rights be worth much in the absence of effective remedies to compensate for past violations and forestall future breaches. With the practical significance of rights being so interconnected with judicial jurisdiction and available remedies, it should occasion no surprise that the same kinds of interests that shape the definition of rights also influence decisions about when parties can sue in court to enforce their rights and about which remedies, if any, courts should award. Yet the interconnections among substantive definitions of rights, jurisdictional doctrines, and the law of remedies – and the penetration of interest-based analysis into the latter two domains – are often overlooked.

Lawyers typically think of constitutional rights litigation as unfolding in three parts. One, the middle part, involves constitutional adjudication on the merits. This is the only aspect about which much of the public has any inkling. But before a court can enter a ruling on the merits of a constitutional challenge, it must make a determination of "justiciability," centrally including whether the party bringing the suit has "standing." If someone claiming a right has not suffered an "injury in fact" and satisfied some other technical requirements, then she has no standing, and a court must dismiss the suit without pronouncing on the constitutional issues that a challenger wants to raise. The third stage is reached only if the party claiming that her constitutional rights have been violated wins on the merits. At the third stage, the court awards an appropriate remedy. Potential remedies would be an injunction ordering a cessation of unconstitutional conduct that harms the challenger, money damages, or, in criminal cases, dismissal of an indictment or release from jail.

Although the Supreme Court often takes governmental interests into account in determining which claims of rights to uphold, the Court sometimes elects to accommodate governmental interests not by defining rights narrowly, but instead through doctrines that limit remedies or restrict standing. Accordingly, it is at least a practical and quite possibly a conceptual error to think we can understand constitutional rights without locating them, and the processes by which they are defined, as aspects of a triadic relationship that also includes remedial and standing rules.

The relationships among constitutional rights, standing, and judicial remedies to enforce rights are best described by an Equilibration Thesis: Although rights, remedies, and standing can be distinguished analytically, courts frequently confront the merits, remedial, and justiciability issues that a lawsuit presents as an integrated unit. When faced with a situation in which they believe that the values underlying constitutional rights are not adequately realized in practice, courts might take any or all of the steps of expanding rights, relaxing barriers to particular types of remedies, or broadening standing. Conversely, when courts regard the social costs of the existing bundle of rights, remedies, and standing rules as excessive, they may consider calibrating adjustments to any part of the package. Insofar as theorizing about constitutional rights ignores the interconnections among rights, standing, and remedies, it has misunderstood its subject matter.[1]

LIMITATIONS OF REMEDIES TO REDUCE THE SOCIAL COSTS OF RIGHTS

The most famous, and probably most notorious, example of the Supreme Court's restriction of judicial remedies as a means of reducing the social costs (or harm to governmental interests) that a substantive right would entail otherwise comes from *Brown* v. *Board of Education*.[2] After holding that single-race schools violate the

---

[1] In a pioneering article exploring the interconnections among rights, standing, and remedies, Professor Daryl Levinson coined the phrase "remedial deterrence" to describe situations in which the Supreme Court defines rights narrowly in order to avoid the remedial implications of a broader definition. *See* Daryl J. Levinson, *Rights Essentialism and Remedial Equilibration*, 99 COLUM. L. REV. 857, 884–85 (1999). But Levinson is unclear regarding what he means by the term "remedial." Among his central examples is *Washington* v. *Davis*, 426 U.S. 229 (1976), discussed in Chapter 3, in which the Court spoke candidly about what it regarded as the disturbing implications of finding that a statute's racially disparate impact triggered strict judicial scrutiny in the absence of racially discriminatory intent. In my view, Levinson's analysis of *Washington* v. *Davis* is substantially correct. Indeed, it substantially overlaps with the analysis that I advanced in Chapter 3. But his use of the term "remedial deterrence" seems to me to be misleading. As used in legal parlance, the term "remedy" typically refers to the specific types of relief for a constitutional violation that a court can award, and among which it sometimes must choose, including damages, injunctions, writs of mandamus, declaratory judgments, and reversals of criminal convictions. As I hope will become clear, there are benefits to reserving the terms "remedy" and "remedial" to forms of relief that are available, if any are, to enforce a right after the right has been defined. I therefore use the terms in this narrower, more precise sense than Professor Levinson does.

[2] 347 U.S. 483 (1954).

Constitution in a ruling known to lawyers as *Brown I*, the Court scheduled a further argument on what the remedy for continuing violations ought to be. A separate decision in *Brown II*, which came roughly a year later, held that desegregation need not occur immediately, but only with "all deliberate speed."[3] The practical effect was that children attending segregated public schools had a constitutional right to desegregated schooling but no remedy to enforce that right, at least in the short term.

In the *Brown* case, Court papers released decades later reveal that rights and remedies were expressly linked in the minds of the Justices. Some would not have gone along with the desegregation mandate in *Brown I* without assurances that southern schools would not be forced to desegregate immediately.[4] From the perspective of the Justices who took that position, the costs of the right-remedy package would have been too high otherwise: A demand for immediate desegregation would have risked too much anger among too many southern whites, too much resistance to and even defiance of judicial orders, and too much violence. In light of subsequent history, it is doubtful whether the Court's decision to postpone anti-segregation injunctions achieved the beneficial results that some of the Justices anticipated.[5] But there is always a risk of mistake when the Justices base their substantive and remedial rulings on empirical predictions, as they do with great frequency.[6]

Brown's decision to frame remedial entitlements with social costs in mind is notorious, not merely famous, because it appeared to condone bigoted resistance to judicial authority. But the Court has held throughout its history that the issuance of injunctions that order parties to alter an ongoing course of conduct is a matter of "equitable discretion," and that courts in exercising their equitable discretion should balance private against public interests.[7] In that balance, the social costs that otherwise would flow from the recognition of a right can be ameliorated – and the practical value of the formally recognized right correspondingly diminished – by a refusal to grant injunctive relief.

---

[3]   349 U.S. 294, 301 (1955).

[4]   *See, e.g.*, Michael J. Klarman, FROM JIM CROW TO CIVIL RIGHTS: THE SUPREME COURT AND THE STRUGGLE FOR RACIAL EQUALITY 313–14 (2004).

[5]   *See, e.g., id.* at 320.

[6]   See, e.g., Richard H. Fallon, JR., IMPLEMENTING THE CONSTITUTION 31 (2001); see also Dan M. Kahan, *The Supreme Court, 2010 Term – Foreword: Neutral Principles, Motivated Cognition, and Some Problems for Constitutional Law*, 125 HARV. L. REV. 1, 39–40 (2011) (explaining that it is "commonplace for courts to assess 'predictive judgments' based in part on empirical data," id. at 39, but noting that this makes the courts susceptible to errors caused by motivated reasoning).

[7]   *See, e.g., Winter v. Nat. Res. Def. Council, Inc.*, 555 U.S. 7, 24 (2008) (explaining the four-part test for a preliminary injunction and emphasizing that courts must consider the effect on each party and give "particular regard for the public consequences in employing the extraordinary remedy" (quoting *Weinberger v. Romero-Barcelo*, 456 U.S. 305, 312 (1982))); *eBay Inc. v. MercExchange, L.L.C.*, 547 U.S. 388, 391 (2006) (explaining the same for permanent injunctions); Samuel L. Bray, *The Supreme Court and the New Equity*, 68 VAND. L. REV. 997, 1039–41 (2015) (arguing that discretion is a "theme in the Court's [recent] treatment of equitable principles," *id.* at 1039, and noting that this view is "deeply rooted in the tradition of equity," *id.* at 1040).

In considering the wisdom of allowing courts to adjust remedies so that they fail to protect constitutional rights fully and immediately, we should keep in mind that courts can, and sometimes do, specify the remedies for rights violations with the aim of ensuring the broadest feasible definition and enforcement of rights over the long term. In *Brown*, for example, the Supreme Court appears to have thought that school desegregation would proceed more smoothly and successfully in the long run if courts did not fan the flames of Southern resistance by insisting that it must occur immediately.

A different kind of example of the Court's limiting remedies with the goal of enhancing rights comes from *Miranda v. Arizona*. There, the Court decided to make both its ruling and the exclusionary remedy that it established substantially non-retroactive: Neither applied to cases involving custodial confessions in which the trial had already been completed, or had even commenced, at the time of the *Miranda* decision.[8] If the Court could not have withheld judicial relief from those criminal suspects who confessed without *Miranda* warnings and whose trials began before *Miranda* was decided, the social costs of releasing many confessed, violent criminals would almost certainly have made promulgation of the *Miranda* rule a practical impossibility. Perhaps partly to impose a restraint on the recognition of new rights of criminal defendants, the Supreme Court has subsequently held that freshly recognized rights must apply to all defendants whose convictions have not yet become final at the time of a pathbreaking decision.[9] But the Court has not retreated from the historic rule that the issuance of injunctive remedies should depend on a balancing of private and public interests.

The Supreme Court has adopted a similar strategy of selectively withholding remedies even for long-settled rights in cases involving constitutionally mandated procedures in criminal cases. The Court routinely denies relief in "harmless error" cases in which trial courts' erroneous rulings on constitutional issues almost certainly had no effect on the outcome.[10] The Court has also developed a number of exceptions to the exclusionary rule, which ordinarily mandates that the fruits of unconstitutional police searches cannot be introduced into evidence. One exception allows admission of evidence when police officers act in "good faith" reliance on a search warrant that a judge or magistrate should not have issued under the

---

[8]   *Johnson v. New Jersey*, 384 U.S. 719, 732 (1966).

[9]   *See Griffith v. Kentucky*, 479 U.S. 314, 328 (1987).

[10] On the origins and defensibility of the harmless error rule, see Daniel J. Meltzer, *Harmless Error and Constitutional Remedies*, 61 U. Chi. L. Rev. 1 (1994); *see also United States v. Gonzalez-Lopez*, 548 U.S. 140, 150 (2006) (holding that the erroneous deprivation of a defendant's choice of counsel constitutes a "structural defect" to which harmless error analysis does not apply); *Arizona v. Fulminante*, 499 U.S. 279, 280 (1991) (holding that harmless error analysis is required in instances of erroneously admitted coerced confessions, a class of so-called "trial errors" which are to be distinguished from the more narrow class of "structural errors" which "defy analysis by harmless-error standards"). For a recent, iconoclastic argument that "harmless error" should be conceptualized as a substantive rather than a remedial doctrine, see Dan Epps, *Harmless Errors and Substantial Rights*, 131 Harv. L. Rev. 2119 (2018).

Fourth Amendment or, more generally, when police act in accordance with binding judicial precedent that is later deemed erroneous.[11] Another exception permits prosecutors to use illegally obtained evidence to "impeach" the testimony of a criminal defendant who testifies to his or her own innocence (as distinguished from introducing the evidence as direct proof of guilt).[12] Commenting on these developments some years ago now, Professor Carol Steiker noted that an increasingly conservative Supreme Court, in seeking to reduce what it regarded as the excessive social costs of rights established by the earlier, more liberal Warren Court, had "left relatively intact [the Warren Court's] instructions to police officers about proper police practices . . . but radically changed the consequences of violating those instructions."[13]

The Supreme Court also seeks to temper the social costs of upholding claims of constitutional right by limiting the availability of money damages as a remedy for constitutional violations. The two most important limitations stem from the doctrines of sovereign and official immunity.

The doctrine of sovereign immunity holds that the United States cannot be sued without its consent and that, with rare exceptions, neither can the states.[14] As a practical matter, the doctrine has little bite in suits for injunctions. A plaintiff who seeks injunctive relief can typically avoid the sovereign immunity bar by suing a state or federal official, rather than the government in its own name, to enjoin allegedly unconstitutional conduct.[15] But sovereign immunity almost invariably bars unconsented suits seeking the payment of money damages out of government coffers, even for violations of constitutional rights. In defending state sovereign immunity, in particular, the Supreme Court relies heavily on a controversial interpretation of relevant history, but also cites practical governmental interests and

---

[11] See, e.g., *United States v. Leon*, 468 U.S. 897, 900 (1984) (holding that the exclusionary rule does not apply to evidence obtained by "officers acting in reasonable reliance on a search warrant issued by a detached and neutral magistrate but ultimately found to be unsupported by probable cause"); *Davis v. United States*, 564 U.S. 229, 239 (2011) (extending the good faith exception to illegal police searches conducted in "objectively reasonable reliance on binding judicial precedent"); *see also Herring v. United States*, 555 U.S. 135, 137 (2009) (extending the good faith exception to illegal searches resulting from "isolated" police negligence, such as conduct of a search incident to arrest in reliance on a police database that erroneously indicated an outstanding warrant).

[12] See, e.g., *United States v. Havens*, 446 U.S. 620 (1980); *but see James v. Illinois*, 493 U.S. 307 (1990) (refusing to expand the impeachment exception to instances where prosecutors use illegally obtained evidence to impeach defense witnesses rather than the defendant himself).

[13] Carol S. Steiker, *Counter-Revolution in Constitutional Criminal Procedure? Two Audiences, Two Answers*, 94 MICH. L. REV. 2466, 2504 (1996).

[14] E.g. *Alden v. Maine*, 527 U.S. 706, 754–57 (1999); *Seminole Tribe v. Florida*, 517 U.S. 44, 59 (1996). The most important exception covers suits under statutes that Congress has validly enacted under Section 5 of the Fourteenth Amendment. *See Fitzpatrick v. Bitzer*, 427 U.S. 445, 456 (1976). On the complex doctrine, see Richard H. Fallon, Jr., John F. Manning, Daniel J. Meltzer & David L. Shapiro, HART & WECHSLER'S THE FEDERAL COURTS AND THE FEDERAL SYSTEM 939–81 (7th ed. 2015) [hereinafter HART & WECHSLER].

[15] The leading case is *Ex parte Young*, 209 U.S. 123 (1908). *See generally* HART & WECHSLER, *supra* note 14, at 922–35.

social costs. States, the Court has said, should have flexibility in planning their expenditures and in managing their fiscal priorities.[16] In the Court's view, needing to pay large damages awards could interfere with state budgets and planning.

With sovereign immunity barring suits for damages against the state and federal governments, the victims of constitutional rights violations frequently pursue monetary relief from the official or officials who directly caused them harm, whether it be the police officer who effected an unconstitutional search or the officials who sought to enforce an allegedly unconstitutional statute. When sued for damages for violating constitutional rights, officials enjoy one of two types of so-called official immunity.[17] Officials performing legislative and prosecutorial functions possess "absolute" immunity.[18] They cannot be liable for any constitutional violations that they may commit within the outer perimeter of their official roles. As a practical matter, this means that legislators cannot be sued for damages for enacting unconstitutional statutes nor prosecutors for attempting to enforce unconstitutional laws.

Other officials enjoy "qualified immunity," defined to mean that they cannot be liable for money damages unless they violated "clearly established" constitutional or statutory rights of which "every 'reasonable official'" would have known.[19] In formulating this standard in the important 1982 case of *Harlow* v. *Fitzgerald*,[20] the Supreme Court said expressly that its previous official immunity decisions had attempted "to balance competing values."[21] Continuing in that tradition, the Court sought to adjust the applicable standard in order to achieve policy goals more effectively.

If there is a single foundational assumption in conventional thinking about official immunity doctrines, it is that "[t]he resolution of immunity questions inherently requires a balance between the evils inevitable in any available alternative."[22] On the one hand, it is thought, to deny redress to victims of constitutional violations is not only unfair to them,[23] but also diminishes the significance of constitutional rights by undermining incentives for officials to obey the law.[24] On the other hand, the thinking continues, it would be costly and unfair to hold

---

[16]   See, e.g., *Alden*, 527 U.S. at 750–51.

[17]   See HART & WECHSLER, *supra* note 14, at 1038–39.

[18]   See *id.*

[19]   *Ashcroft* v. *al-Kidd*, 563 U.S. 731, 741 (2011) (quoting *Anderson* v. *Creighton*, 483 U.S. 635, 640 (1987)).

[20]   457 U.S. 800 (1982).

[21]   *Id.* at 807.

[22]   *Id.* at 813–14; see also Paul Gewirtz, *Remedies and Resistance*, 92 YALE L.J. 585, 587 (1983) (characterizing the law of remedies as "a jurisprudence of deficiency, of what is lost between declaring a right and implementing a remedy").

[23]   See *Harlow*, 457 U.S. at 814.

[24]   See, e.g., Mark R. Brown, *Correlating Municipal Liability and Official Immunity under Section 1983*, 1989 U. ILL. L. REV. 625, 630–31; Sheldon Nahmod, *Constitutional Damages and Corrective Justice: A Different View*, 76 VA. L. REV. 997, 1019 (1990) (criticizing the argument that victims should not be compensated for all foreseeable damages caused by unconstitutional conduct).

officials liable out of their own pockets whenever they make erroneous constitutional judgments when making good-faith efforts to serve the public.[25]

If the Equilibration Thesis is correct, however, it refutes the assumption that
official immunity doctrine necessarily depends on a balance of evils. Although it is
undoubtedly true (indeed, almost tautologically so) that official immunity reduces
the value of rights, the conventional analysis goes wrong at the outset if it assumes
that the substantive content of constitutional guarantees and the availability of
damages remedies to enforce them are fixed, and only then asks whether official
immunity should exist as a regrettably necessary expedient. Official immunity is not
a variable among constants but, instead, is one potential variable among others.[26]
Imagine that the consequence of the ruling in *Brown* v. *Board of Education* would
have been to impose damages liability on every state legislator, school board
member, principal, or teacher who had established or enforced rules requiring
racial segregation in public education. The Supreme Court almost certainly
would have concluded that the social costs of a rights-remedies package that
included damages remedies for all victims of past discrimination were intolerably
high. Accordingly, if the Court could not have limited the available remedy, it might
have felt constrained not to uphold a previously unrecognized constitutional right to
non-segregated education in the public schools. A similar analysis would presumably have precluded the Court from issuing its *Miranda* ruling. It would have been
untenable to impose damages liability on every police officer who had failed to
deliver *Miranda* warnings before the Supreme Court had ever signaled that such
warnings might be required or on every judge who had admitted an unwarned
confession into evidence. In the absence of official immunity doctrines, even some
currently well-established constitutional rights and authorizations to sue to enforce
them might *shrink*, and sometimes appropriately so. For example, it is easy to
imagine the Court narrowing its standards for identifying "unreasonable" searches
and seizures prohibited by the Fourth Amendment.

To recognize that limitations on available remedies for constitutional violations
can sometimes, desirably, facilitate the recognition of constitutional rights is of
course not to assert that existing doctrine includes the optimal mix of substantive
rights and remedial limitations. But if substantive rights, remedial and immunity
doctrines, and standing rules are all potentially adjustable components of a package
of rights and enforcement mechanisms that should be viewed, and assessed for
desirability, as a whole, then neither is it accurate to say that official immunity is
at best a distasteful necessity. Instead, the Equilibration Thesis casts official immunity as a potential mechanism for achieving the best overall bundle of rights and
correspondingly calibrated remedies within our constitutional system.

---

[25] *See Harlow*, 457 U.S. at 806, 813–14; *Scheuer* v. *Rhodes*, 416 U.S. 232, 239–40 (1974); *cf.* Peter
H. Schuck, SUING GOVERNMENT: CITIZEN REMEDIES FOR OFFICIAL WRONGS 98–99 (1983).
[26] *See* John C. Jeffries, Jr., *The Right-Remedy Gap in Constitutional Law*, 109 YALE L.J. 87, 99–100
(1999).

One more perspective on the resulting situation requires consideration. Although courts effect trade-offs between rights and remedies, remedies remain sufficiently distinct from rights for us to be able to say about some victims of constitutional violations that they have rights, but they may have no remedies to enforce those rights. In the view of some, in the absence of an individually effective remedy, it would be more apt to say that an aggrieved person, for both practical and conceptual purposes, has no constitutional right at all.

The conceptual version of this argument often relies on the most iconic case in the constitutional canon, *Marbury v. Madison*,[27] which famously proclaimed the principle that for every violation of a right, there must be a remedy.[28] In the absence of a remedy, it is asserted, there can be no right. And doctrines that leave some victims of constitutional rights violations with no effective remedies are therefore incompatible with the concept of a constitutional right and, it is often added, with the ideal of the rule of law.

In considering this argument, we should distinguish between two cases. In the first, there is a right – imagine it is the Fourth Amendment right to freedom from unreasonable searches and seizures – for which no judicial remedies are ever available to anyone under any circumstances. We may remind the police and public officials of the Fourth Amendment right, and ask them to honor it, but courts will not enforce it. In the second case, which we can again imagine involving the Fourth Amendment, judicial remedies are sometimes or even frequently available, but not to a particular person for a particular violation. Perhaps an unreasonable search happened in the past, but it disclosed no evidence of criminal activity. As a result, the victim cannot benefit from the exclusionary rule. Sovereign immunity bars damages relief against the government; official immunity precludes recovery from the official who effected the unconstitutional seizure.

In the first case, in which no judicial remedies were ever available to anyone for the violation of an ostensible right, we should take seriously the possibility that no right worthy of the name existed. Even in this case, however, we should not necessarily rush to the conclusion that the absence of judicially enforceable remedies precludes any conceptually plausible claim that a constitutional right exists at

---

[27] 5 U.S. (1 Cranch) 137 (1803).

[28] *See id.* at 163. The principle traces to the Latin maxim, *ubi jus, ibi remedium*, and it received perhaps its classic statement in the Anglo-American tradition in 3 W. BLACKSTONE, COMMENTARIES *23 ("[W]here there is a legal right, there is also a legal remedy, by suit or action at law, whenever that right is invaded."). Marshall's opinion in *Marbury* quoted Blackstone's formulation, *see* 5 U.S. (1 Cranch) at 163; according to one commentator, Marshall apparently believed the principle "a kind of self-evident matter." William W. Van Alstyne, *A Critical Guide to* Marbury v. Madison, 1969 DUKE L.J. 1, 11. For reasons more of rhetorical structure than substance, however, Marshall's own formulation did not take the classic *ubi jus, ibi remedium* form. Marshall stated instead: "The very essence of civil liberty certainly consists in the right of every individual to claim the protection of the laws, whenever he receives an injury . . . The government of the United States has been emphatically termed a government of laws, and not of men. It will certainly cease to deserve this high appellation, if the laws furnish no remedy for the violation of a vested legal right." 5 U.S. (1 Cranch) at 163.

all. The political question doctrine – which holds that the responsibility for enforcing some rights lies with the legislative or executive branch, not the courts – illustrates one possible exception.[29] We might have rights that are not enforceable by courts, but that other governmental officials have a constitutional duty to uphold. Other branches of government could, in principle, have rights-generating obligations even if courts would not enforce the rights.

However we judge that situation, the issue raised by the principle "for every right, a remedy" differs markedly in the second case that I have imagined, in which judicial enforcement mechanisms are often available, but immunity or other doctrines preclude a particular person from securing any individually effective, compensatory remedy for a single past constitutional violation. When we consider this second situation, the long teaching of our tradition is that individually effective remedies – and especially damages remedies – are not always required for all victims of constitutional rights violations under all circumstances.[30] It is too late in the day to argue that doctrines such as sovereign immunity and official immunity are flatly unconstitutional.[31] Rather, judicial practice in determining which remedies to award under which circumstances has been consistent with, even if it does not explicitly embrace, the kind of interest-based, consequence-sensitive analysis that prevails in the definition of substantive rights. Quite apart from cases in which some victims of rights violations get no individually effective remedy at all, appeal to an interest-based, consequence-sensitive analysis is also necessary to explain legislative discretion to substitute one remedy for another even when the Constitution may require that some remedy must be available. As Professor Henry Hart put it, "Congress necessarily has a wide choice in the selection of remedies, and ... a complaint about [the substitution of one remedy for another that is preferred by the claimant] can rarely be of constitutional dimension."[32]

To make sense of the varying and sometimes uncertain relationship between rights and remedies in the constitutional scheme, we must understand remedies as serving two basic functions. The first is to provide redress to individuals whose rights have been violated. The slogan "for every right, a remedy" reflects this purpose. The second function is related but distinct: to create incentives for governmental officials to respect individual rights, to deter rights violations, and to ensure that nonjudicial governmental officials generally conduct themselves within the bounds of law, even if violations occasionally occur. In effectuating this second function, the

---

[29] For brief discussion of that doctrine, see Chapter 3. For a survey of issues arising under the political question doctrine and of related scholarship, see HART AND WECHSLER, *supra* note 14, at 237–66.

[30] *See, e.g.*, Richard H. Fallon, Jr. & Daniel J. Meltzer, *New Law, Non-Retroactivity, and Constitutional Remedies*, 104 HARV. L. REV. 1731, 1779–97 (1991).

[31] It is a different question whether the Supreme Court might have overstepped constitutional bounds in extending those doctrines as far as it has. *See, e.g.*, William Baude, *Is Qualified Immunity Unlawful?*, 106 CALIF. L. REV. 45 (2018).

[32] Henry M. Hart, Jr., *The Power of Congress to Limit the Jurisdiction of Federal Courts: An Exercise in Dialectic*, 66 HARV. L. REV. 1362, 1366 (1953).

Court must take account of public interests in governmental adherence to law and promotion of the rule of law, but it must also weigh the immediate public or social costs that might attend the award of a remedy, particularly when the remedy sought is money damages. The public, rule-of-law interest in providing constitutional remedies is obviously reflected in doctrines, such as the Fourth Amendment exclusionary rule, that create deterrent remedies – remedies designed not to redress individual wrongs but to furnish incentives for officials generally to respect constitutional norms.[33] But more traditional remedies, including injunctions and even damages, also serve a systemic function of creating deterrent pressure to avoid future lawbreaking.

Of the two functions performed by constitutional remedies, providing effective remediation to individual victims is the more familiar, but ensuring governmental faithfulness to law is, if not the more fundamental, at least the more unyielding. Whatever may be the case with respect to denying individually effective remedies to some victims of constitutional violations, it would be intolerable to have a general regime of public administration that was systematically unanswerable for violations of constitutional rights, as identified from a relatively detached and independent judicial perspective.

Recognizing that two values, rather than one, underlie the law of constitutional remedies explains much of the traditional doctrine, including the phenomenon of congressional discretion to withdraw or deny particular remedies that Henry Hart emphasized. Within a historically defensible yet normatively appealing account of our constitutional tradition, the aspiration to effective individual remediation for every constitutional violation represents an important remedial aspiration, but not an unqualified command. Its force may vary with the nature of the constitutional violation for which a remedy is sought. For example, our constitutional tradition recognizes a stronger interest in relief from continuing coercion – for instance, in reversing an unconstitutional conviction, or enjoining an ongoing pattern of constitutional rights violations against a particular person – than in obtaining damages relief for a relatively isolated instance of past misconduct. Whatever the weight of the individual interest, however, the remedial calculus also must include a second principle, which demands an overall structure of remedies adequate to preserve separation-of-powers values, meaningful individual rights, and a regime of government under law.

These two remedial principles complement, and are readily subsumed under, the Equilibration Thesis. They highlight some of the most important interests that the Supreme Court should have in mind when assessing the comparative merits of alternative packages of rights and remedies.

[33] See generally Daniel J. Meltzer, *Deterring Constitutional Violations by Law Enforcement Officials: Plaintiffs and Defendants as Private Attorneys General*, 88 COLUM. L. REV. 247, 253–78 (1988).

LIMITING STANDING TO REDUCE THE COSTS OF RIGHTS
AND REMEDIES

Although the Supreme Court has not articulated the requirements of standing doctrine with perfect consistency, it almost invariably states three demands attributable to Article III:

> [T]o satisfy Article III's standing requirements, a plaintiff must show (1) it has suffered an "injury in fact" that is (a) concrete and particularized and (b) actual or imminent, not conjectural or hypothetical; (2) the injury is fairly traceable to the challenged action of the defendant; and (3) it is likely, as opposed to merely speculative, that the injury will be redressed by a favorable decision.[34]

The Supreme Court can adopt, and sometimes has adopted, a relaxed interpretation of these requirements in order to permit the effective enforcement of constitutional rights. The Warren Court did so, for example, in *Flast v. Cohen*,[35] which held that all taxpayers suffered a cognizable injury when their tax dollars were used to support religious institutions in alleged violation of the Establishment Clause. The Court has taken a comparably broad view of actionable injuries in cases involving challenges to affirmative action in admissions to higher education. Excluded white students who want to challenge affirmative action programs would often find it difficult if not impossible to prove that their rejections were "fairly traceable" to a racial preference. Even in the absence of affirmative action, any particular white candidate might have been denied admission anyway. In response to this situation, the Court held in *Regents of the University of California v. Bakke*[36] that the plaintiff Allan Bakke suffered a redressable injury from the University's denial to him of the opportunity to compete for every slot in its entering class.[37] A subsequent case made the Court's rationale even more explicit: "The 'injury in fact' in an equal protection case of this variety is the denial of equal treatment resulting from the imposition of [a barrier that makes it more difficult for the members of a group to obtain a benefit], not the ultimate inability to obtain the benefit."[38]

More commonly, however, the Court deploys the requirements of standing doctrine to alleviate what it would otherwise regard as the excessive social costs of injunctive remedies for constitutional rights violations. An especially vivid example of this use of standing comes from *City of Los Angeles v. Lyons*.[39] After being stopped

---

[34] *Friends of the Earth, Inc. v. Laidlaw Envtl. Servs. (TOC), Inc.*, 528 U.S. 167, 180–81 (2000); *see also Spokeo, Inc. v. Robins*, 136 S. Ct. 1540, 1547 (2016) (reciting these requirements); *Clapper v. Amnesty Int'l USA*, 568 U.S. 398, 409 (2013) (same).

[35] 392 U.S. 83 (1968).

[36] 438 U.S. 265 (1978).

[37] *Id.* at 280 n.14.

[38] *Ne. Fla. Chapter of the Associated Gen. Contractors of Am. v. City of Jacksonville*, 508 U.S. 656, 666 (1993).

[39] 461 U.S. 95 (1983).

for a traffic violation, Adolph Lyons was subjected to a life-threatening chokehold by Los Angeles police, allegedly as part of a policy that had caused the death of sixteen people within the previous eight years.[40] When Lyons responded with a federal civil rights action in which he sought both damages and injunctive relief, the Supreme Court allowed the suit for damages, but it held that he lacked standing to sue for an injunction restricting police use of chokeholds. According to the Court, by the time that Lyons filed his suit, he no longer suffered any continuing injury that equitable relief could redress, and it was "no more than speculation" that he faced a sufficient threat of being choked by the police again to establish standing on that basis.[41] Although Lyons could seek damages for his past injury, the threat that he might be subjected to another chokehold in the future was not sufficiently imminent to warrant standing to seek an injunction.[42]

The Court's decision to uphold Lyons's standing to sue for damages, but not for an injunction, reveals volumes. In assessing whether an injunction could issue under traditional equitable principles, the Court said expressly that "[r]ecognition of the need for a proper balance between state and federal authority counsels restraint in the issuance of injunctions against state officers engaged in the administration of the States' criminal laws."[43] It is hard not to believe that similar concerns about the peculiar intrusiveness of injunctive remedies on decision-making by executive officials also influenced the Court's rulings with respect to standing. It would be one thing for a court to say that a particular choking on a particular occasion violated the Constitution, another for a court to issue an injunction comprehensively pre-scribing when police employment of chokeholds would and would not be permis-sible in the myriad of situations that police might encounter when apprehending criminal suspects. In light of what the Court took to be the social costs of federal judicial interference with local law enforcement discretion in dealing with poten-tially dangerous individuals, the majority opinion adjudged damages to be a less disruptive and, therefore, a more acceptable remedy than an injunction. The Court may have erred in its calculation, but the risk of error is endemic to judicial – and indeed to all human – decision-making.

The connection between standing and remedies that emerges from *Lyons* has broad relevance. Standing issues almost never arise in suits for damages.[44] If someone has suffered a sufficiently palpable injury in the past to have

---

[40] See *id.* at 115–16 (Marshall, J., dissenting).

[41] *Id.* at 108–09 (majority opinion).

[42] *Id.* at 105, 109.

[43] *Id.* at 112.

[44] *Cf. Texas v. Lesage,* 528 U.S. 18, 21 (1999) (per curiam) (holding that a rejected applicant challenging an affirmative action program had established "no cognizable injury warranting [damages] relief" when it was undisputed that he would not have been admitted in the absence of the program, even though an applicant would have standing to sue for injunctive relief based simply on "the inability to compete on an equal footing" (quoting *Ne. Fla. Chapter,* 508 U.S. at 666)). For discussion, see Ashutosh Bhagwat, *Injury without Harm:* Texas v. Lesage *and the Strange World of Article III Injuries,* 28 HASTINGS CONST. L.Q. 445, 453–54 (2001).

a plausible claim to damages, damages will redress the injury. By contrast, standing and other justiciability issues occur with relative frequency in suits for injunctions, which depend on assessments of the likelihood of future harms. Especially when plaintiffs seek injunctions that would require changes in the policies or practices of complex institutions – such as police departments, prisons, or agencies responsible for national security – courts understandably grow doubtful about their competence to weigh costs and benefits and to lay down appropriate standards of behavior for contexts that they may little understand or cannot foresee. Issues about the appropriate judicial role within the framework of constitutional federalism and the separation of powers also arise.[45] As *Lyons* illustrates, even when a court can decide a claim on the merits (and potentially award damages), there may be a further concern about the acceptability of injunctive remedies that would tie officials' hands in unforeseen future circumstances, and that concern may manifest itself in justiciability doctrine.[46]

To offer just one more example, the Supreme Court rather transparently deployed standing doctrine as a cost-sensitive equilibrating device in *Clapper* v. *Amnesty International USA*,[47] a case with potential national security implications. The plaintiffs in *Clapper* were US citizens residing in the United States who sought judicial invalidation of an amendment to the Foreign Intelligence Surveillance Act. The amendment permitted the Attorney General and Director of National Intelligence, with the authorization of the Foreign Intelligence Surveillance Court, to direct the interception of communications involving non-Americans "reasonably believed to be located outside the United States [in order] to acquire foreign intelligence information."[48] The plaintiffs alleged that their personal and professional relationships with parties abroad made it likely that their communications would be intercepted, and that they would therefore suffer injury to their interests in privacy, under the revised statute. Writing for the Court, Justice Alito denied standing based on the plaintiffs' failure to establish that an injury in fact was "certainly impending" in light, among other things, of the opacity of the Government's criteria for seeking foreign-security wiretaps.[49] He concluded, in addition, that the plaintiffs had not adequately established that any injury they might suffer would be causally traceable to the challenged amendment since

---

[45]   See, e.g., William A. Fletcher, *The Discretionary Constitution: Institutional Remedies and Judicial Legitimacy*, 91 YALE L.J. 635, 637, 644–45 (1982); Paul J. Mishkin, *Federal Courts as State Reformers*, 35 WASH. & LEE L. REV. 949, 964–65 (1978); Robert F. Nagel, *Separation of Powers and the Scope of Federal Equitable Remedies*, 30 STAN. L. REV. 661, 674–75 (1978).

[46]   *Lyons*, 461 U.S. at 109; *see also Friends of the Earth* v. *Laidlaw Envtl. Servs. (TOC)*, 528 U.S. 167, 185 (2000) ("[A] plaintiff must demonstrate standing separately for each form of relief sought.").

[47]   568 U.S. 398 (2013).

[48]   *Id.* at 404–05 (quoting 50 U.S.C. § 1181a(a) (2012)). The amendment required "minimization procedures" to restrict the collection of information about persons within the United States. *Id.* at 405 (quoting 50 U.S.C. § 1181a(g)(2)(A)(ii) (2012)).

[49]   *See id.* at 401 ("[R]espondents' theory of *future* injury is too speculative to satisfy the well-established requirement that threatened injury must be 'certainly impending.'").

"[t]he Government has numerous other methods of conducting surveillance, none of which is challenged here."[50]

As four dissenting Justices pointed out, although some of the Court's past decisions had referred to "certainly impending" injury as a necessary condition for standing, future injury is seldom if ever "absolutely certain," and the "federal courts frequently entertain actions for injunctions and for declaratory relief aimed at preventing future activities that are reasonably likely or highly likely ... to take place."[51] Because the plaintiffs had averred that their work as lawyers, scholars, and journalists required them to communicate with people abroad whom the government believed to be affiliated with terrorist groups, the dissenters thought the likelihood of injury – in the form of interception of private communications – large enough to permit standing.[52]

With the majority and dissenting opinions citing different cases to support their judgments about the appropriate standard for determining standing – and with even the majority acknowledging in a footnote that "[o]ur cases do not uniformly require plaintiffs to demonstrate that it is literally certain that the harms they identify will come about"[53] – an additional distinction that Justice Alito cited in his majority opinion takes on enhanced significance: "[W]e have often found a lack of standing in cases in which the Judiciary has been requested to review actions of the political branches in the fields of intelligence gathering and foreign affairs."[54]

In light of the supporting authority that the Court cited, among other cases, that assertion seems unquestionably true. As *Clapper* illustrates, the Supreme Court regards national security concerns – and the social costs of allowing remedies for constitutional privacy rights – as relevant to standing inquiries.[55] In other words, the Court varies the stringency of its standing analysis in response to the perceived social cost of allowing cases that implicate national security interests to proceed. A denial of standing forecloses any demand for an injunctive remedy that might even possibly damage national security.

Corroborating evidence for the hypothesis that worries about remedies influence standing determinations comes from the Court's 2014 decision in *Susan B. Anthony*

50 *Id.* at 412–13.
51 *See id.* at 431 (Breyer, J., dissenting).
52 *See id.* at 425–31.
53 *See id.* at 414 n.5 (majority opinion). The majority went on to say that it had sometimes "found standing based on a 'substantial risk' that harm will occur." *Id.* The footnote then continued: "[T]o the extent that the 'substantial risk' standard is relevant and is distinct from the 'certainly impending' requirement, respondents fall short of even that standard, in light of the attenuated chain of inferences necessary to find harm here." *Id.*
54 *Id.* at 409 (first citing *United States v. Richardson*, 418 U.S. 166, 167–70 (1974); then citing *Schlesinger v. Reservists Comm. to Stop the War*, 418 U.S. 208, 209–11 (1974); and then citing *Laird v. Tatum*, 408 U.S. 1, 11–16 (1972)).
55 *See also* Jonathan Remy Nash, *Standing's Expected Value*, 111 MICH. L. REV. 1283, 1297–98 (2013) (suggesting that, based on language in the Court's opinion, "the holding in *Clapper* should at least be somewhat limited to its facts," *id.* at 1298).

List v. *Driehaus*.[56] *Susan B. Anthony List* upheld the standing of two advocacy groups to seek an injunction against enforcement of a statute alleged to violate the First Amendment by forbidding knowingly false statements about the voting records of political candidates. Anticipating that the statute might be enforced in future campaigns, the Court unanimously ruled that "a plaintiff satisfies the injury-in-fact requirement where he alleges 'an intention to engage in [conduct] arguably affected with a constitutional interest, but proscribed by a statute, and there exists a credible threat of prosecution.'"[57] *Susan B. Anthony List* leaves little room for doubt that it is easier for a plaintiff to establish a credible threat of prosecution than to establish a credible threat of being subjected to allegedly unconstitutional surveillance.[58]

An unusually clear demonstration of the interconnections among the Supreme Court's merits, remedial, and standing inquiries – and its use of standing doctrine as an alternative to merits rulings in weighing individual interests against countervailing social interests – comes from *Allen* v. *Wright*.[59] In *Allen*, the parents of black public school children complained that government officials subjected them to "stigmatic injury, or denigration" by failing to enforce laws denying tax benefits to racially discriminatory private schools.[60] Deeming the asserted injury too "abstract," the Supreme Court denied standing.[61] By contrast, the Court upheld standing in *Heckler* v. *Mathews*,[62] in which male plaintiffs challenged a provision of the Social Security Act under which women received higher benefits than men.[63] Because a severability clause provided that women should receive the same lesser awards as men if a court found the disparity unconstitutional, the plaintiffs could achieve no material benefit from a decision in their favor.[64] The Court upheld standing nonetheless, based on the notion that the disparate treatment injured the men by "perpetuating 'archaic and stereotypic notions.'"[65]

Distinctions between the asserted stigmatization injury that was deemed too abstract in *Allen* and that which was deemed actionable in *Heckler* are too thin to carry much credibility. When the Court denies claims to standing by plaintiffs such as those in *Allen* while upholding claims such as those in *Heckler*, it makes "a judgment based not on any fact" of injury that is discernible through empirical or

---

[56] 134 S. Ct. 2334 (2014).
[57] *Id.* at 2342 (quoting *Babbitt* v. *Farm Workers*, 442 U.S. 289, 298 (1979)).
[58] The *Susan B. Anthony List* opinion blandly described *Clapper* as having recognized that "[a]n allegation of future injury may suffice [for standing] if the threatened injury is 'certainly impending,' or there is a 'substantial risk' that the harm will occur." *Id.* at 2341 (quoting *Clapper*, 568 U.S. at 414 n.5).
[59] 468 U.S 737 (1984).
[60] *Id.* at 753–54.
[61] *Id.* at 755–56.
[62] 465 U.S. 728 (1984).
[63] *Id.* at 735.
[64] *Id.* at 734, 736–37.
[65] *Id.* at 739 (quoting *Miss. Univ. for Women* v. *Hogan*, 458 U.S. 718, 725 (1982)).

psychological inquiry, but on other considerations.[66] As others have emphasized, it seems likely that the Supreme Court's central, underlying concern in cases such as *Allen* and *Heckler* involves the substantive merits of the plaintiffs' underlying claims.[67] In *Heckler*, equal protection norms gave the plaintiffs a right to challenge a law that directly classified them on the basis of sex and, based on that classification, accorded them less favored treatment than women. In *Allen*, by contrast, it is at least more doubtful that equal protection norms gave the aggrieved parents a legal right to have government officials enforce the tax laws in a particular way against third-parties. If so, the holding that the *Allen* plaintiffs lacked standing could be seen as a straightforward surrogate for a holding that the plaintiffs had asserted no cognizable violation of their personal constitutional rights. The interests and concerns that bore on the standing issue and the merits issue were identical and interchangeable.

In addition, the question whether plaintiffs have a substantive right inevitably bleeds into questions about constitutionally and practically acceptable remedies. In *Heckler*, the Court was asked to enjoin the direct enforcement by government officials of a facially discriminatory law. In *Allen*, by contrast, the Court was asked to grant an injunction intruding on the executive's traditional discretion about whether and how to enforce the law, not against the plaintiff but against the public generally. In a number of opinions, sometimes for the Court and sometimes for himself, Justice Scalia argued repeatedly that injunctions compelling the executive to enforce the law against third parties represent unconstitutional interferences with the President's power to "take Care that the Laws [are] faithfully executed."[68] Although I do not believe that this categorical claim ultimately deserves to be accepted,[69] injunctions directing the executive to enforce the law against third parties raise distinctive, sometimes troublesome issues – potentially dispositive in the minds of some Justices – involving practically and constitutionally acceptable remedies.[70]

---

[66] Cass R. Sunstein, *What's Standing after* Lujan? *Of Citizen Suits, "Injuries," and Article III*, 91 MICH. L. REV. 163, 189 (1992).

[67] *See, e.g.,* William A. Fletcher, *The Structure of Standing*, 98 YALE. L.J. 221, 239 (1988) (" The essence of a standing inquiry is thus the meaning of the specific statutory or constitutional provision upon which the plaintiff relies. . .").

[68] U.S. CONST. art. II, § 3; *see, e.g., FEC v. Akins*, 524 U.S. 11, 36 (1998) (Scalia, J., dissenting); *Lujan v. Defenders of Wildlife*, 504 U.S. 555, 577 (1992); *see also* Antonin Scalia, *The Doctrine of Standing as an Essential Element of the Separation of Powers*, 17 SUFFOLK U. L. REV. 881, 894 (1983) (arguing that standing law should exclude courts from the "undemocratic role of prescribing how the other two branches should function in order to serve the interest *of the majority itself*"). For critical commentary, see Gene R. Nichol, Jr., *Justice Scalia, Standing, and Public Law Litigation*, 42 DUKE L.J. 1141, 1142–43 (1993).

[69] *Cf.* Cass R. Sunstein, *Standing and the Privatization of Public Law*, 88 COLUM. L. REV. 1432, 1471 (1988) (terming the Take Care Clause "a duty, not a license" and finding "no usurpation of executive prerogatives in a judicial decision" enforcing the President's duty). The Supreme Court has sometimes upheld standing in cases in which plaintiffs have sought orders requiring executive officials to enforce the law. *See, e.g., Massachusetts v. EPA*, 549 U.S. 497 (2007) (suit to require the EPA to regulate greenhouse gas emissions).

[70] The Supreme Court has resisted suits seeking to compel enforcement of the law against third parties in other contexts, most notably through its insistence that agency decisions not to take enforcement

If the Justices are troubled about the appropriateness of courts issuing injunctions in particular cases or types of cases, the amorphous character of the concept of injury makes it almost inevitable that those concerns will sometimes penetrate the Court's standing analysis.[71] For Justices who believe an injunctive remedy to be practically undesirable or even unacceptable, an obvious solution to the looming remedial dilemma is to determine that the plaintiff has not shown an injury in fact.

As we now come to the end of a long argument, the intricacy of the details should not obscure my central thesis about the interconnections among constitutional rights, judicial remedies, and justiciability doctrines such as those that govern standing to sue. Prior chapters have argued that constitutional rights are constructs that are built out of and limited by judicial assessments of competing individual and governmental interests. Consistent with that thesis, we should now further recognize that judicial appraisal of competing interests and judicial efforts to achieve an optimal accommodation do not focus on the definition of rights alone. Constitutional rights are enmeshed in packages of rights, remedies, and justiciability rules that allow courts additional opportunities to accommodate and manage the competing interests and social costs that the judicial enforcement of rights inescapably implicates.

In advancing this claim, I have not sought to demonstrate – nor do I believe – that the Supreme Court has always employed its equilibrating powers wisely. A number of the Court's decisions seem to me to undervalue the individual interests at stake, a few to overvalue those interests. But my aim here has not been to offer normative assessments at the level of individual cases. It has been to vindicate the core analytical claim of the Equilibration Thesis by describing and illustrating the mechanisms of interconnection among justiciability, rights-defining, and remedial doctrines. When confronted with the prospect of results that it deems unacceptable, the Court responds by making an adjustment designed to bring about a new, better doctrinal alignment, but the choice about which doctrine to adjust is often optional, not a matter of legal necessity. The Court may respond to an apprehension that substantive rights are too broad by curbing available remedies or by limiting standing. When confronting the prospect of awarding remedies that it deems practically unacceptable, the Court may of course adjust applicable remedial doctrine, but it may also, alternatively, redefine the underlying substantive right in narrower terms or raise the justiciability threshold for enforcing the right.

---

action are discretionary and thus not generally reviewable under the Administrative Procedure Act. See *Heckler* v. *Chaney*, 470 U.S. 821, 831–32 (1985).

[71] See Douglas Laycock, *The Triumph of Equity*, 56 LAW & CONTEMP. PROBS., Summer 1993, at 53, 64 (1993) (noting that because the value of non-economic rights is often impossible to quantify, the only plausible remedy in suits to enforce non-economic rights will often be an injunction).

FACIAL AND AS-APPLIED CHALLENGES

A further mechanism for adjusting the social costs and benefits of judicially recognized constitutional rights inheres in doctrines regulating the availability of "facial," as distinguished from "as-applied," challenges to statutes. The doctrine governing facial and as-applied challenges is tangled. Even the terminology is controversial. As a first approximation, however, a facial challenge asks a court to examine, adjudge the constitutionality of, and invalidate a statutory provision as applied to all possible cases. By contrast, as-applied challenges ask a court to hold only that a statute cannot validly be applied to the particular person before the court and the particular conduct in which that person has engaged or wishes to engage.[72]

It sometimes makes good sense to restrict challengers to bringing as-applied challenges. Suppose I am arrested for driving 80 miles per hour on a Massachusetts highway where the speed limit is 55. In defending myself against a speeding charge, imagine I argue that the law setting the speed limit is facially invalid because the Constitution would not permit Massachusetts to apply it to an FBI agent pursuing a fleeing terrorist suspect. Further suppose that the Massachusetts statute would indeed be invalid as applied to an FBI agent under those circumstances. Even so, it would make no practical sense for me to succeed in a facial challenge. Constitutional litigation should not proceed on the basis of bizarre hypotheticals. The state speed limit statute would be constitutionally valid as applied to me, and my constitutional attack on the statute therefore should, and would, fail.

Now consider a different kind of case, framed by the strict scrutiny test and many of the other tests that effectively define preferred or fundamental constitutional rights. By its very nature, the strict scrutiny formula calls for the strict scrutiny of statutes, not particular applications of statutes to particular people. Otherwise the requirement of "narrow tailoring" would make no sense. Rational basis review also seems to require courts to scrutinize statutes on their faces, though not strictly, by asking whether a statute is rationally related to a legitimate governmental interest.[73]

With both strict scrutiny and rational basis review requiring courts to test the validity of statutes, not individual applications of statutes to particular people on particular occasions, it would seem obvious that facial challenges must occur frequently, not infrequently. Yet it is easy to cite Supreme Court opinions that flatly deny this seemingly obvious conclusion. The Justices recurrently insist that facial challenges are and ought to be rare.[74]

---

[72] *See* Richard H. Fallon, Jr., *Fact and Fiction about Facial Challenges*, 99 CALIF. L. REV. 915, 923 (2011).

[73] Accordingly, the Supreme Court sometimes invalidates statutes pursuant to the rational basis test. *See, e.g., Lawrence v. Texas*, 539 U.S. 558 (2003); *Romer v. Evans*, 517 U.S. 620 (1996); *U.S. Dep't of Agric. v. Moreno*, 413 U.S. 528 (1973).

[74] *Wash. State Grange v. Wash. State Republican Party*, 552 U.S. 442, 450 (2008) ("[F]acial challenges are disfavored. . ."); *Sabri v. United States*, 541 U.S. 600, 608 (2004) ("recalling that facial challenges are best when infrequent").

A leading modern case that exemplifies the conventional view about the rarity of facial challenges is *United States* v. *Salerno*.[75] In *Salerno*, the Supreme Court rejected arguments that the Bail Reform Act of 1984, which mandates pretrial detention without bail for some people accused of federal crimes, violates the Due Process Clause of the Fifth Amendment and the Excessive Bail Clause of the Eighth Amendment.[76] Chief Justice Rehnquist's opinion for the Court explained why the facial challenge must fail in language that has framed much of the subsequent debate about the availability of facial challenges:

> A facial challenge to a legislative Act is, of course, the most difficult challenge to mount successfully, since the challenger must establish that *no set of circumstances exists under which the Act would be valid*. The fact that the Bail Reform Act might operate unconstitutionally under some conceivable set of circumstances is insufficient to render it wholly invalid, since we have not recognized an "overbreadth" doctrine outside the limited context of the First Amendment.[77]

If both strict judicial scrutiny and rational basis review require courts to examine statutes on their faces in order to rule on constitutional challenges, then the *Salerno* analysis, and the conventional wisdom that *Salerno* embodies, seem stunning – and stunningly wrong. And empirical study has exposed the error, even though the Supreme Court sometimes continues to repeat it. A survey of all constitutional cases decided by the Court in its 2009, 2004, 1999, 1994, 1989, and 1984 Terms revealed that the Court adjudicated more facial challenges than it did as-applied challenges in each of those years.[78] The overall success rate for facial challenges was also higher than that for as-applied challenges.[79]

Perhaps unsurprisingly, however, there is a good deal more to be said. Otherwise the myth that facial challenges are rare and disfavored and that they seldom succeed could not have taken hold. The key to unraveling the mystery will lie in recognizing that here, as elsewhere, constitutional adjudication reflects a complex weighing of competing rights-supporting and governmental interests that include avoidance of social costs.

Even though strict scrutiny inescapably requires courts to examine statutes on their faces, courts can, and frequently do, apply calibrating mechanisms even after concluding that a statute, as written, either fails strict scrutiny or would likely fail strict scrutiny if it were applied without exception to all cases within its sweep. The most important mediating device is the doctrine of "severability."[80] Pursuant to severability principles, the Supreme Court will, when reasonably possible, "sever" statutes, or excise some of their invalid parts or applications, in order to "save" the

---

[75] 481 U.S. 739 (1987).
[76] *See id.* at 745–51.
[77] *Id.* at 745 (emphasis added).
[78] *See* Fallon, *supra* note 72, at 941.
[79] *See id.* (finding success in 44 percent of facial challenges and 38 percent of as-applied challenges).
[80] On severability doctrine, see HART & WECHSLER, *supra* note 14, at 169–75.

statutes from complete invalidation (and thus, for example, leave Massachusetts with no valid speed limit just because it could not enforce its speed limit against an FBI agent chasing a suspected terrorist). In less technical parlance, the Court will effectively fix the constitutional defect that strict judicial scrutiny reveals by paring down a statute so that it ceases to fail the narrow tailoring requirement.

In order to gain an intuitive grasp of the technical legal idea of "severability," we can start with two ideas. The first, tracing to the foundational case of *Marbury v. Madison*,[81] is that a constitutionally invalid law is not a law at all. It is a legal nullity. The other idea, which practical necessity makes equally fundamental, is that laws are capable of being divided up into constitutionally valid and constitutionally invalid parts or applications. Unfortunately, the legal notion of severability is vague, protean, even mysterious. But it operates straightforwardly when a law has multiple, linguistically distinguishable parts. Suppose a law says, "It shall be a crime, punishable by ten years in prison, to (a) threaten to kill the president or (b) criticize the president." Part (b) is clearly unconstitutional. Part (a) would be just as clearly constitutionally valid if it stood alone, independently of Part (b). Rather than treating (a) and (b) as a package, a reviewing court would hold that although (b) is invalid, (a) and (b) can be separated or severed, and the valid (a) can continue to be enforced.

The notion of severability grows more mysterious when we consider statutes that do not have multiple, and therefore presumptively severable, linguistic units.[82] Consider a hypothetical case, similar to the one that I introduced above, involving the Massachusetts speed limit. Suppose, most improbably, that an FBI agent was arrested and prosecuted for speeding while chasing a suspected terrorist. Under the Constitution's Supremacy Clause,[83] the Massachusetts speed limit could not validly be applied to a federal official acting within the scope of federally conferred authority. So recognizing, a judge would dismiss the prosecution. But suppose, after the dismissal, I was arrested for speeding and tried to argue that the Massachusetts statute was "no law at all" because it was invalid as applied to the FBI agent. In response, a court would again invoke the severability doctrine. Even though the anti-speeding statute does not have linguistically separable parts – one applying to FBI agents, the other to the rest of us – the court would say that the statute's rare invalid *applications* could be severed from its valid ones and that the statute, once its invalid applications were severed, was therefore not "no law at all" within the meaning of *Marbury*.

Although the notion of separability helps to explain why courts sometimes feel justified in rebuffing facial challenges, it may raise a new puzzle, involving how facial challenges could ever be allowed. To express the worry only slightly

---

[81] 5 U.S. (1 Cranch) 137 (1803).

[82] For a conceptualization of how the notion of separability applies to such statutes, see Richard H. Fallon, Jr., *As-Applied and Facial Challenges and Third-Party Standing*, 113 HARV. L. REV. 1321, 1331–33 (2000).

[83] U.S. CONST. art. VI, cl. 2.

differently, once separability enters the picture, it might appear that a facial challenge could never succeed against a statute with even a single valid application – which, it will be recalled, is the position that Chief Justice Rehnquist took in the *Salerno* case. And it might further appear that the strict judicial scrutiny test, which looms so large in constitutional doctrine, would be considerably defanged by *Salerno's* seeming rejection of facial challenge against statutes with even a single valid application – if we could even imagine how strict scrutiny could be applied in the first place if the Supreme Court consistently enforced the *Salerno* approach. (If a statute could always be separated into individual applications, the very idea of there being a single statute for courts to scrutinize strictly might seem to vanish before our eyes.)

Clearly, however, the Supreme Court does not believe that all statutes are always separable. It implicitly acknowledges as much when it distinguishes between facial challenges – which sometimes result in facial invalidations of statutes – and as-applied challenges. What remains to be worked out is how the various pieces of the doctrinal puzzle fit together.

In confronting that challenge, we should recognize candidly that the law is muddled. As is often the case with conceptual muddles, however, the problem inheres less in the Supreme Court's actual practices than in its attempts to describe those practices. We can start to make sense of what the Court typically does, even though it sometimes misdescribes the norms that it applies, by recognizing that all constitutional challenges to statutes begin as as-applied challenges. In order to have standing to assert a constitutional claim, a challenger must always argue that she would be harmed by a statute's application and that the Constitution gives her a right not to have the statute enforced against her.[84]

As we have seen illustrated throughout this book, however, a challenger who asserts a claim of constitutional right will often, perhaps typically, back up that claim by pointing to a test, such as the judge-made strict scrutiny test, that applies to statutes, not applications of statutes. Accordingly, let us now suppose that a court, in a case to which strict scrutiny applies, actually or provisionally determines that the statute as written could not survive strict scrutiny. Separability doctrine becomes pertinent when, but only when, the Court concludes that a statute would not be narrowly tailored to a compelling governmental interest unless it could be validly separated.

When separability doctrine becomes relevant in this way, it is at least misleading and possibly mistaken for the Supreme Court to assert – as it sometimes does – that a "presumption of severability" applies in all cases.[85] Under tests such as strict judicial scrutiny, which inherently require courts to assess statutes' facial validity, the Court cannot simply presume severability without being able to

---

[84] *See* Fallon, *supra* note 82, at 1336–39.
[85] *See* Michael C. Dorf, *Facial Challenges to State and Federal Statutes*, 46 STAN. L. REV. 235, 250 (1994).

articulate how severing should occur. Rather, in order to sever or separate a statute, the Court needs to identify an articulable line along which a statute could be severed such that, as so severed, it would survive strict judicial scrutiny as narrowly tailored to a compelling governmental interest. In other words, if there is an obvious and articulable line of severability, such that the Court can say that part of the statute would survive strict scrutiny if the remainder were severed, then the Court can and should reject the facial challenge by saying that severing of the statute along the identified line would cure the narrow tailoring problem. After the severing, a more narrowly tailored statute would remain and, as severed, would survive strict scrutiny. But if there is no obvious line of severing – and if the Court's effort to identify one would seem more like "rewriting" than trimming – then a facial challenge will and should succeed.

Two examples will illustrate this distinction, rough and ready though it is. The first involves a case in which the Supreme Court indicated that the lower court should have severed a statute, rather than invalidated it. In *Ayotte v. Planned Parenthood of Northern New England*,[86] the Court reviewed a lower court ruling that a state statute requiring minors to notify their parents before obtaining an abortion was facially unconstitutional because it failed to provide an exception for medical emergencies. In an opinion by Justice O'Connor, the Court unanimously agreed that the statute was invalid under its precedents, which had held that parental notification statutes must include emergency exceptions to pass constitutional muster.[87] But it was error, Justice O'Connor wrote, for the lower court to have invalidated the statute on its face, without "contemplat[ing] relief more finely drawn."[88] In *Ayotte*, "background constitutional rules"[89] made it plain that the statute could survive constitutional scrutiny if invalidated only as applied to emergency cases – in other words, if it were severed in a way that left the statute intact except in its application to emergency situations. Accordingly, the Court held that partial invalidation, not total invalidation, was the appropriate "remedy,"[90] as long as "New Hampshire's legislature intended the statute to be susceptible to such a remedy,"[91] presumably pursuant to applicable separability principles.

By contrast with *Ayotte*, when the Supreme Court has applied the strict scrutiny test to rule for challengers to the constitutionality of affirmative action policies, the Justices have invariably invalidated the challenged policies on their faces.[92] Not all affirmative action schemes fail strict scrutiny, at least in the context of higher

---

[86]   546 U.S. 320 (2006).
[87]   *Id.* at 327–28.
[88]   *Id.* at 331.
[89]   *Id.* at 329.
[90]   *Id.* at 330–31.
[91]   *Id.* at 331.
[92]   *See, e.g., Gratz v. Bollinger*, 539 U.S. 244 (2003); *Regents of the Univ. of Cal. v. Bakke*, 438 U.S. 265 (1978).

education. The Court has upheld some.[93] But when challenged policies accord too much significance to race in the Court's view, the Justices have seen no way to "save" the policies in question that would not involve replacing them with entirely new policies. The severing of a statute, the Justices insist, must not require such a creative or unconstrained rewriting as to constitute "quintessentially legislative,"[94] rather than judicial, work.[95] It could perhaps go without saying that the degree of "rewriting" that courts can perform in severing a statute is a question of judgment, not governed by hard rule.[96] Clearly, however, the Supreme Court generally feels no obligation to sever statutes in imaginative ways not suggested either by the language of a challenged law or, as in *Ayotte*, by "background constitutional rules."[97] (In the hypothetical case of an FBI agent exceeding the Massachusetts speed limit, the Court could hold that after severance of applications that the Supremacy Clause makes invalid, the statute would easily satisfy rational basis review as applied to me or any other speeding driver.)

The Court's stated anxiety about overstepping the bounds of a properly judicial role reveals a tension that the Justices may experience acutely. On the one hand, the Court says, its function is to vindicate the rights of individuals, not to pronounce more generally on the validity of statutes. In doing so, it signals a preference for as-applied over facial challenges to statutes. On the other hand, the Court insists that the rewriting of statutes so that they could be applied to some cases but not to others would itself be a quintessentially legislative function. In criticizing judicial rewriting of statutes, the Court implies that it must judge the validity of statutes on their faces, as they were written. There is a genuine dissonance if not a contradiction here, one built into the judicial role. It may not have any wholly adequate resolution.

Nevertheless, when we sort out some of the confusion that attends the distinction between as-applied and facial challenges, and look with clear eyes at what the Supreme Court actually does, we can see that facial invalidations are common, not uncommon. To put the point slightly differently, much and even most of the

---

[93]   See, e.g., *Fisher v. Univ. of Tex. at Austin*, 136 S. Ct. 2198 (2016); *Grutter v. Bollinger*, 539 U.S. 306 (2003).

[94]   *Ayotte*, 546 U.S. at 329.

[95]   See *Reno v. ACLU*, 521 U.S. 844, 884–85 (1997) ("This Court 'will not rewrite a . . . law to conform it to constitutional requirements.'" (omission in original) (quoting *Virginia v. Am. Bookseller's Assn.*, 484 U.S. 383, 397 (1988))); *United States v. Nat'l Treasury Emps. Union*, 513 U.S. 454, 479–80 (1985) (citing "[o]ur obligation to avoid judicial legislation," *id.* at 479, as a ground for declining to adopt a saving construction); *Aptheker v. Sec'y of State*, 378 U.S. 500, 515–16 (1964) (declining to perform a "substantial rewriting" of a statute, *id.* at 515).

[96]   For a relatively recent case apparently testing the outer limits of permissible judicial action to save an otherwise unconstitutional statute, see *United States v. Booker*, 543 U.S. 220 (2005), in which the Court, by 5–4, cured an identified constitutional defect in statutorily mandated sentences under the federal Sentencing Guidelines by rendering the Guidelines "effectively advisory," *id.* at 245. See also *Skilling v. United States*, 561 U.S. 358, 422 (2010) (Scalia, J., concurring in part and concurring in the judgment) (protesting that the majority's "paring down" of a statute to save it from unconstitutional vagueness was "clearly beyond judicial power").

[97]   546 U.S. at 329.

time, the Court's claim that it disfavors facial challenges will not wash. But sometimes that claim does wash – namely, in those cases in which the Court sees or
foresees that it can save a statute that otherwise would fail strict judicial scrutiny or
another applicable constitutional test by separating it. In those cases, we can see the
Court's stated preference for as-applied challenges and its reliance on separability
doctrine as mechanisms – similar to others that this book has explored – for
equilibrating the social costs and benefits of constitutional rights and the available
remedies for their enforcement.

7

The Core of an Uneasy Case for Judicial Review

In the debates of the 1950s that preceded the development of strict judicial scrutiny in the 1960s, a central concern involved the justification, if any, for judicial balancing of competing values and interests that it was also the function of elected officials to weigh. Complicating the challenge was the bitter experience of the *Lochner* era, which seemed to dictate that any justification must incorporate and rationalize a double standard, pursuant to which economic interests received virtually no judicial protection. Although strict scrutiny responded relatively successfully to other challenges confronting the Court in the 1950s and 1960s, including that of defining a level of protection for preferred rights intermediate between absolutism and open-ended balancing, it left issues about the ultimate justification for judicial second-guessing of legislative judgments substantially unaddressed.

The question thus lingers: Why should we ask courts to redo the job of weighing and balancing competing individual and governmental interests, not all of which are plainly visible on the Constitution's surface, subject to the proviso that economic interests should count for little? Or, perhaps alternatively, are courts justified in taking on a role that requires as many value judgments as the application of strict judicial scrutiny? The issue, to be clear, is not whether the Supreme Court can get away with doing so much interest-balancing. As political scientists have argued, judicial review is in an important sense "politically constructed." It has thrived over time only because political leaders, supported by the public, have wanted it to exist in roughly the form that it does.[1] If they did not approve of judicial review, political leaders and the public would have found ways to weaken it – whether by defying judicial rulings, impeaching Justices who strayed too far from mainstream opinion, stripping the Supreme Court of jurisdiction over selected categories of cases, or "packing" it by increasing its size and letting presidents appoint new members who

---

[1] *See*, e.g., Keith Whittington, POLITICAL FOUNDATIONS OF JUDICIAL SUPREMACY: THE PRESIDENCY, THE SUPREME COURT, AND CONSTITUTIONAL LEADERSHIP IN U.S. HISTORY 4, 9 (2007) (explaining thesis that "judicial supremacy" is "politically constructed"); Mark A. Graber, *Constructing Judicial Review*, 8 ANN. REV. POL. SCI. 425, 425 (2005) (reviewing emerging body of political science literature that frames judicial review as an institution constructed by the political branches).

would reliably vote in "acceptable" ways. But none of these strategies has found favor. Among the considerations that have influenced both elite and public attitudes, judicial review provides incumbent officials with a hedge against their successors' severely adverse treatment of their legislative accomplishments and possibly themselves after they are out of office. Elected officials may also find it politically advantageous to leave the resolution of some contentious issues, though surely not all of them, to the courts.

Nevertheless, the political motivations that have helped to entrench judicial review do not provide it with a normative justification (any more than the political motivations that help to sustain other power-sharing agreements among elites suffice to legitimate those agreements.) Our question, accordingly, is whether judicial review, in roughly the form in which it is practiced in the United States, can be defended successfully on grounds of political morality, including reasonable consistency with democratic theory.

In addressing that issue, it is not enough to say that the Constitution contemplates judicial review. Available evidence suggests that the Founding generation predominantly anticipated judicial review of legislation, but expected it to be much more deferential than under strict scrutiny and other searching, modern tests. According to a recurring description, it was widely assumed among the Founding generation that the Supreme Court would invalidate statutes only when the legislature had made a "clear mistake" about constitutional permissibility.[2]

Even if the Founding generation did not contemplate the robust judicial review that we have today, courts might be justified in aggressively scrutinizing legislative enactments if modern constitutional rights and applicable tests for protecting them emerged relatively directly from the original meaning of constitutional language. Under those circumstances, judges and Justices would have opportunities for detached historical study that those engaged in other occupations would not. And courts, in enforcing original meanings, could claim to be doing no more and no less than the law required. But our constitutional practice is not predominantly originalist.[3] Constitutional adjudication in the Supreme Court does not consist

---

[2] *See, e.g.,* Sylvia Snowiss, JUDICIAL REVIEW AND THE LAW OF THE CONSTITUTION 13–89 (1990); Dean Alfange, Jr., Marbury v. Madison *and Original Understandings of Judicial Review: In Defense of Traditional Wisdom,* 1993 SUP. CT. REV. 329, 342–49; William R. Casto, *James Iredell and the American Origins of Judicial Review,* 27 CONN. L. REV. 329, 341–48 (1995); Michael J. Klarman, *How Great Were the "Great" Marshall Court Decisions?,* 87 VA. L. REV. 1111, 1120–21 (2001); Gordon S. Wood, *The Origins of Judicial Review Revisited, or How the Marshall Court Made More Out of Less,* 56 WASH. & LEE. L. REV. 787, 796–99 (1999); *see also* Barry Friedman, THE WILL OF THE PEOPLE (2009); Larry D. Kramer, THE PEOPLE THEMSELVES: POPULAR CONSTITUTIONALISM AND JUDICIAL REVIEW (2004); Robert G. McCloskey, THE AMERICAN SUPREME COURT (5th ed. 2010). In the history of American constitutional theory, the most famous defense of the rule of clear mistake is James B. Thayer, *The Origin and Scope of the American Doctrine of Constitutional Law,* 7 HARV. L. REV. 129 (1893).

[3] *See, e.g.,* David A. Strauss, THE LIVING CONSTITUTION (2010); Richard H. Fallon, Jr., *Constitutional Precedent Viewed through the Lens of Hartian Positivist Jurisprudence,* 86 N.C. L. REV. 1107 (2008).

principally of historical inquiry, even though historical inquiry plays a role. Close examination of the judicial function first in developing and then in applying strict judicial scrutiny belies pretensions to the contrary.

If we reject originalist defenses of the kind of judicial review that the modern Supreme Court practices, the most familiar remaining argument holds that courts have a special, justifying aptitude for making moral judgments – for example, that courts are peculiarly well designed to function as "forum[s] of principle."[4] But this argument turns out to be difficult to sustain as well, as the political theorist Jeremy Waldron has prominently argued.[5] In any reasonably democratic society that satis-fies four "quite demanding" but "not unrealistic" conditions, Waldron maintains, there is no reason to think that courts will perform better than legislatures in correctly identifying and defining citizens' moral rights against the government.[6] Waldron's most important conditions are that legislators take questions involving individual rights seriously and that "reasonable disagreement" exists about those questions' correct resolution.[7] His argument also assumes that a society has both representative political institutions and courts that are in "reasonably good order."[8] (He does not challenge judicial review of action by executive and bureaucratic officials,[9] who may often have less opportunity for debate and deliberation before they act in ways that might put rights at risk.) When these conditions are met, Waldron asserts, the fact that courts and legislatures differ in their assessments provides no ground for thinking courts more likely to be correct.

Waldron's assumptions about prevailing societal conditions are optimistic ones. Where they are not satisfied, he acknowledges that judicial review might be justified in response to "pathologies" in electoral politics and legislative decision-making.[10] I shall briefly consider pathology-based justifications for judicial review toward the end of this chapter. First, however, I want to take up Waldron's more challenging argument that judicial review could not be justified if our political institutions were in "reasonably good order" and if legislators strove conscientiously to respect indi-vidual rights. In response, I argue that something approximating the two-tiered scheme of judicial review that emerged in the 1950s and the 1960s makes sense, even on the assumption that our politics are reasonably well-ordered, as I believe that they have often been in the past and hope that they will be in the future.

Because Waldron's argument depends heavily on the assumption that debates about constitutional rights are largely debates about moral rights,[11] a number of

---

[4]   Ronald Dworkin, A MATTER OF PRINCIPLE 69–71 (1985).
[5]   Jeremy Waldron, *The Core of the Case against Judicial Review*, 115 YALE L.J. 1346 (2006) [hereinafter Waldron, *The Core Case*]; *see also* Jeremy Waldron, LAW AND DISAGREEMENT 211–312 (1999).
[6]   Waldron, *The Core Case, supra* note 5, at 1401–02.
[7]   *Id.* at 1369; *see id.* at 1364–69.
[8]   *Id.* at 1360; *see also id.* at 1360–64.
[9]   *See id.* at 1353–54.
[10] *Id.* at 1406.
[11] *See id.* at 1367, 1385–86 & 1385 n.110.

complexities attend its application to US constitutional law. Implicit rules of our constitutional practice impose significant restrictions on the rights that courts can recognize. Nonetheless, once we acknowledge that constitutional rights emerge from an identification and then a weighing of competing individual and governmental interests, assertions that courts should be presumed better than legislatures at determining whether legislation violates individual rights have a troublingly elitist cast. Virtually without exception, judges and Justices are well-educated members of the upper or upper-middle classes who have been socialized to accept professional norms.[12] The preference for having a small number of lawyers in robes resolve contested questions of political morality almost inevitably reflects some form of skepticism about majoritarianism,[13] frequently coupled with idealized portraits of the few who wield judicial power. As Waldron points out, moreover, courts have an understandable tendency to confront issues that are fundamentally moral in legalistic, logic-chopping terms in which head-on engagement with contending moral considerations sometimes gets almost wholly washed out.[14] In the view of many, *Roe* v. *Wade*[15] – in which the Court rather summarily invoked the strict scrutiny formula and then, equally brusquely, announced that state interests in protecting fetal life become compelling at the point of fetal viability but are not compelling before that point, with no real supporting argument – stands as Exhibit One for this proposition.[16] Even among those who agree with *Roe*'s result, almost no one seems satisfied with its reasoning.[17] Other examples abound.

To defeat Waldron's challenge – which depends on premises not terribly different from those that Justice Frankfurter embraced in rejecting the idea that the judiciary should aggressively protect "preferred" rights during the 1950s – supporters of judicial review need a non-originalist argument that does not rely on the premise that judges have superior, across-the-board moral acumen. I believe that such an argument exists, but also that it is complex, qualified, and contingent. Even if disposed to defend robust judicial review of the kind exhibited in strict judicial scrutiny, we should come to terms with difficulties in the

---

[12]   See John Ferejohn, *Independent Judges, Dependent Judiciary: Explaining Judicial Independence*, 72 S. CAL. L. REV. 353, 369 (1999) (noting that judges "are likely to bring to their work the perceptions of an upper middle class, educated, largely male, and largely white elite"); *see also* Paul Brest, *Who Decides?*, 58 S. CAL. L. REV. 661, 664 (1985).

[13]   See Kramer, *supra* note 2, at 241–46; Richard D. Parker, "HERE, THE PEOPLE RULE": A CONSTITUTIONAL POPULIST MANIFESTO 56–58 (1994).

[14]   See Waldron, *The Core Case*, *supra* note 5, at 1383–85.

[15]   410 U.S. 113 (1973).

[16]   See John Hart Ely, *The Wages of Crying Wolf: A Comment on* Roe v. Wade, 82 YALE L.J. 920, 924 (1973) (asserting that the Court's analysis "seems to mistake a definition for a syllogism"); Waldron, *The Core Case*, *supra* note 5, at 1383 (noting that the fifty-page opinion in *Roe* devoted only a few paragraphs to the moral issues at stake and that "the 'reasoning' is thread-bare.").

[17]   See WHAT ROE V. WADE SHOULD HAVE SAID 22 (Jack Balkin ed., 2005) ("It is hardly surprising that critics of a constitutional right to abortion would find much to criticize in [*Roe*]. But supporters of the abortion right over the years have also found them wanting.").

supporting arguments, and we should be open to changes in how judicial review is practiced in some cases.

In a nutshell, the best case for judicial review in politically and morally healthy societies depends on what Waldron calls "outcome-related" reasons, but it does not rely – as he imagines – on the idea that courts are more likely than legislatures to make correct decisions about how to define the morally grounded rights that the Constitution protects. The argument rests instead on the subtly different ground that legislatures and courts should *both* be enlisted in protecting fundamental or pre-ferred rights. More precisely, both should have veto powers over legislation that might reasonably be thought to violate the kind of fundamental, constitutionally secured moral rights that strict scrutiny and similarly robust judicial tests protect.[18] The supporting premise should be that it is worse, morally speaking, to define constitutional rights too narrowly than too broadly and that we should, therefore, charge the Supreme Court with imposing its definition of protected rights when its definition is more expansive than that of Congress or a state legislature. In a phrase, the best defense of judicial review is that it is presumptively better for constitutional rights to be over-protected than under-protected in circumstances of reasonable disagreement about how rights should be defined and that courts, as well as legislatures, should therefore be enlisted to protect individual rights.

CHALLENGES AND COMPLEXITIES

Although this argument is easy to state in outline form, developing it requires engagement with a number of complex issues. The first complexity arises from Waldron's emphasis on the phenomenon of reasonable disagreement about issues involving moral rights – about whether, for example, there is a moral right to engage in hate speech, to procure an abortion, or not to be classified on the basis of race in connection with an affirmative action program. We should recognize not only that there is disagreement about these questions, as is undeniably the case, but also that reasonable and rational people may come to different conclusions from those that we reach, sometimes after conscientious engagement with facts and arguments that we think decisive.[19] From the recognition of reasonable

---

[18] For an earlier defense of a similar position, see Frank B. Cross, *Institutions and Enforcement of the Bill of Rights*, 85 CORNELL L. REV. 1529, 1576 (2000) (arguing that judicial review may be justified even if a judiciary lacks "any intrinsic advantage in constitutional interpretation and enforcement" because "adding an additional check on government action will enhance the liberty the Bill of Rights offers.").

[19] John Rawls, POLITICAL LIBERALISM 54–58 (1993). Rawls used the term "the burdens of judgment" to refer to "the many hazards involved in the correct (and conscientious) exercise of our powers of reason and judgment," *id.* at 56, which give rise to "reasonable disagreement," *id.* at 55, and explain why "it is not to be expected that conscientious persons with full powers of reason, even after free discussion, will all arrive at the same conclusion," *id.* at 58. To say that a decision is subject to the burdens of judgment is not to say that there can be no right answer, *see id.* (noting that some reasonably disputable judgments "may be true"), but it is to acknowledge that knock-down arguments cannot always be expected.

disagreement, some slide immediately to the conclusion that moral questions have no right or wrong, or even no better or worse, answers. This conclusion would be fatal to my argument, and quite possibly to any argument, in favor of judicial review. If there are no better or worse answers to moral questions, then I obviously could not argue that a system with judicial review is likely to produce morally better outcomes than a system without judicial review. (Neither, however, could someone who denied that there are morally better and worse outcomes argue against judicial review on the ground that it is fairer to resolve disputable questions through majoritarian processes. This imagined ground for argument presupposes that there is a correct answer to at least one moral question, involving whether it is fair to entrust judges with the power of judicial review.)

Although it is admittedly difficult to give an account of precisely what makes moral judgments right or wrong, and I shall not attempt to provide such an account here, the deep structures of our moral thought and vocabulary presuppose objective correctness. When I say that murder is wrong, I mean that murder is wrong, full stop. Slaughtering Jews may have been morally acceptable from the perspective of the Nazis, but insofar as we are making moral rather than sociological judgments, we need to judge – on the basis of reflection and argument – how we and everyone else *ought* to think about the matter.[20] At first blush, the claim that our moral judgments are about what is right or wrong for everyone may sound arrogant and imperial. But common sense about the nature of morality insists that it cannot be "relative" in a sense that could make the slaughtering of Jews right for the Nazis, given their views or preferences, but wrong for you or me, given ours.

Although there is no complete consensus, most moral philosophers now seem to embrace the reflective equilibrium methodology that I described in Chapter 3 as the best model of moral reasoning.[21] When employing that methodology, we track back and forth between, and make necessary adjustments to reconcile, our intuitions about proper outcomes in particular cases and our beliefs about generally applicable moral principles. Two points about this method deserve emphasis, in part because they are easily misunderstood. First, employment of the method furnishes no guarantee of correct outcomes. Different people beginning with different moral commitments will reach different conclusions. But, second, the aim of the method is not mere consistency at the level of personal beliefs. To the contrary, the goal of moral inquiry is to reach correct, objectively justified conclusions. As a matter of

[20]   See Ronald Dworkin, *Objectivity and Truth: You'd Better Believe It*, 25 PHIL. & PUB. AFF. 87, 92 (1996) (describing as "the view you and I and most other people have" the belief that "genocide in Bosnia is wrong, immoral, wicked, odious … [and] moreover, that our opinions are not just subjective reactions to the idea of genocide, but opinions about its actual moral character. We think, in other words, that it is an objective matter – a matter of how things really are – that genocide is wrong.").

[21]   See Jeff McMahan, *Moral Intuition*, in THE BLACKWELL GUIDE TO ETHICAL THEORY (Hugh LaFollette & Ingmar Persson, eds., 2013) 103, 110 (characterizing the Rawlsian reflective equilibrium methodology as "[t]he most commonly endorsed method of moral inquiry among contemporary moral philosophers.").

general epistemology, we think beliefs reliable when they are arrived at using good methods for forming beliefs about matters of the relevant kind under good conditions for doing so. With respect to matters of moral right and wrong, reflective-equilibrium reasoning is as good a method as we have.[22] We need to start with the beliefs that we hold, then subject them to critical scrutiny. (If starting with our own beliefs does not seem promising, try to imagine a better way of beginning. Even if tempted by the view that I should start with someone else's beliefs, I would still, necessarily, be beginning with *my* belief that someone else's substantive views were more likely to be correct than mine.)

Professor Waldron, I should hasten to add, does not rest his argument against judicial review on morally relativist or skeptical premises.[23] Rather, assuming that moral questions can have correct answers, he targets and seeks to refute a particular argument supporting judicial review – an argument maintaining that courts are better than legislatures at resolving the moral issues that arise in the adjudication of constitutional rights disputes. According to Waldron, claims for courts' comparatively greater competence fail either because courts do not in fact possess specifically asserted advantages or, alternatively, because any judicial advantage is offset by a judicial disadvantage. Among the advantages of legislatures in comparison with courts, he includes their tendency to focus directly on underlying moral considerations.[24] Courts, he says, too often become preoccupied with issues of textual exegesis and interpretive methodology that distract them from the issues that we ought to care about most.[25]

The core of Waldron's argument thus comes to this: We have no good reason to think that courts will be better than legislatures at correctly identifying the rights that either courts or legislatures morally ought to recognize. And if not, it is simply fairer to let the people's elected representatives in Congress and the state legislatures decide than to repose the power of decision-making exclusively in an elite, non-elected judiciary.

Whatever its force as directed against arguments that courts are likely to be better moral decision-makers than legislatures, Waldron's argument, like others of a similar tenor, overlooks the possibility that we might have good, outcome-related reasons to enlist both the legislature and the courts in protecting individual rights. More specifically, we have good reason to want to create multiple veto points so that governmental action cannot occur if *either* the Supreme Court *or* the legislature thinks that it would violate individual rights of fundamental importance.[26] The one

[22] *See, e.g.,* T. M. Scanlon, Being Realistic about Reasons 77–84 (2014).
[23] Waldron's core case against judicial review involves societies in which the rights-skeptical position is merely "an outlier." Waldron, *The Core Case, supra* note 5, at 1365.
[24] *See id.* at 1384–85.
[25] *See id.* at 1381–82.
[26] *See* Cross, *supra* note 18, at 1576 (explaining that "the multiple vetoes concept relies on the benefit of adding judicial review on top of congressional and executive action."). Other scholars have argued that regardless of whether courts are more likely to identify rights correctly than are legislatures,

important proviso, echoing from the disastrous experience of the *Lochner* era, is that there must be assurances of limitations concerning the kinds of rights or interests that courts will deem fundamental.

Two analogies suggest the force of my argument for a judicial veto power. One comes from the federal jury system in criminal cases, under which a defendant cannot be convicted without the unanimous agreement of the jury,[27] and each of the twelve jurors must vote to acquit unless persuaded that the defendant has been proven guilty "beyond a reasonable doubt."[28] If the concern were simply to get correct judgments about whether the accused has committed a crime, decisions by majority vote, pursuant to a preponderance of the evidence standard, would produce more accurate outcomes.[29] Instead, we skew the system in a pro-defendant direction based on the premise that errors resulting in mistaken convictions of the innocent are morally worse, and thus more important to avoid, than erroneous acquittals of the guilty.[30] In other words, we care less about minimizing the overall number of errors than about minimizing the errors in a particular direction – a situation that might also obtain with respect to judgments involving individual rights.[31] With judgments of whether people have constitutional rights as with determinations of whether they have committed crimes, we might think it worse to err in one direction than in the other.

An even closer analogy involves the multipart system of lawmaking created by the United States Constitution, which has parallels in the constitutions of some other nations. As a matter of structural design, the Constitution makes it difficult for majorities to legislate. Separate majorities of both houses of a bicameral legislature are required, and the President also possesses a veto power. The underlying premise, plainly, is that it is presumptively worse for legislation to be enacted than not

judicial review might be defended on the ground that it creates an additional barrier to the enactment or enforcement of legislation. *See, e.g.*, Richard A. Epstein, *The Independence of Judges: The Uses and Limitations of Public Choice Theory*, 1990 BYU L. Rev. 827, 846; Julia D. Mahoney, *Kelo's Legacy: Eminent Domain and the Future of Property Rights*, 2005 Sup. Ct. Rev. 103, 129–31; Kermit Roosevelt III, *Constitutional Calcification: How the Law Becomes What the Court Does*, 91 Va. L. Rev. 1649, 1704 & n.182 (2005).

[27] The analogy of multiple jurors having vetoes to the vetoing effect of judicial review is admittedly not perfect. Whereas the Supreme Court can conclusively nullify an enactment that it believes to be unconstitutional (at least in the absence of a constitutional amendment), a single dissenting juror cannot absolutely block a conviction, due to the possibility of a retrial in which a conviction might subsequently be obtained.

[28] *In re Winship*, 397 U.S. 358, 363 (1970) (quoting *Davis v. United States*, 160 U.S. 469, 493 (1895)).

[29] *See* Larry Laudan, Truth, Error, and Criminal Law: An Essay in Legal Epistemology 29–30 (2006) (examining traditional principles of criminal law to show that standards such as the requirement of proof beyond a reasonable doubt are designed to ensure that errors "will be predominantly false acquittals rather than false convictions.").

[30] *See id.* at 63 (collecting authorities that so assert).

[31] *See* Cross, *supra* note 18, at 1592 (arguing that "false negatives (underenforcement of constitutional freedoms) are both more serious and more likely to occur than false positives (overenforcement of constitutional freedoms)" and calling "for a decision rule that does not necessarily minimize all mistakes but rather minimizes false negatives.").

enacted, largely because of the threat that legislation might violate individual rights, and that multiple veto points should therefore exist.

This argument for judicial review obviously depends heavily on an assumption that legislative action is more likely to violate fundamental rights than is legislative inaction. This is a commonly held assumption that underlies a variety of familiar governmental structures, including bicameralism requirements and provisions for presidential vetoes. Nevertheless, the assumption that governmental action is more likely to violate rights than governmental inaction is certainly open to challenge. Indeed, I believe that it is both possible and important to identify categories of cases in which that assumption does not hold. I shall return to this concern shortly and propose that our existing structure of judicial review should be revised modestly in light of it.

First, however, we need to address a related complexity. Although it is reasonable in principle to believe it better to err on the side of too much rather than too little protection of fundamental rights, an argument that supports judicial review on this basis obviously risks proving too much. If multiple vetoes are good, why stop with the legislature, the President, and the courts? Why not establish other institutions with veto powers or insist on unanimous consent before any legislation can be enacted? Furthermore, why limit the veto power to what I have referred to as fundamental rights? Why not protect every liberty interest in the same way?

Any good answer to questions such as these must have two related parts. First, in striving for a reasonable balance, the strategy of assigning vetoes to multiple institutions makes most sense insofar as the recipient institutions possess distinctive perspectives tending to make them more sensitive than others to some morally pertinent considerations.[32] A reason to give the President a veto over legislative action is that the executive and legislative branches will likely have different, potentially valuable vantage points from which to assess competing interests and values. Similarly, a reason to give courts a veto power is that courts are likely to have a perspective that may make them more sensitive than legislatures to some possible rights violations even if the evidence on whether that perspective is better overall may be inconclusive.[33] Perhaps most obviously, courts typically decide cases upon

---

[32] My argument in this paragraph parallels the argument for federal habeas corpus review of state criminal convictions advanced in Robert M. Cover & T. Alexander Aleinikoff, *Dialectical Federalism: Habeas Corpus and the Court*, 86 YALE L.J. 1035 (1977). The authors defend federal review not on the ground that federal courts are more likely than state courts to define constitutional rights correctly, but on the basis that jurisdictional redundancy is especially desirable because state and federal courts are likely to have different perspectives on how rights ought to be defined. *Id.* at 1046–54.

[33] *See, e.g.*, Jonathan R. Siegel, *The Institutional Case for Judicial Review*, 97 IOWA L. REV. 1147 (2012). Although "there are a large number of obviously nontotalitarian societies – Great Britain, New Zealand, the Netherlands, Sweden, and France, for example – that survive quite nicely without" robust, American-style judicial review, those countries tend to be less protective than the United States of claimed rights involving "criminal procedure, freedom of the press when it is irresponsible, freedom of speech for the truly evil (Nazis, Klansmen, and child pornographers, for example), and

concrete facts, some of which even highly competent legislators may not have foreseen. Furthermore, a distinguishing feature of judges' professional training and mission involves a solicitude for rights as they have historically been understood. Historic understandings may of course have been wrong in some, even many, instances.[34] Nevertheless, judges' professionally ingrained instincts and processes of judgment are likely to differ from those of legislators and to be better adapted to reflecting such imperfect wisdom about the content of rights as our legal tradition embodies.[35] In the context of historic understandings of and anxieties about judicial power, courts can also be asked and expected to discharge their reviewing functions with reasonable restraint.

Second, even insofar as the courts are concerned, limits on judicial second-guessing of legislative judgments need to be established. Although it is easy to think of cases in which the costs of under-enforcing rights would seem much worse than those of overprotection, no sound approach could wholly discount the costs of errors in either direction.[36] Most of us may think it worse to convict one innocent defendant than to let three or five or perhaps nine guilty persons go free, but we do not structure the criminal process on the assumption that it would be better to let thousands escape accountability than to risk ever punishing a single innocent.

We need to take account, moreover, of rights or interests that require legislative action for their protection – those that are not threatened by governmental action, but instead provide sometimes imperative justifications for the government to legislate. As prior chapters have emphasized, among our Constitution's strategies for protecting individual interests, including the kinds of interests from which rights derive, is to vest power in the legislative branch. The US Constitution creates relatively few "positive" rights to benefits and opportunities that did not already exist within the common law framework that generally prevailed at the time of the Constitution's ratification. Accordingly, any scheme of judicial review that could be defended successfully would need limiting mechanisms to avoid frustration of

---

a strong separation between church and state." Frederick Schauer, *Judicial Supremacy and the Modest Constitution*, 92 CALIF. L. REV. 1045, 1066 n.100 (2004). According to Schauer, "[i]t may be wrong for the United States to be so divergent, but setting these countries out as models suggests a willingness to accept fewer defendant's rights, free speech rights, free press rights, and separation of church and state rights than exist in the United States." *Id.; see also* Frank B. Cross, *The Relevance of Law in Human Rights Protection*, 19 INT'L REV. L. & ECON. 87, 92–93 (1999) (concluding on the basis of empirical data that "[j]udicial independence" is "significantly associated with greater political freedom, suggesting a prominent role for the law and courts in the protection of freedom.").

[34] *See generally* Adrian Vermeule, *Common Law Constitutionalism and the Limits of Reason*, 107 COLUM. L. REV. 1482 (2007) (skeptically probing arguments that the historic survival of common law decision rules attests to their likely wisdom).

[35] *See generally* David A. Strauss, *Common Law Constitutional Interpretation*, 63 U. CHI. L. REV. 877 (1996) (defending judicial review partly on Burkean grounds).

[36] *But cf.* Cross, *supra* note 18, at 1577–78 (arguing that "even a wildly incompetent court would have a constitutional benefit as a backstop to screen out unconstitutional legislation.").

governmental efforts to protect important individual interests by enacting legislation.

In sum, for a defense of judicial review to succeed, it is not enough to establish, in principle, that errors that result in the under-enforcement of fundamental rights are often more troubling than errors that result in overprotection, and that judicial review may provide a distinctively valuable hedge against errors of under-enforcement. To defend a robust regime of judicial review, we need to go on to establish that its central defining features are sensibly designed to defend the right kinds of rights in ways appropriate to the nature of the interests at stake.

DEFENDING STRICT SCRUTINY AND THE STRUCTURE OF JUDICIAL REVIEW

With this turn in the argument, questions about the wisdom of a tiered, analytically sequenced scheme of judicial review move back to the center stage that they occupied during the 1950s.

Preferred Rights and Tiers of Scrutiny

If we think about rights as protecting interests in the way that Chapter 3 laid out, we could imagine a myriad of possible protective structures, including ones that tailor the precise form of judicial review very particularly, and possibly uniquely, to the importance of the right or interests in question in any particular case. But reason and experience counsel strongly against too complexly differentiated an approach. There are famous disputes about how best to describe the prevailing scheme of judicial review during the *Lochner* era. But the most salient point is that too aggressive judicial review to protect too many kinds of interests, centrally including interests in freedom from unwanted governmental regulation of businesses and the economy, produced disastrous consequences.

If we ask why, the answer has many aspects, some conceptual and some historically contingent. But it is crucial to recognize that the Supreme Court came to grief as a result of efforts to protect one set of economic interests, through the enforcement of judicially protected constitutional rights, against governmental efforts to promote another set of interests that most Americans had come to adjudge at least equally important.

That judgment, which any effective defense of the modern scheme of judicial review needs to embrace, was well justified. With the political branches of the government needing flexibility in order to discharge their interest-protecting function effectively, the post-*Lochner* Supreme Court was right to distinguish between "ordinary" liberty interests, on the one hand, and preferred or fundamental rights, on the other hand. Although the decision to create a substantially two-tiered structure of judicial review occurred in a particular historical moment, it has stood up well to the challenges of ensuing years. In light of reasonable disagreement about precisely how best to weigh or value many particular liberty interests – notably including asserted interests in freedom of contract – a relatively clear, disciplining standard of judicial review was desirable to stop too much varied and unpredictable judicial second-guessing of legislative judgments about how to distribute the benefits and burdens of economic life. To take classic examples, worker safety laws restrict the liberty interests of employers and some employees, but benefit others. Environmental laws that burden liberty interests also do so in order to promote competing interests. Reasonable people can disagree about how exactly the balance should be struck. Within broad bounds, however, the community's political representatives should not be hamstrung in their efforts to enact worker-safety and environmental legislation, any more than they should be aggressively second-guessed by courts when they set the speed limit at 55 rather than at 45, as some might prefer, or at 60 or 65 miles per hour. If the legislature goes too far, as it surely can, the corrective should ordinarily come through elections and politics. One can undoubtedly cavil about exactly how deferential to legislative judgment rational basis review ought to be. But the basic design choice to distinguish fundamental rights from mere liberty interests and to accord only minimal judicial protection to the latter seems well justified, as does the exclusion of nearly all claims of economic rights from the upper tier.

For a long season in the post-*Lochner* era of strict judicial scrutiny in the United States, the assignment of economic interests to second-tier status provoked little opposition. The lessons of history seemed too strong. Some pressure to deviate from the equilibrium came from the political left during the 1960s and 1970s, when commentators argued powerfully for recognition of fundamental constitutional rights to welfare and education.[37] As the most insightful of these commentators noticed, however, recognition of "positive" rights to education, welfare, and the like – at least in the absence of substantial implementing legislation – would overtax courts' practical competence.[38] If courts were to identify a fundamental right to welfare, for example, implementing the right would not only require complex judgments about appropriate institutional design, but also implicate a host of issues involving tax policy (to finance the required benefits) and comparative resource allocation, involving the competing claims of interests in education and national defense. As I have emphasized, governmental powers exist to protect vital human

[37] See, e.g., Frank I. Michelman, *The Supreme Court, 1968 Term – Foreword: On Protecting the Poor through the Fourteenth Amendment*, 83 HARV. L. REV. 7 (1969) [hereinafter Protecting the Poor]; Frank I. Michelman, *In Pursuit of Constitutional Welfare Rights: One View of Rawls' Theory of Justice*, 121 U. PA. L. REV. 962 (1973); Laurence H. Tribe, *Unraveling National League of Cities: The New Federalism and Affirmative Rights to Essential Government Services*, 90 HARV. L. REV. 1065 (1977); see also Goodwin Liu, *Rethinking Constitutional Welfare Rights*, 61 STAN. L. REV. 203 (2008); id. at 205 n.5 (collecting sources).

[38] See, e.g., Michelman, *Protecting the Poor, supra* note 37, at 39; Lawrence G. Sager, *Justice in Plain Clothes: Reflections on the Thinness of Constitutional Law*, 88 Nw. U. L. REV. 410, 419–20 (1993); Lawrence Gene Sager, *Fair Measure: The Legal Status of Underenforced Constitutional Norms*, 91 HARV. L. REV. 1212, 1217–18 (1978).

interests. Within broad bounds, however, substantial judicial deference to legislative judgments about whether to create and then how to define statutory rights to affirmative governmental assistance makes sound structural sense. There may be an important role for courts in ensuring procedural fairness and nondiscrimination in the distribution of benefits. But such a role should acknowledge legislative primacy in converting interests in education, welfare, and health care into statutory, not constitutional, rights.

More recently, philosophical libertarians have increasingly maintained that all liberty interests are important and that traditional economic liberties, including asserted rights to freedom of contract, deserve substantial judicial safeguards.[39] In my judgment, that view is deeply mistaken as a philosophical matter. If rights reflect interests – as I have argued throughout this book – libertarian arguments that people have pre-political rights to freedom from economic regulation stumble into fallacy at the ground level. As generations of legal and philosophical thinkers have recognized, the world does not come naturally divided up into property and property rights.[40] Law must decide who owns what: today's capitalists, descendants of Native Americans who were forcibly evicted from lands that others now claim, or the government on behalf of the citizenry collectively? Having done so, law must further decide whether the ownership of land includes a right to exclude airplanes from flying overhead or to operate a factory the noxious emanations from which make neighbors' enjoyment of their adjoining property a practical impossibility. For my own part, I believe strongly in a scheme of regulated capitalism, but solely and simply because regulated capitalism seems as a practical matter to serve human interests better than other forms of economic organization. And "regulated capitalism" implies substantial judicial deference to legislative judgments about how property and liberty rights should be defined and regulated.

Economic libertarians will reject this argument as superficial. In reply, I must acknowledge that a deep engagement would require volumes that would largely only repeat what other volumes have said already. But I would also emphasize, once more, that recognition that rights reflect interests implies the necessity for consequence-sensitive balancing of competing interests. And when discussion occurs on those terms, history and experience – including the calamity of the *Lochner* era, culminating in the Court-packing threat of 1937 and the ensuing "switch in time that saved the nine"[41] – teach that searching judicial review of legislation defining and adjusting the benefits and burdens of economic life is a recipe for disaster. Correctly

---

[39] *See, e.g.*, Randy E. Barnett, Restoring the Lost Constitution: The Presumption of Liberty (2004); Richard A. Epstein, Takings: Private Property and the Power of Eminent Domain (1985).

[40] *See, e.g.*, Felix S. Cohen, *Transcendental Nonsense and the Functional Approach*, 35 Colum. L. Rev. 809, 815–16 (1935); Morris R. Cohen, *Property and Sovereignty*, 13 Cornell L.Q. 8, 11–12 (1927); *see also* Liam Murphy & Thomas Nagel, The Myth of Ownership: Taxes and Justice 31–37, 64–66 (2002).

[41] On the Supreme Court's hostile stance toward New Deal legislation in the years preceding 1937, President Roosevelt's proposed Court-packing plan, and the effect of a seeming judicial reversal on the

grasping that rights are constructs designed to protect underlying interests, a majority of the electorate might well conclude, for example, that the balance of interests urgently requires the creation of statutory rights to education, health care, and safe working conditions that would require associated infringements on non-fundamental liberty interests, especially involving economic matters.

Having taken this view about economic liberties and interests, should we now reconsider whether courts should be trusted to exercise moral judgment in identifying other kinds of fundamental rights any infringement of which should trigger elevated judicial scrutiny? No. As experience has shown, the lesson from the *Lochner* era does not generalize so broadly. To the contrary, when enough kinds of cases are brought into view, almost no one believes that the Supreme Court, if it is to engage in judicial review at all, should abandon strict scrutiny in all cases. Indeed, almost no one insists consistently that the identification of triggering rights should be rigidly limited by the language or original history of particular constitutional provisions. For example, nearly everyone accepts that the Free Speech Clause creates rights against the president and the judicial branch as well as against Congress (even though it begins by saying "Congress shall make no law "), affords protection to association in addition to speech (even though it makes no express reference to association), and extends to corporations in at least some facets of their operations (even if the Founding generation viewed corporations as possessing only such rights as their charters granted them).

At this point another question arises: In embracing an assertive judicial role in identifying preferred or fundamental rights, must we assume that courts at least have a special moral expertise that justifies them in determining which non-economic rights and interests require special judicial solicitude? I think not. We should ask judges to make the requisite judgment not because their general capacity for moral reasoning is a cut above that of legislators or the public, but because judges could not act as a veto-gate in protecting fundamental rights if they could not determine which rights are sufficiently fundamental to merit special judicial solicitude. Ceding responsibility to judges to determine which rights are fundamental and which are not is thus part and parcel of the decision to create a two-tiered scheme of judicial review. Although that decision may depend on the premise that judges have a distinctive and valuable perspective to bring to bear, it does not need to rely on the stronger proposition that courts have a generally superior capacity for moral reasoning.

The Scope of Review in Fundamental Rights Cases: Strict Scrutiny Revisited

We now come to questions involving the stringency of the protection that judicial review should afford to fundamental rights. The precise form that searching review

plan's ultimate defeat, see, *e.g.*, Barry Friedman, The Will of the People: How Public Opinion Has Influenced the Supreme Court and Shaped the Meaning of the Constitution 2 195–236 (2009); William E. Leuchtenburg, The Supreme Court Reborn: The Constitutional Revolution in the Age of Roosevelt (1995).

ought to take is undoubtedly debatable. As Chapter 1 emphasized, strict scrutiny is a generic response to a partly, but only a partly, generic problem. So recognizing does not rule out different, more particularized tests. Although much more might be said about those tests, a number of which Chapter 4 canvased, here I shall focus on strict scrutiny because of its outsized importance as a mechanism for identifying and enforcing fundamental rights.

As Chapter 2 emphasized, the Supreme Court has never definitively determined whether strict scrutiny should embody a nearly categorical prohibition or a weighted balancing test. It should now be easy to see why. Although strict scrutiny addresses a problem that is generic in one sense, involving how to give meaningfully robust but not absolute protection to important constitutional rights, the challenges that arise in different cases of alleged infringement of fundamental rights are highly diverse. Different candidates to count as triggering rights reflect a multiplicity of interests. Competing governmental interests vary comparably. Questions of narrow tailoring can take an endless range of forms.

Under these circumstances, the Supreme Court's failure to achieve clear consistency on whether strict scrutiny should reflect a nearly categorical prohibition or a prescription for weighted balancing has meant that the formula functions as a sliding scale. It is extremely rights-protective in some cases, less so in others. An important question thus arises involving how we should judge this state of affairs.

Relative to the alternatives, the sliding-scale approach has much to commend it. Allowing strict scrutiny to operate along a sliding scale permits case-by-case decision-making that is sensitive, within a bounded range, to the varied moral importance of particular claimed rights and of the interests that compete with them in particular cases. A comparison with the converging judgment of other liberal democracies lends support to this conclusion. In seeking a framework for judicial protection of constitutional rights that is not absolutist but is nevertheless more stringent than mere balancing, other nations have increasingly adopted forms of "proportionality" analysis.[42] As intimated in Chapter 2, I believe that the American formulation of the strict scrutiny test conveys rhetorical signals, which are healthy, that fundamental rights demand more stringent protection in all cases than proportionality analysis necessarily demands. Nevertheless, a sliding-scale version of strict scrutiny does so without precluding an appropriate modicum of flexibility, analogous but not identical to that which exists under proportionality review. The American approach also reflects convergent practice in making the infringement of a relatively fundamental right or interest a predicate for meaningful judicial review.

In sum, strict judicial scrutiny seems to me to be reasonably defensible as falling into the middle range of a continuum on which both polar regions ought to be

---

[42] *See* Alec Stone Sweet & Jud Mathews, *Proportionality Balancing and Global Constitutionalism*, 47 COLUM. J. TRANSNAT'L L. 72, 74 (2008); *see also* Carlos Bernal Pulido, *The Migration of Proportionality Across Europe*, 11 N.Z. J. PUB. & INT'L L. 483, 499–500 (2013); Moshe Cohen-Eliya & Iddo Porat, *Proportionality and the Culture of Justification*, 59 AM. J. COMP. L. 463, 465 (2011).

avoided. More specifically, strict scrutiny is flexible to more or less the right degree. While avoiding either absolutism or mere balancing, strict judicial scrutiny can take either a more or a less stringent form.

IS JUDICIAL REVIEW UNFAIR?

One last objection to judicial review in general, and to the substantially two-tiered scheme that the Supreme Court has evolved in particular, remains to be confronted. Having dismissed the outcome-based case in favor of judicial review, Waldron advances "process-based" arguments purporting to establish that judicial review is unfair and "illegitimate" in any society that meets his four conditions, centrally including the legislature's seriousness about protecting constitutional rights.[43] In essence, he claims that judicial review deprives political majorities of the right to democratic self-governance on important issues. This process-based objection might possibly be overcome, he acknowledges, if courts were likely to be better than legislatures at resolving disputed questions about moral rights.[44] But having adjudged the outcome-related case for judicial review to be "at best inconclusive,"[45] Waldron concludes that the fairness-based argument in favor of majority decision by politically accountable legislatures ought to prevail.[46] If Waldron's normative arguments were valid, they would retain their bite even if political leaders prefer to have relatively aggressive judicial review for their own self-interested reasons. In that case, politically accountable decision-makers should have to take full political and moral responsibility for decisions about people's moral and constitutional rights.

But Waldron's fairness- or process-based arguments against judicial review fall with his argument that there are no good, outcome-based reasons to have courts second-guess legislative judgments about individual rights. It is almost too plain for argument that the fairness of procedures for protecting rights depends on the nature of the substantive ends that the procedures are designed to promote. For example, it is not unfair to use non-majoritarian voting procedures in criminal trials. To accord each juror the power to veto a guilty verdict is wholly justifiable in view of the goals of the criminal justice system. Similarly, if judicial review promotes morally better outcomes than would exclusive legislative definitions of disputed rights, then reliance on judicial review is not unfair within the context of an otherwise largely democratic government.

Nor, Waldron to the contrary notwithstanding, does judicial review necessarily lack "legitimacy."[47] As Waldron uses the term, a political regime is legitimate insofar

---

[43] See Waldron, *The Core Case, supra* note 5, at 1386–95.
[44] See *id.* at 1375.
[45] *Id.*
[46] See *id.* at 1375–76.
[47] See *id.* at 1386–93.

as its design and composition provide good reasons for those who disagree with particular laws and decisions nevertheless to respect and obey them. In arguing against judicial review, Waldron frequently equates "political legitimacy" with "democratic legitimacy." When decisions emerge from processes in which everyone has a voice and a vote, he argues, even the losers have reason to accede to the outcome on the ground that their views were fairly taken into account.[48] We do not, he believes, have comparably good reason to respect Supreme Court decisions with which we disagree.

Although Waldron is correct that democratic legitimacy is important, he fails to acknowledge that political legitimacy – which is a broader concept – can have multiple sources.[49] No less than fairness, political legitimacy is relative to the ends that an institution seeks to achieve. One possible ground for the political legitimacy of a decision is that it emerged from open processes in which all citizens had equal voice and votes. But there are grounds for political legitimacy besides the majority-decision principle. Another good reason to respect a decision and to regard it as deserving obedience is that it issued from a process designed to reach generally sensible substantive decisions while making infringements of individual rights as unlikely as reasonably possible. When the diversity of potential sources of political legitimacy comes into view, what Waldron can claim to have established convincingly is, at most, that judicial review lacks the specifically democratic form of legitimacy that adheres to decisions reached through majoritarian processes. When other sources of political legitimacy enter the calculus, the possibility emerges that judicial review might actually promote, not detract from, the overall legitimacy of our regime of government if it provides important assurances against rights violations. To put the point more assertively, if judicial review reduces the likelihood that important rights will be infringed, then it may actually enhance, rather than undermine, the overall political legitimacy of constitutional government in the United States.

THE PATHOLOGY-BASED CASE FOR JUDICIAL REVIEW

So far my argument has assumed that Waldron's four "quite demanding" but "not unrealistic" conditions obtain in the United States[50] and that judicial review should be defended on the assumption that courts have no greater moral acumen than legislators in identifying fundamental rights. Notably, however, Waldron acknowledges that severe defects in the politics of some societies might justify reliance on judicial review as a partial corrective. He writes that judicial review might be necessary to counteract "legislative pathologies relating to sex, race, or religion in

[48] *See id.* at 1386–89.
[49] On the various senses of "legitimacy," including moral or political legitimacy, see Richard H. Fallon, Jr., LAW AND LEGITIMACY IN THE SUPREME COURT 20–46 (2018).
[50] Waldron, *The Core Case, supra* note 5, at 1401–02.

particular countries."[51] He adds that "hasty or sectarian legislating is [also] not part of the normal theory of what legislatures are set up to do" and notices arguments that the United States may fall short of being reasonably well ordered in this respect as well.[52] If the United States fails to satisfy the conditions that Waldron postulates, judicial review might be justifiable on what he calls "non-core" grounds.[53] Under those circumstances, the challenge would be to establish that courts, and especially the Supreme Court, would be less prone to infection by relevant pathologies than the citizens and legislators whose judgments judicial review sometimes displaces.

I take no pleasure – no one should – in adducing evidence that our prevailing political and legislative cultures in the United States are not reasonably well-ordered in Waldron's sense. But we should not dismiss that possibility either. Electoral politics are notoriously and increasingly riven by suspicion, partisanship, and ill will. Close and nonpartisan observers deem Congress a broken institution, where short-term political interests, mostly defined along partisan lines, tend to dominate.[54] According to numerous accounts, modern members of Congress typically take scant interest in constitutional issues presented by the legislation that they debate and enact.[55] Apart from promoting ideological interests, most focus predominantly on warding off challengers and securing reelection.[56]

By contrast, conditions in the judicial branch look relatively better, at least for now. The legal system churns up an endless flow of "easy" questions,[57] nearly all of which I assume courts decide fairly, correctly, and without hint of corruption. There are also difficult cases. With respect to these, purported realists claim that the Justices of the Supreme Court, in particular, routinely follow political agendas without regard for law.[58] Based on the available evidence, I would reject this claim.[59] Among other indicators, the Justices reach unanimous judgments in

---

[51] *Id.* at 1352.

[52] *Id.* at 1386.

[53] *Id.*

[54] *See* Thomas E. Mann & Norman J. Ornstein, It's Even Worse Than It Looks: How the American Constitutional System Collided with the New Politics of Extremism (2012); Thomas E. Mann & Norman J. Ornstein, The Broken Branch: How Congress Is Failing America and How to Get It Back on Track (2006).

[55] See Neal Devins, *Why Congress Does Not Challenge Judicial Supremacy*, 58 Wm. & Mary L. Rev. 1495, 1515–24 (2017); Frederick Schauer, The Annoying Constitution: Implications for the Allocation of Interpretive Authority, 58 Wm. & Mary. L. Rev. 1689, 1707 (2017).

[56] *See* David R. Mayhew, Congress: The Electoral Connection 16–17, 43–44 (2d ed. 2004).

[57] *See generally* Frederick Schauer, *Easy Cases*, 58 S. Cal. L. Rev. 399 (1985).

[58] *See, e.g.,* Jeffrey A. Segal & Harold J. Spaeth, The Supreme Court and the Attitudinal Model Revisited 372–76 (2002) (giving statistics showing the Chief Justices, especially recently, assign cases favorably to their ideological allies – which is most salient in important cases, "guarantee[ing] . . . the opinion will conform as closely as possible to the chief's personal policy preferences," *id.* at 377); Richard A. Posner, *The Supreme Court, 2004 Term – Foreword: A Political Court*, 119 Harv. L. Rev. 31, 34 (2005) (arguing that the Supreme Court is a "political body" when deciding constitutional cases).

[59] *See* Richard H. Fallon, Jr., *Constitutional Constraints*, 97 Calif. L. Rev. 975, 1002–24 (2009).

many cases – in 62 percent during the 2013 Term,[60] for example. To cite just one more bit of evidence, an examination of the coalitions of Justices that invalidated fifty-three federal laws between 1980 and 2004 revealed that more than 70 percent had a bipartisan composition and that "more than [60%] ... [were] inconsistent with a model of policy-motivated judging, either because they were joined by both liberal and conservative justices or because they reached results that are difficult to place in ideological space."[61]

In describing the judicial branch as taking its constitutional obligations seriously, I would not paint an entirely sanguine picture. The modern constitutional era is characterized by both high methodological self-consciousness and widespread hermeneutic suspicion.[62] Critics recurrently point to cases in which both liberal and conservative Justices deviate from previously embraced methodological principles – such as those requiring fidelity to the original public meaning of constitutional language, or alternatively to judicial precedent – in high stakes, ideologically salient cases. For example, conservative Justices who sometimes champion originalism have voted to invalidate affirmative action programs, despite the absence of evidence that relevant constitutional provisions were originally understood or intended to preclude preferences for racial minorities.[63] On the other side, liberals who castigate their conservative colleagues for overturning broad swaths of precedent in some cases[64] have readily jettisoned precedents in order to find protected rights to sexual intimacy outside of marriage[65] and to same-sex marriage.[66]

Appointments processes aimed at pushing the Court in an ideologically defined direction raise the prospect of increasing polarization, which should also provoke unease. Even if judicial review might otherwise be justified as a hedge against legislative pathologies, no sound reason of political morality calls for placing the

[60] Cass R. Sunstein, *Unanimity and Disagreement on the Supreme Court*, 100 CORNELL L. REV. 769, 784 (2015).

[61] Thomas M. Keck, *Party, Policy, or Duty: Why Does the Supreme Court Invalidate Federal Statutes?*, 101 AM. POL. SCI. REV. 321, 324, 336 (2007).

[62] See Duncan Kennedy, *The Hermeneutic of Suspicion in Contemporary American Legal Thought*, 25 LAW & CRITIQUE 91, 116 (2014).

[63] See, e.g., Cass R. Sunstein, RADICALS IN ROBES: WHY EXTREME RIGHT-WING COURTS ARE WRONG FOR AMERICA 137–42 (2005) (arguing the history of the Fourteenth Amendment provides no foundation for deeming affirmative action unconstitutional); Jed Rubenfeld, Essay, *Affirmative Action*, 107 YALE L.J. 427, 431–32 (1997) (citing the Freedmen's Bureau Acts as examples of nineteenth century "statutes expressly refer[ring] to color in the allotment of federal benefits"); Stephen A. Siegel, *The Federal Government's Power to Enact Color-Conscious Laws: An Originalist Inquiry*, 92 NW. U. L. REV. 477, 513–25, 549–65 (1998) (detailing color-conscious lawmaking, benign and invidious, in both the Founding and Reconstruction eras).

[64] See, e.g., *Citizens United* v. *FEC*, 558 U.S. 310, 395–96 (2010) (Stevens, J., concurring in part and dissenting in part) (criticizing the majority for "reject[ing] a century of history" and "blaz[ing] through our precedents, overruling or disavowing a body of case law.").

[65] See *Lawrence* v. *Texas*, 539 U.S. 558, 586 (2003) (Scalia, J., dissenting) (criticizing the majority for hypocrisy in its "17-year crusade to overrule *Bowers* v. *Hardwick*" after castigating those trying to overrule *Roe* v. *Wade* in *Planned Parenthood* v. *Casey*).

[66] See *Obergefell* v. *Hodges*, 135 S. Ct. 2584 (2015).

power to thwart the policies of politically accountable officials in a tribunal composed of ideological extremists, individually nominated and confirmed to advance sometimes dueling political agendas. That said, if we were to adjudge our political processes too disordered to afford fair protection to fundamental rights, judicial review might be justified, however precariously, as a corrective. If so, moreover, judges would be justified in reweighing interests that the legislature should have weighed because there would be no other plausible way for judges and Justices to identify and enforce constitutional rights. As Chapter 5 argued, distinguishing between acceptable moral judgment and forbidden animus, prejudice, or (as we might now add) pathology is itself a morally inflected exercise.

ADJUSTING JUDICIAL REVIEW

Although my double-safeguard defense of judicial review fits the main outlines of modern American judicial practice, several matters of detail deserve attention. To begin with, my argument for multiple veto opportunities to protect fundamental rights would ordinarily provide no foundation for judicial review of congressional action to protect congressionally defined rights under Section 5 of the Fourteenth Amendment.[67] To be concrete, if Congress enacts statutes designed to protect a broader right to the free exercise of religion than the Supreme Court has found to exist, and if no one's fundamental rights are threatened, then my argument for searching judicial review, which emphasizes that it is better for constitutional rights to be over-enforced than under-enforced, would not apply.[68]

Nor would my argument, which is premised on the desirability of a double-safeguard for rights, establish the desirability of judicial review to protect any structural constitutional norms that do not directly safeguard fundamental rights (including norms of constitutional federalism).[69] Nothing in my argument

---

[67] The Supreme Court has recently engaged in close oversight of congressional efforts to "enforce" the Fourteenth Amendment based on its judgment that Congress may not define the Constitution's substantive guarantees more broadly than the Court has defined them. *See City of Boerne v. Flores*, 521 U.S. 507, 519 (1997) (holding that by attempting to provide more protection to free exercise rights than had the Supreme Court, Congress exceeded its Section 5 powers, since "[l]egislation which alters the meaning of the Free Exercise Clause cannot be said to be enforcing the Clause."). The Court once took a more relaxed approach, positing that Congress's powers under Section 5 mirrored the broad reach of its powers under the Necessary and Proper Clause as articulated in *McCulloch v. Maryland*, 17 U.S. (4 Wheat.) 316 (1819). *See Katzenbach v. Morgan*, 384 U.S. 641, 651 (1966) (holding that "the *McCulloch v. Maryland* standard is the measure of what constitutes 'appropriate legislation' under § 5," which is "a positive grant of legislative power authorizing Congress to exercise its discretion in determining whether and what legislation is needed to secure the guarantees of the Fourteenth Amendment.").

[68] *Cf. Katzenbach*, 384 U.S. 651 n.10 ("We emphasize that Congress' power under § 5 is limited to adopting measures to enforce the guarantees of the Amendment; § 5 grants Congress no power to restrict, abrogate, or dilute these guarantees.").

[69] *Cf.* Jesse H. Choper, JUDICIAL REVIEW AND THE NATIONAL POLITICAL PROCESS (1980) (arguing that judicial review is appropriate in cases involving individual rights, but not in those involving federalism issues or the respective powers of Congress and the President). It is frequently argued that judicial

precludes judicial review to enforce structural constitutional norms. It is possible that courts might have special expertise in resolving relatively technical issues involving federalism and the separation of powers that do not turn directly on judgments about moral rights. If so, judicial review would be justified in such cases. Nevertheless, the case for judicial review would need to depend on arguments other than those that I have advanced.

A more nettlesome issue concerning the implications of my argument arises when claims of fundamental rights are plausibly (even if not correctly) asserted on both sides of a lawsuit. For example, Congress might think certain "accommodations" of religious institutions or believers necessary to protect their fundamental right to religious freedom, whereas those burdened by an accommodation – for example, employees whose jobs are put at risk when a law exempts their religious employers from otherwise applicable anti-discrimination mandates – might contend that Congress has violated their fundamental right not to be compelled to support religious practice or belief.[70] Or a legislature might conclude that prohibitions against hate speech are necessary to afford vulnerable minority groups the equal protection of the laws, while opponents claim that a prohibition against hate speech interferes with the fundamental right to freedom of expression.[71] In cases in which the legislature has determined which of two competing fundamental rights claims deserves to prevail, my veto-gates argument might appear to imply that there is no good reason to want judicial review. If upholding the claim of one party risks under-protecting a fundamental right of the other, why should we privilege a judicial veto over a contrary legislative judgment except on the assumption that the judicial determination is more likely to be correct?

One possible reason might be that a relevant pathology has afflicted the legislative branch. If so, judicial power to make controlling decisions might be justified on the ground that courts are likely to be more reliable in identifying relevant moral and legal rights – not because judges have special moral acumen, but because their ordinary acumen is less likely to have been compromised.

review of separation-of-powers and federalism issues is appropriate because the ultimate purpose of the separation of powers and federalism is to protect rights.

70   *Cf. Corp. of the Presiding Bishop of the Church of Jesus Christ of Latter-day Saints v. Amos*, 483 U.S. 327 (1987) (upholding a federal law exempting religious organizations from an otherwise applicable prohibition against employment discrimination on the basis of religion even though the effect of this exemption was to allow employees to be dismissed based on their religious practices and beliefs).

71   *Cf. R.A.V. v. City of St. Paul*, 505 U.S. 377, 391 (1992) (striking down a city ordinance prohibiting bias-motivated crime because "[t]he First Amendment does not permit St. Paul to impose special prohibitions on those speakers who express views on disfavored subjects"); *Am. Booksellers Ass'n v. Hudnut*, 771 F.2d 323, 329 (7th Cir. 1985) (declaring unconstitutional on free expression grounds a city's antipornography ordinance even while accepting the ordinance's premise that pornography that subordinates women "leads to affront and lower pay at work, insult and injury at home, [and] battery and rape on the streets"); Frank I. Michelman, *Conceptions of Democracy in American Constitutional Argument: The Case of Pornography Regulation*, 56 TENN. L. REV. 291, 307–09 (1989) (noting *Hudnut*'s refusal to balance the interest in free expression against the "women's claims to liberty and equal protection" infringed by unregulated pornography).

But even if we shrink from the conclusion that our politics and legislatures have sunk into pathology, we should think carefully about how to appraise assertions that a lawsuit involves competing claims of fundamental rights such that a ruling in favor of either side might result in under-enforcement of a fundamental right possessed by the other. The challenge emerges from the now-familiar distinction between abstract rights and triggering rights. It seems likely that abstract rights – which are identified largely without regard to competing interests and considerations – will frequently be at stake on both sides of constitutional disputes. Using this measure, we could say, for example, that fundamental rights under the Free Exercise and Establishment Clauses are both at risk when religious practitioners seek exemptions from statutes that otherwise would apply to them, or that free speech and equal protection rights are both at stake in cases involving hate speech. But if we focus instead on judicially defined triggering rights, serious concerns about collisions of fundamental rights, or the under-enforcement of one right whenever another is upheld, diminish sharply, possibly to the vanishing point. For example, there should be few if any cases in which the Free Exercise Clause mandates accommodations that would infringe triggering rights under the Establishment Clause or in which the Equal Protection Clause would create a triggering right to have legislatures enact statutes that would violate the First Amendment. The judicial analysis that leads to the definition of triggering rights virtually guarantees this result. In defining triggering rights, courts routinely take competing interests and consequences into account.

In my view, unless judicially recognized *triggering rights* are at risk on both sides of a dispute, courts should exercise non-deferential review to make sure that the triggering right of whichever party has one (if either does) is not under-enforced. Among the reasons to embrace this conclusion, reliance on triggering rights to determine when the double-safeguard argument for judicial review ceases to apply has signal virtues of simplicity and administrability.[72] Without reliance on triggering rights, how, for example, would a court determine whether fundamental rights really were at stake on both sides of a lawsuit? Yes, the parties might each claim a fundamental right, but how could a court decide that a controversy really posed a conflict without digging deep into the merits of the contending claims? And what standards would it use for doing so? Taking judicially recognized triggering rights as the measure of conflict avoids this otherwise daunting if not intractable conundrum. This approach also maintains continuity with long-settled practice involving the application of strict scrutiny that has worked well enough over the past fifty years to justify continued adherence.

---

[72]   I once embraced a broader view of relevant conflicts. *See* Richard H. Fallon, Jr., *The Core of an Uneasy Case* for *Judicial Review*, 121 HARV. L. REV. 1693, 1730–31 (2008). For criticism of that view, which has moved me to narrow my position about when conflicts of fundamental rights give rise to symmetrical risks of underenforcement, see Mark Tushnet, *How Different Are Waldron's and Fallon's Core Cases For and against Judicial Review?*, 30 OXFORD J. LEGAL STUD. 49 (2010).

CONCLUSION

When all relevant considerations are taken into account, the case for judicial review on the substantially two-tiered model that has prevailed in the United States since the 1950s is uneasy. There are too many questions about whether judges will display good judgment in defining and enforcing fundamental rights – beginning at the triggering rights stage – for the situation to be otherwise. Nevertheless, solid arguments support the basic outlines of the existing regime. Because the legislature should have a large role in weighing individual against governmental interests and in adjusting the benefits and burdens of economic life, rational basis review is appropriate for many if not most cases, especially when legislation is plausibly framed to create rights in order to protect important, constitutionally cognizable interests that otherwise would go unprotected. But some interests and rights are more fundamental than others. Insofar as legislation threatens fundamental rights, a significant judicial role in appraising the validity of legislation becomes defensible on the premise that it is better to err on the side of over- rather than under-enforcement. Strict judicial scrutiny then emerges as a reasonable if not a necessary device for protecting fundamental rights appropriately.

Conclusion

What are constitutional rights? How do they relate to the governmental interests with which they sometimes compete? What do courts do when they enforce constitutional rights?

With regard to the nature of constitutional rights, this book's first conceptual conclusion was that rights are multifarious. In order to understand rights discourse, and not become mystified or enchanted by it, we need to distinguish among abstract, triggering, scrutiny, and ultimate constitutional rights. Only ultimate rights are "trumps."

The book's second important conceptual claim was that constitutional rights are limits on the discretion of the government and its officials to act in particular ways, not categorical privileges to engage in speech or conduct, regardless of competing regulatory interests. To repeat a now-familiar example, the First Amendment constrains the government from engaging in content-based censorship and, thus, bars the government from targeting flag-burning for prohibition. But it does not establish an absolute privilege to burn the flag, even as a form of political protest. The First Amendment imposes no restriction on the government's regulatory discretion that would protect a flag-burner from prosecution under a law that forbade all lighting of fires on public property.

A third, closely related claim was that abstract, triggering, scrutiny, and ultimate rights are all compounded – though in diverse ways, with intermingled contributions by the Framers and by judges – of "interests." Behind rights lie interests. Rights exist to protect individual interests. Importantly, however, governmental powers also exist to protect individual interests. The challenge, first for constitutional designers and then for judges, is to achieve the best package of rights and governmental powers.

In exploring that challenge, I have emphasized that constitutional rights are not Platonic essences. Nor are they historical artifacts, given determinate shape by the Constitution's Framers. History matters, but it is not all that matters. Finally, rights are not, or should not be, defined on the basis of calculations conducted exclusively in terms of utility, pleasure, pain, or any other single currency. The interests that judges must consider are people's interests, which vary greatly in kind and in importance. Sometimes it would be unreasonable to ask particular individuals to sacrifice interests of great importance to them in order to make large numbers of others only marginally better off, even if doing so would increase overall utility. Accordingly, constitutionally cognizable interests need to be identified and appraised with care. Judges and Justices need to make moral judgments, not just quantitative calculations, in order to identify triggering rights to strict scrutiny or the application of other tests and to balance individual rights against competing governmental interests.

My fourth conceptual claim was that constitutional rights are interconnected not only with interests, but also with judicial remedies for rights violations and with standing to sue. Like rights, judicial remedies often carry social costs as well as benefits. Courts must weigh those social costs in determining which remedies to provide. For example, in the aftermath of *Brown* v. *Board of Education*, should the prevailing plaintiffs have had a right to damages, to immediate desegregation, or to desegregation implemented with "all deliberate speed"? In addressing questions such as this, we should understand that rights and remedies are not indissolubly linked in a one-to-one correlation. Courts sometimes need to make hard choices, based on interest-balancing. In some situations, we, as a society, may be best off with relatively broadly defined rights and with limited remedies to enforce those rights. If the social costs of providing individually effective remedies for all constitutional violations became too high, we would likely have either fewer rights or narrower ones than we have today.

Finally, I have argued that a clear-eyed view of the judicial role in constitutional adjudication requires a different defense of judicial review than its champions have usually advanced. In balancing individual and governmental interests, courts largely replicate functions that conscientious legislators would have performed already. When robust judicial review is warranted – as I believe it often is – the best justification will typically not be that courts should enforce original constitutional understandings or that they possess special capacities for enlightened moral judgment. It is that fundamental rights (as abstractly defined) deserve a double safeguard against unjustified infringement. On the premise that the under-enforcement of fundamental rights is ordinarily worse than their over-enforcement, courts justifiably possess a kind of veto power over legislation that, in their judgment, threatens fundamental rights unduly.

As Chapter 7 made clear, this defense of judicial review is contingent and uneasy. There are many ways in which judges might botch their assignments, as the Supreme Court did during the *Lochner* era. But my qualified argument in support of American-style judicial review is of a piece with the rest of the book, which emphasizes the irreducibly practical functions of the courts, and especially the Supreme Court, in identifying and balancing sometimes competing individual and governmental interests.

If judges and especially Supreme Court Justices absorbed this book's lessons about the complex relations between rights and interests, as embodied in the Constitution's text and refracted through history, they would emerge empowered. They would have a clearer grasp of the options open to them in determining which triggering, scrutiny, and ultimate rights to recognize and which remedies to provide. But judges and Justices also would, or should, be chastened by recognizing the precariousness of the moral justification for charging them with the interest-balancing functions that they inescapably perform. Although judges and Justices wear robes, they are not oracles, and they should not slip into self-delusion on this score.

For concerned citizens who are not judges, the book's arguments should furnish an antidote to lazy, stylized assumptions that partisans have too often relied on in constitutional debate. Readers should emerge as better critics, including self-critics, and as more informed appraisers of judicial and political discourse about constitutional law. This point holds nearly across the political spectrum. If originalists take seriously the lessons that a close examination of strict judicial scrutiny teaches, they will need either to renounce strict scrutiny as a pillar of constitutional analysis – which few prominent originalists have recommended – or revise their theories to acknowledge the limits of historical research in determining modern constitutional outcomes.

Those who claim that the Supreme Court is a "forum of principle" and that rights are "trumps" would also need to modify, or at least clarify, their claims. To apply the strict scrutiny formula, the Court must make practical, predictive, interest-balancing judgments. The Justices define rights in light of competing governmental interests. Interests in providing remedies for constitutional rights violations yield, and ought to yield, in some cases. Among those who rally instinctively to arguments exalting rights over interests, and have not thought through what rights are and how they relate to interests, there should be less sanctimony and more sober thinking about questions involving the optimal, forward-looking design of packages of rights and remedies.

To give just one more example, "living constitutionalists" who take this book's message to heart should recognize that their slogan is only a slogan. The practical challenge of constitutional adjudication is to bring competing considerations into a tenable balance. Living constitutionalist judges and Justices need to think simultaneously about abstract rights and the interests that underlie them, governmental interests that excessively broad enforcement of rights could put at risk, optimal design of the judicial tests (such as strict judicial scrutiny) from which ultimately enforceable constitutional rights emerge, and appropriately available judicial remedies. The Constitution would not live very successfully for very long if the Justices of the Supreme Court indulged their unfiltered intuitions about rights and fairness without taking complex connections among different kinds of rights and different kinds of constitutionally cognizable interests into account.

No book could dissolve all disagreements about constitutional rights. Unlike some, this book has not tried. If it has succeeded, however, it will have clarified what constitutional rights are. It will also have illuminated the choices that judges and Justices confront – whether aware or unawares, whether honestly or disingenuously – when they resolve disputed cases.

Index